Pakistan's Spy Agencies

Pakistan's Spy Agencies

Challenges of Civilian Control over Intelligence Agencies Bureaucratic and Military Stakeholderism, Dematerialization of Civilian Intelligence, and War of Strength

Musa Khan Jalalzai

Vij Books India Pvt Ltd

New Delhi (India)

Published by

Vij Books India Pvt Ltd
(Publishers, Distributors & Importers)
2/19, Ansari Road
Delhi – 110 002
Phones: 91-11-43596460, 91-11-47340674
Mobile: 98110 94883
e-mail: contact@vijpublishing.com
www.vijbooks.com

Contents

Introduction

………..The BBC journalist M Ilyas Khan confirmed atrocities of Pakistan army in his BBC News report: "In May 2016, for example, an attack on a military post in the Teti Madakhel area of North Waziristan triggered a manhunt by troops who rounded up the entire population of a village. An eyewitness who watched the operation from the wheat field nearby and whose brother was among those detained told the BBC that the soldiers beat everyone with batons and threw mud in children's mouths when they cried. A pregnant woman was one of two people who died during torture, her son said in video testimony. At least one man remains missing". (BBC News, Dera Ismail Khan, 02 June 2019).

Pakistan today presents an excruciating picture of ethnic faultlines. The complex reciprocation among the internal and external forces, fashioning Pakistan today, call on to an in-depth evaluation of their influence on the country's future-in the context of both continued state stability and Pakistan's potential to jump-start broader security priorities in the region. Pakistani politicians, economists, and research scholars have written numerous research papers to find out an immediate panacea to its fractured physique, but policy makers and military junta have also been mixed up in a complex web of debt trap, ethnic faultlines, and corruption, to that end, they have been unable to smash the strong web of challenges encompassing their way to aggrandisement.

Pakistani analyst and writer, Dr. Muhammad Taqi has added a murky picture to the country's deteriorating political and economic crisis: "Pakistan's economy is in a virtual free-fall and the blame for it rests squarely with the army, which had upset the applecart of democracy by engineering former Prime Minister Nawaz Sharif's ouster in 2017". Now, as the country is staggering on the brink, Military establishment manifested no interest in the deteriorating health of the Islamic Republic as it has already established its own military republic of 10 million retired and working military friends that exports fear and consternation to India and Afghanistan. The military state of Pakistan is intelligent and competent in managing its own economy, industry, health sector, education, food, medical industry, banking system, property development, and poverty. Moreover, a little while back, Lt. Gen. P.R Shankar, (Retd) (Bharat Shakti, June 22, 2019) painted a consternating picture of the Islamic Republic of Pakistan's relationship with neighbouring states:

> "Pakistan has poor relations along all its borders. Indo-Pak relations are poor. Well known Pakistani meddling for strategic space is fundamental to the collapse of Afghanistan. Good Taliban, Bad Taliban, Afghan Taliban, Pakistani Taliban, State actors, Non-State actors (sponsored and non-sponsored), and Pashtun movements along and Durand Line will keep Pakistan on its toes and take a toll on its purse. A Shia Iran and a Sunni Pakistan will always be uneasy neighbours. Stoking transnational Baluch, Pashtun and Kashmiri population will ensure permanent border instability. Pakistan's strategic attraction to Afghanistan is like a drug addict to poppy. Hostile and unsettled borders extract long term costs and promote Pakistani State failure".

The imbalance of Pakistan's civil-military relations since the abolishing of Nawaz Sharif's government caused increasingly misperceptions about the changing role of military in politics, while Pakistan's intelligence agencies have been regularly communicating with political parties to improve the image of the army after it used unrestrained power in FATA and Baluchistan operations, in which more than one million Pashtuns and Balochs were forced to leave their houses. The current democratic administration under Prime Minister Imran Khan needs to address these systemic challenges, though the need for institutional reform and building a process-driven approach. The eruption of violence in Baluchistan and the excessive use of force by the army demonstrate this lack of strategy.

The country maintains 32 secret agencies working under different democratic, political and military stakeholders who used them for their own interests. The rapid aggrandisement and evolution of the strategic, political, and economic environment in Pakistan since 2001, has furthered the quest for information on security issues and operational mechanism of intelligence agencies. In the wake of recent series of sectarian and terrorist attacks on civilian and military installations, and growing security concerns has been a wave of new security regulation and unlimited power aimed at expanding intelligence powers across the country.

Established in 1948, the ISI was tasked with acquiring intelligence of strategic interests and assessing the intensity of foreign threats, but political and military stakeholders used the agency adversely and painted a consternating picture of its working environment. The best intelligence agency with its excellent and professional security approach is now dancing to different tangos. The civilian intelligence agency-Intelligence Bureau (IB) has been gradually neglected due to the consecutive military rule and weak democratic governments. The Intelligence Bureau (IB) was established by the British Army Major General Sir. Charles MacGregor, who at that time was Quartermaster General and head of the Intelligence Department for the British Indian Army at Shimla in 1885. Appointment for IB's Director-General is made by the Prime Minister and confirmed by the President. The IB, which was patterned after the IB of British India, used to be largely a police organisation, but the post of Director-General (DG), IB, is no longer tenable only by police officers as it was in the past. Serving and retired military officers are being appointed in increasing numbers to senior posts in the IB, including to the post of DG. In 1990s, the IB remained actively involved to curb sectarianism and the fundamentalism in the country. Many of its operations were directed towards infiltration, conducting espionage, counterespionage, and providing key information on terrorist organizations.

The successive governments have been using the agency against opponents, writers, and journalists in Pakistan since 1970s, while former Prime Ministers Benazir Bhutto and Nawaz Sharif painted a controversial picture of its operational mechanism. I am not going to highlight the whole historical journey of the agency but wish to describe its modernistic way of operation under democratic governments. In 2017, a list of over 37 lawmakers suspected of having links with banned terrorist and sectarian outfits was openly circulated by the agency to win the favour of Prime Minister Nawaz Sharif. The list first came to light when a private television channel (ARY News) aired a report claiming that former Prime Minister Nawaz Sharif had directed the IB on July 10 to keep watch on the listed legislators, mostly belonging to the PML-N. On 26 September 2017, DG IB Aftab Sultan came under scathing criticism from PTI Chief Imran Khan for visiting London to further put heads together with former PM Nawaz Sharif. In October 2017, the 37 parliamentarians staged a walkout from National Assembly after the Intelligence Bureau (IB) report accused them of having links with terrorist organizations. While yelling in parliament, Federal Minister Riaz Peerzada said that the government should launch an investigation into the matter and unveil the name of the person who prepared the report. Thus, the IB became a controversial agency, and several whistleblowers and double-crossers asserted one.

On 26 September 2017, Dawn newspaper reported a serving Assistant Sub-Inspector of Intelligence Bureau (ASIIB), Malik Mukhtar Ahmed Shahzad's accusation against his senior officers of not taking action against terrorism suspects, and filed a petition before the Islamabad High Court (IHC) requesting it to refer the matter to the Inter-Services Intelligence (ISI) for a thorough probe. The newspaper reported. Dawn also reported Islamabad High Court Registrar's Office fixation of the petition before Justice Aamer Farooq who referred the case to IHC Chief Justice Mohammad Anwar Khan Kasi, with a note that the matter needed to be transferred to Justice Shaukat Aziz Siddiqui since an identical matter was pending in his court. In the petition filed through his counsel Masroor Shah, Mr. Shahzad said he joined the IB in 2007, and that he "reported against various terrorist groups having roots in Uzbekistan, Iran, Afghanistan, Syria and India". The ASI told the court he reported against terrorist groups from various countries, but no action was taken:

"However, to the petitioner's utter dismay, no action was ever been taken by IB in this respect despite concrete evidence provided to it in the form of the intelligence reports", the petition says. "Upon thorough intelligence gathering process, it transpired that certain high officials of the IB themselves are directly involved with the terrorist organizations having linkages with hostile enemy intelligence agencies" the petition reads. It goes on to say that the matter was even reported to the IB director general, who also did not take any steps. It says some IB officials travelled to Israel and had direct links with Afghan intelligence which, it was found later, had links with another terrorist group from Kazakhstan. "These terrorists used to disguise themselves as citrus dealers in Kot-Momin and Bhalwal, Sargodha. The business was a mere camouflage," the petition said.

Moreover, the petition revealed that the son of Joint Director IB (Punjab) had established links with these terror groups. The petition uncovered that some officials of Afghan and Iranian intelligence used to take refuge in the places of the citrus dealers. The petition named certain IB's officials who were on the payroll of foreign intelligence agencies which included a Joint Director General, Directors and Deputy Directors. The petitioner said: "Senior IB officials also facilitate Afghan nationals in getting Pakistani nationality. Mr. Shahzad said he "has been running from pillar to post including approaching the Prime Minister of Pakistan to raise this issue of national security and protection of lives of the citizen of this country but in vain." The petitioner requested the court that the issue of connivance, complacency and involvement of official of IB and other senior bureaucrats raised in the petition may graciously be entrusted to ISI for investigation. Dawn reported that the Intelligence Bureau (IB) also came under attack by a Joint Investigation Team (JIT) consisting of officials from ISI, Military Intelligence and officials from other departments for 'hampering the investigation' into the assets of former Prime Minister Nawaz Sharif's family. The Intelligence Bureau (IB) was accused by one of its own spies of "protecting" terrorists. That petition prompted misunderstandings between the ISI and the IB.

The unending resultant tussle between civilian and military intelligence agencies forced former Prime Minister Nawaz Sharif to restructure the IB and make it more effective to counter ISI's influence in political institutions. The Prime Minister allocated huge funds to the IB to recruit and employ more agents to meet the country's internal and external challenges. The greatest challenge Nawaz Sharif faced was on the national security front, where he failed to take control of the security policy of Kashmir and Afghanistan. The miltablishment was not happy with his democratic intentions. The Intelligence Bureau is the country's main civilian intelligence agency that functions under the direct control of the Prime Minister, tackling terrorism, insurgency and extremism. Over the last four decades, the ISI operated in changing security environment, but the agency mostly targeted democracy and political parties, strengthened miltablishment and its illegal business.

The intelligence community of Pakistan was once described by the daily Frontier Post (May 18, 1994) as an invisible government and by the Daily Dawn (April 25, 1994 as secret godfathers consist of the Intelligence Bureau (IB) and the ISI. While the IB comes under the Interior Minister, the ISI is part of the Ministry of Defence (MOD). Each wing of the Armed Forces maintains its own intelligence directorate. After the PTI Chief Imran Khan became Prime Minister, the IB started dancing to his tango. Analyst Azaz Syed (28 September 2018) noted some developments within the intelligence infrastructure as Prime Minister Imran Khan restructured the agency and fitted it to the recurrent nature of his charleston:

> "Amid a major reshuffle within the premier civilian intelligence outfit, the Intelligence Bureau (IB) has been directed to concentrate on fighting corruption instead of countering terrorism, The Friday Times has learnt. Although IB chief Dr. Suleman Khan denied this development while talking to TFT, sources within the agency insist that they have been tasked to bring forward corruption cases against prominent political figures and pay attention to these areas. "There are other agencies and organisations which were trained for anti-

corruption efforts. IB should not do this. Its expertise is in countering terrorism and its focus should not be redirected towards corruption," said Ehsan Ghani, a recently retired former chief of the IB while talking to TFT. Dr. Suleman, who has also served the agency in Khyber Pakhtunkhwa, is counted among those who played a vital role in countering terrorism in the province with the help of the police and the Counter-Terrorism Department (CTD). Now, sources say, he has agreed to shelve counterterrorism as a subject of the agency, as another agency has been tasked to deal with it. Dr. Suleman was appointed chief of the agency by former Prime Minister Shahid Khaqan Abbasi on the recommendation of Aftab Sultan, the then IB chief. But in a conversation with TFT, Dr. Suleman denied this. "I come from a background of counter-terrorism, how can I abandon something I have worked on for years"?

The third most important agency-having something on the ball during the Musharaf, Zardari and Nawaz Sharif government was Federal Investigation Agency (FIA). FIA has also been playing political role for different governments since 1970s. The FIA's main objective was to protect the nation's interests and defend Pakistan, to uphold and enforce law in the country. The Federal Investigation Agency (FIA) was established on 13 January 1975, after being codified in the Constitution with the passing of the FIA Act in 1974. The FIA is headed by Director-General who is appointed by the Prime Minister and confirmed by the President. Appointment for the Director of FIA either comes from the high-ranking officials of police or the civil bureaucracy. The DG FIA reports to the Interior Secretary of Pakistan.

Civilian control over intelligence agencies and oversight in Pakistan is a challenging issue, the reason that intelligence agencies in Pakistan operating without oversight. On 04 November 2013, Dawn reported recommendations of the Senate Standing Committee on Human Rights which "recommended an effective role of parliament in monitoring the Inter-Services Intelligence (ISI) agency and putting it under civilian control. The report was unanimously adopted by the committee and presented in the house. The committee unanimously approved recommendations on 05 September 2013 and voiced for setting up a bicameral intelligence and security committee to suggest ways of addressing the issue of enforced disappearance of citizens".

In July 2008, the PPP government notified the Interior Ministry to take control of ISI but had to backtrack within 24 hours when the military establishment expressed its displeasure. Senator Farhatullah Babar of the PPP was the convener of the three-member committee which prepared the report. After that constant failure, now every agency in the country is above the law and they are free to detain, kidnap and harass civilians in many ways. Former President General Pervez Musharraf and General Raheel Sharif committed war crimes in FATA, Baluchistan and Waziristan by killing innocent people there. They sold their countrymen to the CIA and tortured children and women. General Shahid Aziz once unveiled secret business of General Musharraf in a TV interview with journalist Hamid Mir, in which he admitted that Pakistan army killed thousands of Pashtuns, Afghans and Balochs.

The way military intelligence operated over the past decades was not a traditional or cultural pattern. Instead of tackling national security challenges, the ISI, along with Military Intelligence (MI) and the IB unnecessarily concentrated on making political alliances and countering democratic forces within the country. When the intelligence war among military and civilian agencies intensified, the blame-game became the focus of literary debates in newspapers and electronic media. Democratic forces stood behind civilian intelligence agencies, while pro-establishment forces supported the ISI and its undemocratic business. In 2014, officials from the ISI had their phone calls eavesdropped at the height of civil-military tension.

On 13 September 2013, Dawn newspaper reported allegations of the Directorate General of Inter-Services Intelligence (ISI) against the 34 civilian inspectors who filed petitions with the Islamabad High Court (IHC) that they were compromising national security and hampered the smooth functioning of the organisation as well. In August that year, the ISI inspector Abdul Rahim filed a petition with the IHC saying that contrary to the court restraining orders the Directorate of ISI had posted him to Sui in Balochistan and also evicted him from the official residence in Islamabad.

However, Mr. Justice Shaukat Aziz Siddiqui suspended the posting orders of Mr. Rahim but also restrained the ISI from evicting him from the official residence as well. Moreover, before this petition, on 01 July 2013, Dawn newspaper reported a petition of the promotion case of civilian officers against the ISI Directorate. The litigation related to the service matter of several civilian officials working within offices of Inter-Services Intelligence (ISI) indicated that it was difficult for them to reach even BPS-21-grade in their entire service. Because of this, the names of civilian officials cannot even be considered for the post of Director General which is a BPS-22 position.

However, that year, three more petitions were also filed with the Islamabad High Court (IHC) by the civilian officials of the Inter-Services Intelligence (ISI). All but, 30 civilian officials of the ISI Directorates filed their petition against the agency Directorate-stating that a civilian official working in ISI offices hardly gets only one-time promotion during his entire 25 years of service. Reports indicated more than 325 officers were working in BPS-17 to 21 in the five different cadres of the ISI. Out of the 325, only one officer enjoyed BPS-21. Seven others were in BPS-20 and were working as Deputy Directors. Lt-General (retired) Talat Masood said despite being a civilian organisation, there was hardly any oversight of the civilian governments over the ISI.

The perspicacity that ISI is a number-1 intelligence agency in South Asia is not accurate; the agency is weak, and its national security approach has been controversial since years. It collects intelligence in an untraditional manner, which leads policymakers on the wrong direction. Its intelligence officers are not so greatly educated and unable to use intelligence technology properly or establish strong networks within different communities. There are thousands of volunteer informers who work for the agency in different environments but don't even know the basic knowledge of intelligence information technic. Their purveyed low-quality intelligence information leads policymakers on wrong direction-the reason that they view Afghanistan and India with hostile military glasses. The second underwhelming thing is that military and civilian officers working within the agency have adopted two cultures of intelligence collection and analysis. In view of the fact that for civilian officers, working in a militarised agency with a military way of operation and administration, is an exasperating task. The ISI collects intelligence information on militarised manner, analyse it on militarised manner, and disseminates it within specific circles.

The rivalry between the IB and ISI boiled over in June 2017, when a Joint Investigation Team (JIT) probing alleged money-laundering of the Sharif family made a written complaint to the Supreme Court that the IB was wiretapping JIT members, including the ISI and military intelligence personnel. The JIT further reported that the IB was hampering its inquiries, adding that military-led intelligence agencies were not on "good terms" with the IB. More worrisome was that IB was collecting intelligence information on members of the JIT from the National Database and Registration Authority (NADRA) and presented it to Prime Minister Nawaz Sharif to use it against them. The shortcomings of the civilian security apparatus are numerous as well.

First, it should be acknowledged that Pakistani agencies view the myriad threats to the country differently. While the ISI may view a particular group or an individual to be an asset, local police may view them as a threat. The Inter-Services Intelligence is not responsive to civilian control despite the fact that the organization is constitutionally accountable to the Prime Minister. Most of the officers come from the army on secondment, which means that their promotions, professional achievement, and ultimate loyalty rest with the army. Civilian officers within the agency have limited knowledge of intelligence operations and secret alliances. They are powerless and neglected.

Dawn newspaper published an article of journalist Almeida, which said that some in Pakistan's civilian government confronted military officials at a top-secret national security Committee meeting. They said that they were being asked to do more to crack down on armed groups, yet, whenever law-enforcement agencies took action, "the security establishment…worked behind the scenes to set the arrested free". He reported that the civilians warned that Pakistan risked international isolation if the security establishment didn't crackdown on terrorist groups operating from Pakistan. After these leaks, the National Security Council and its committee became controversial. Pakistan's Chief Executive General Pervez Musharraf formally established the National Security Council on 21 August 2002. Under Article 152A of the Pakistan Constitution, the President of Pakistan and the Prime Minister of Pakistan serve as Chairman and Vice-Chairman respectively. The Council remains unpopular and resented by leading political parties and liberal politicians pointing to the fact that the NSC primarily takes on the oligarchic structure of high-ranking military retirees and elite civilian officials close to the military.

On April 29, Major General Asif Ghafoor, the spokesman for the Pakistani army's Inter-Services Public Relations (ISPR) expressed his institution's dissatisfaction over the government's probe into the leak that put military and the civilian government on a collision course. "Notification on Dawn Leak is incomplete and not in line with recommendations by the Inquiry Board. "Notification is rejected," Ghafoor said on Twitter. When Ghafoor was writing this tweet, he probably had no idea it would anger many people in Pakistan. Journalist Almeida's story came out at a particularly sensitive time for Islamabad, as its ties with New Delhi deteriorated following tensions on the Kashmir border. Indian Prime Minister Narendra Modi vowed in a speech that he would work to isolate Pakistan internationally due to its alleged support to Islamic militants in Kashmir.

Pakistani establishment never allowed controlling the hydra of intelligence agencies to introduce security sector reforms, and fit it to the fight against radicalization, terrorism and jihadism. Consequentially, the agencies strategies became militarised and became a tool of miltablishment to harass politician and those who write against the corruption of military Generals. Scholar Frederic Grare (18 December 2015) noted some aspects of the business of military establishment in his well-written paper: "Despite more than eight years of continued civilian power, Pakistan can be labeled as a transitional democracy at best. True, the country has experienced two successive and relatively democratic elections in February 2008 and May 2013, and the mainstream political parties-essentially the Pakistan Muslim League Nawaz faction (PML-N) and the Pakistan People's Party (PPP)--are no longer willing to let themselves be played off the other by the military, thereby limiting the margin of maneuver of the security establishment...Today, as much as in the past, "operations against dissenting politicians, objective intellectuals, and other activists, are still carried out through systematic harassment, disinformation campaigns, fictitious trials, kidnap, torture, and assassinations", as demonstrated by the de facto genocide in Balochistan."

The consecutive militarisation and Talibanisation of society, and instability led to the catastrophe of disintegration and failure of the state institutions, which was further inflamed by the US so-called war on terrorism, and involvement of NATO forces in Afghanistan. Pakistan's weak and unprofessional diplomatic approach towards Afghanistan prompted deep crisis, including the closure of trade routes and a diplomatic impasse. According to the Constitution of Pakistan, every democratic government is answerable to the people of Pakistan. In reality, they are actually answerable to the Army headquarters in Rawalpindi. Every single Prime Minister in Pakistan can only do his or her job smoothly if they completely surrender defense, interior, strategic decisions and foreign policy to the Army.

It means the rules for civilian governments are pre-decided and they have been told to go by the book and not cross the red lines defined by the defense establishment. This makes it a "State within a State" that, instead of ruling the country from the front, prefers that the politicians and civilian governments implement their decisions and exercise power. On 22 September 2015, I put in writing that radicalised elements within the army can facilitate the access of Taliban, the ISIS and Lashkar-e-Taiba to steal material of dirty bomb. My predictions become a reality when military intelligence and ISI arrested Dr. Wasim Akram and Brigadier Raja Rizwan (retd), who the ISPR described as an employee of a "sensitive organisation. Dr. Wasim was working as a nuclear scientist at the Kahuta Nuclear Research Labs, Pakistan's main uranium enrichment facility.

Over the last two decades, the role and scale of Pakistan's intelligence agencies has grown over and above their prescribed functions, to the degree that their operations, often undercover and at odds even with each other, have earned them the repute of being a "State within a State". In most parts of the country, intelligence information collection faces numerous difficulties since the Taliban and other militant groups returned to important strategic locations. Having faced serious difficulties in dealing with insurgent forces in Balochistan and Waziristan, the agencies started translating their anger into the killing and kidnapping of innocent civilians with impunity. They needed to adopt a professional mechanism in countering insurgency in Waziristan.

On 06 October 2016, Dawn newspaper reported an unprecedented warning of the civilian government to the military leadership of a growing international isolation of Pakistan and sought consensus on several key actions by the state. First, DG of ISI Gen Rizwan Akhtar, accompanied by National Security Adviser General Nasser Janjua, was instructed to travel the four provinces with a message for provincial apex committees and ISI sector commanders. The message warned that military-led intelligence agencies must not interfere when law enforcement acts against militant groups that were banned or until now considered off-limits for civilian action. Second, former Prime Minister Nawaz Sharif directed that fresh attempts be made to conclude the Pathankot investigation and restart the stalled Mumbai attacks-related trials in a Rawalpindi anti-terrorism court. Those decisions, taken after an extraordinary verbal confrontation between Punjab Chief Minister Shahbaz Sharif and the DG ISI appeared to indicate a high-stakes new approach by the PML-N government. However, during the meeting, Gen Akhtar offered that the government should arrest whomever it deems necessary, but Shahbaz Sharif said: "When action is taken against certain groups by civilian authorities, military intelligence work behind the scene to set the arrested free. Dawn reported".

In July 2019, Prime Minister Imran Khan supported Shahbaz Sharif's allegations against the agencies during his official visit to the United States and admitted the presence of 30000-40000 armed terrorists in his country. The agencies established links with fundamentalist parties such as the Jamaat-e-Islami and its offshoots, the Tablighi Jamaat and Markaz Dawa-al Irshad. This interaction also allowed the Islamic fundamentalist parties in Pakistan to extend influence over armed forces personnel. The U.S. Country Reports on Terrorism described Pakistan as a "Terrorist safe haven" where terrorists are able to organize, plan, raise funds, communicate, and recruit fighters, while the ISI, has often been accused of playing a role in major terrorist attacks across India including terrorism in Kashmir. President Hamid Karzai was regularly reiterating allegations that militants operating training camps in Pakistan used it as a launch platform to attack targets in Afghanistan.

Pakistan's relations with Afghanistan have been in strain due to the former Chief Executive General Musharraf short-sighted policies since 2001. The General shamelessly genuflected to the United States demands of it's so called war on terrorism, and accepted all terms and conditions of allowing US and NATO forces to bomb Afghanistan from their bases inside Pakistan. By virtue of Musharraf's short-sighted policies, Pakistan was pushed into the Afghan quagmire. Pervez Musharraf came under instant U.S. and NATO pressure to act against Al-Qaeda leader Osama bin Laden, who was hiding in Pakistan. In an interview aired by a private channel in 2018, Mr. Musharraf acknowledged that terrorists were trained in Pakistan. "We trained Taliban and sent them to fight against Russia. Taliban, Haqqani, Osama bin Laden and Zawahiri were our heroes then," he said.

The arrest of Afghan Ambassador Mullah Abdul Salam Zaeef by Pakistan's law enforcement agencies further caused misunderstanding between the people of Afghanistan and Pakistan that a close and friendly neighbour intentionally violated international diplomatic principles. No doubt, ISI had a prolexit list of friends in Afghanistan, but military dictator General Musharraf acted differently. Former Afghan Ambassador was arrested and handed to US agencies by Pakistan. He was humiliated by the CIA in the presence of officials in Islamabad. John F. Burns 04 January 2002) published a detailed story of his humiliation and torture in New York Times. Pakistani analyst Ayaz Amir (daily Dawn. 22 September 2006) also noted some aspects of his painful instant:

"We know, to our lasting shame, how our overlords, dazzled by American power, and afraid of God knows what, handed over the ex-Taliban ambassador, Mullah Abdus Salam Zaeef, to the Americans in January 2002—in violation of every last comma of international law. But until now we have not been privy to the details: how exactly did the handing-over take place? Now to satisfy our curiosity, and perhaps outrage our feelings, comes Mullah Zaeef's own account, published in Pashto and parts of which have been translated into Urdu by the Express newspaper. To say that the account is eye-opening would be an understatement. It is harrowing and mind-blowing. Can anyone bend so low as our government did? And can behaviour be as wretched as that displayed by American military personnel into whose custody Zaeef was given? On the morning of January 2, 2002, three officials of a secret agency arrived at Zaeef's house in Islamabad with this message: "Your Excellency, you are no more excellency." One of them said no one can resist American power or words to that effect. "America wants to question you. We are going to hand you over to the Americans so that their purpose is served, and Pakistan is saved from a big danger." Zaeef could have been forgiven for feeling stunned. From the "guardians of Islam" this was the last thing that he expected, that for the sake of a few "coins" (his words) he would be delivered as a "gift" to the Americans. Under heavy escort he was taken to Peshawar, kept there for a few days and then pushed into his nightmare. Blindfolded and handcuffed, he was driven to a place where a helicopter was waiting, its engines running. Someone said, "Khuda hafiz" (God preserve you).

Ayaz Amir also reported his torture and noted Pakistan's constraints as well. This was Pakistan's bigger mistake that changed the attitude of every Afghan about the country. Mullah Abdul Salam Zaeef, the Taliban Government's Ambassador to Pakistan in his book "My Life with the Taliban" has described his heartbreaking story:

"When we arrived in Peshawar I was taken to a lavishly-fitted office. A Pakistani flag stood on the desk, and a picture of Mohammad Ali Jinnah hung at the back of the room. A Pashtun man was sitting behind the desk. He got up, introduced himself and welcomed me. His head was shaved — seemingly his only feature of note — and he was of an average size and weight. He walked over to me and said that he was the head of the bureau. I was in the devil's workshop, the regional head office of the ISI. He told me I was a close friend —a guest — and one that they cared about a great deal. I wasn't sure what he meant, since it was pretty clear that I was dear to them only because they could get a good sum of money for me when they sold me. Their trade was people, just as with goats, the higher the price for the goat, the happier the owner. In the twenty-first century, there aren't many places left where you can still buy and sell people, but Pakistan remains a hub for this trade. I prayed after dinner with the ISI officer, and then was brought to a holding-cell for detainees.........Finally, after days in my cell; a man came, tears flowing down his cheeks. He fainted as his grief and shame overcame him. He was the last person I saw in that room. I never learnt his name, but soon after—perhaps four hours after he left — I was handed over to the Americans. Even before I reached the helicopter, I was suddenly attacked from all sides. People kicked me, shouted at me, and my clothes were cut with knives. They ripped the black cloth from my face and for the first time, I could see where I was. Pakistani and American soldiers stood around me. The Pakistani soldiers were all staring as the Americans hit me and tore the remaining clothes off from my body. Eventually, I was completely naked, and the Pakistani soldiers — the defenders of the Holy Qur'an — shamelessly watched me with smiles on their faces, saluting this disgraceful action of the Americans".

The ISI established relationship with numerous groups and political organizations in Afghanistan but its persisting policy inside the country caused distrust. The ISI wants Indian intelligence to curtail its presence in Afghanistan but doesn't want to undermine its own networks. The agency never tolerated the Indian RAW presence in Afghanistan, the reason that its role in managing several anti-India proxy networks was also unmistakable. On 07 May 2018; Javid Ahmad in his article revealed so many new things about the ISI role in Afghanistan:

"In Afghanistan, ISI's Afghan operations are undertaken by at least three units. The first is Directorate S, the principal covert action arm that directs and oversees the Afghan policy, including militant and terrorist outfits and their operations. The second unit is the Special Service Group (SSG), also known as the Pakistani SS, and is the army's Special Forces element that was established in the 1950s as a hedge against the communists. Today, some SSG units effectively operate as ISI's paramilitary wing and have fought alongside the Taliban until 2001. In other instances, SSG advisors have allegedly been embedded with Taliban fighters to provide tactical military advice, including on special operations, surveillance, and reconnaissance. In fact, encountering ISI operatives fighting alongside the Taliban in Afghanistan has become a common occurrence that no longer surprise Afghan and American forces. The third ISI unit is the Afghan Logistics Cell, a transport network inside Pakistan facilitated by members of Pakistan's Frontier Corps that provide logistical support to the Taliban and their families. This includes space, weapons, vehicles, protection, money, identity cards and safe passage.

Such ISI support networks have been designed to break Afghanistan into pieces and then remold it into a pliant state. The objective is to complicate Afghanistan's security landscape and drive its political climate into uncharted constitutional territory to create a vacuum, which inevitably places the Taliban in the driving seat. These support actions have visibly made the group more effective. However, the Pakistani mantra is that they maintain contacts with the Taliban but exercise no control over them".

Musa Khan Jalalzai

March 2020, London

Pakistan's Intelligence Agencies: Stakeholders, Crisis of Confidence and lack of Modern Intelligence Mechanism

Writing on Pakistan's secret agencies is no longer a wearisome and laborious piece of work as great deal of information is available in newspaper, journals, and books. Any author, or journalist who wants to find out secret information in libraries, or archives, he must be aware of the fact that there are no intelligence operations files in archives in Pakistan. However, discussion about the military operations in FATA and Waziristan is also forbidden on print and electronic media. If we look at the process of election in 2018, the way intelligence agencies and the army with all speed managed the results reflected influence of the army and agencies in politics. Scholar Rai Mansoor Imtiaz (14 November 2019) in his recent analysis elucidated the role of military and intelligence in election process:

"The military launched two far-right religious parties for the 2018 elections: Tehrik e Labyk Pakistan (TLP) and Allah-o-Akbar-Party (AAP). Although neither party won any seats in the National Assembly (NA), they made a significant dent in the baralevi-sunni and Wahabi (religious sects) vote bank of the PML-N in many electoral constituencies of Punjab as well as in other provinces. It can be seen that TLP caused the defeat of the PML-N in many NA seats in Punjab, since the margin of defeat was less than the votes polled by the TLP candidates". Pakistani intelligence agencies have been playing various political and sectarian roles instead of safeguarding security interests of the country since 1980s.[1] The key point that cannot be denied is the agencies have often supported sectarian organization in elections.[2] There are multifarious agencies operating under the command of military, political and bureaucratic stakeholders who scamper and whisk their horses on different missions to bring Gallus-Gallus.[3]

As the key providers of information relevant to national security threats, agencies are essential components of every state security system.[4] The need for intelligence (Florina Cristiana Matei and Carolyn Halladay-2019) is a fact of life for modern governments. Few states take the view that they can dispense with a foreign intelligence service and none is sufficiently immune from terrorism or the inquisitiveness of its neighbours to forgo an internal security service.[5] The fact is; intelligence is crucial to the survival of the state and the mandate of a security intelligence service defines the tasks that the service has to perform, and provides the guiding principles by which the service conducts its operations and measures effectiveness. In the wake of recent series of sectarian and terrorist attacks on civilian and military installations in Pakistan, and growing security concerns has been a wave of new security regulation and unlimited power aimed at expanding intelligence powers across the country.[6]

The underwhelming development was the authorization of preventive investigation powers in protecting domestic security. The army is a prominent player in the country's politics, particularly regarding domestic security, foreign policy and economic affairs, but never shared its billions of dollar annual revenue with the poor state. Its control of political theatre is causing wide-ranging clash of interests.[7] Dr. Julian Richards, an author of four books and a number of papers and book chapters on a range of security and intelligence issues have contributed a chapter on Pakistan's intelligence agencies in the book (The Image of the Enemy: Intelligence Analysis of Adversaries Since 1945), in which he reviewed some weak aspects of Pakistan's intelligence infrastructure that operates in different directions.[8] He also highlighted successful intelligence operations of ISI and IB in 1965 and 1971 wars, which have been warranted by Indian army generals, but he still believes that the ISI's operational mechanism needs more refinement:

> "There is some evidence that a growing preoccupation with domestic affairs led to a damaging lack of resources allocated to military intelligence during the 1965 war with India. Over the ensuing years, the ISI continued to flourish under both civilian and military regimes and became very much the predominant intelligence actor in Pakistan. It involved itself increasingly in gathering intelligence on internal insurrections in Balochistan, and the North West Frontier Province (now Khyber Pakhtunkhwa province), in orchestrating military and logistical assistance to proxy forces in Afghanistan and Kashmir, in helping to nurture the Taliban as a strategic force in Afghanistan, in establishing a network of spies and intelligence activities throughout India, and in interfering a domestic election within Pakistan, notably in 1990 when the situation was looking unfavourable to the military-bureaucratic center of power. By the turn of the twenty first century, the ISI had again become a strategic partner of the United States in the so-called war on terrorism, resuming its role of the 1980s, albeit on built on sometimes shaky level of trust".[9]

Any civilian or military government that wants to professionalize its intelligence infrastructure, and prevent it from decaying, needs statecraft, which is comprised of economic power, and a strong military force and mature diplomacy.[10] The case is quite different in India and Pakistan, where emerging contradictions in the state system, ethnic and sectarian divide, and failure of intelligence and internal security strategies generated a countrywide debate, in which experts deeply criticised the waste of financial resources by their intelligence agencies in an unnecessary proxy war in South Asia. The biggest Indian intelligence failure occurred in 1999 in the Kargil war between India and Pakistan, in which RAW failed to report infiltration of Pakistan army intelligence units into the region.[11]

Indian analyst Prem Mahadevan in his research paper (2011) spotlighted important aspects of intelligence failures in Kargil war.

He is on the opinion that Pakistani forces crossed Indian border while Indian intelligence was unable to spotlight their locations: "During the summer of 1999, India and Pakistan fought a 10-week limited war in Kargil, a remote area of Kashmir. Fighting broke out in May, when Indian troops discovered that a number of armed men had crossed the Line of Control (LOC) and entrenched themselves on the Indian side. Over the following weeks, the Indian army learned that these gunmen were not Islamist guerrillas, as it had first assumed, but Pakistani soldiers in Mufti. A security crisis erupted, with allegation of 'failure' being thrown at the Indian intelligence agencies."[12]

The Mumbai attacks (2008) unveiled a number of terrorist tactics that prevailed in the country. Those tactics and the way terrorists targeted civilians and the police were new to RAW and the IB. Once again, in Delhi policy makers began debating with the assumption that counterterrorism operations had been influenced by weak intelligence analyses in the country. They also raised the question of check and balance, while the bureaucratic and political involvement further added to their pain. The exponentially growing politicisation, radicalisation and sectarian divides within ranks of all Indian intelligence agencies including RAW and the IB, and violence against Muslims across the country painted a negative picture of the unprofessional intelligence approach to the national security of India.[13]

The Kargil Review Committee found that human intelligence aspect of Indian intelligence agencies was weak. During the Kargil war, RAW succeeded in intercepting the telephone conversation between General Musharraf and his then Chief of General Staff Lt Gen Aziz, which provided crucial evidence to international media that the operation was being controlled from military headquarters in Rawalpindi. Experts perceived it as a major intelligence success, but the Kargil Review Committee criticised RAW and military intelligence for their failure related to the absence of updated and accurate intelligence information on the induction and deinduction of military battalions, and the lack of expertise to spotlight Pakistan's military battalions in the Kargil area in 1998. After the 1965 and 1971 wars between Pakistan and India, the ISI succeeded in establishing intelligence networks across India to better understand the intention of its traditional enemy.[14]

The perception that the Indian agencies decide whatever they want without restricting themselves to the advisory role causing misunderstanding between the citizens and the state. Political rivalries, poor coordination, sectarian and political affiliations, uncorroborated reports, and lack of motivation are issues that need the immediate attention of policy makers. Moreover, numerous intelligence committees like the Henderson-Brook Committee on the Indo-China war and India's defeat in 1962; B S Raghavan IAS Committee on the failure of intelligence during the 1965 Indo-Pak war; L P Singh Committee; K.S Nair Committee; the 1999 Kargil Review Committee; and the Ram Pradhan Committee on the intelligence failure during the 2008 terrorist attacks in Mumbai have taken place after every big perceived intelligence failure.[15]

Notwithstanding the establishment of several investigation committees into the failure of intelligence in yesteryears, and the reform packages passed by parliament, the RAW, IB and military intelligence are still dancing to different tangos, and never been able to respond to a series of terrorist attacks (14 February 2019) in Kashmir. Janani Krishnaswamy (2013) in her research paper on the causes of Indian intelligence failure diverted public attention to the starting point of failures:

> "Why do our secret intelligence agencies fail repeatedly? It is because of (a) lack of adequate intelligence, (b) dearth of trained manpower in the intelligence sector, (c) lack of proper intelligence sharing between the center and the state, (d) lack of action on available intelligence, (e) the current state of political instability or (f) the lack of sensible intelligence reforms? In the aftermath of the terrorist attack at Dilsukhnagar in Hyderabad, India's secret intelligence agencies were subjected to an intense inspection. Heated political debates over the construction of the National Counterterrorism Centre (NCTC), a controversial anti-terror hub that was proposed in the aftermath of 26/11 attacks, was stirred up after five years. Are such organisation reforms sufficient to fix the problems of the intelligence

community? Intelligence reviews committees and politicians constantly assess the performance of intelligence agencies and underline numerous failures within the intelligence system."[16]

Pakistan army and its intelligence agencies are facing the same challenges on domestic and international fronts. It spends huge budget on military buildup, and luxurious enjoyment of generals. The fund the military receives from the state budget is in addition to the revenue it gets from its large business operations. Notwithstanding being rich itself, the army continues to be a burden on the country's weak economy. Political instability is endemic to Pakistan with governments alternating between legitimacy and illegitimacy and political leadership propped by the Army, does not have a free hand. That kind of government has never been able to handle economic crisis.[17] Writer and analyst Muhammad Taqi (13 March 2019) has painted an underwhelming picture of the army role in politics in a nutshell: "The problem with the army's obsession with becoming the sole arbiter of national interest and security is that it has arrogated itself the right to dictate domestic and foreign policies to suit that rather nebulous creed in which Pakistan and Islam are somehow in perpetual danger and the army is the only saviour they have. These twin delusions of paranoia and grandeur are actually feigned and self-serving to justify the outfit's chokehold on the country and its resources".[18]

The complex reciprocation among the internal and external forces fashioning Pakistan today call on to an in-depth evaluation of their influence on the country's future- in the context of both continued state stability and Pakistan's potential to jump-start broader security priorities in the region. The country maintains 32 secret agencies working under different political and bureaucratic stakeholders but failing to maintain domestic stability and support the culture of intelligence sharing on law enforcement level. Established in 1948, the ISI was tasked with acquiring intelligence of strategic interests and assessing the intensity of foreign threats, but, unfortunately, ISI was tasked by General Zia to vanquish political leadership, make alliances and recruit jihadists for Kashmir and Afghanistan. Civilian intelligence agency (Intelligence Bureau) has been gradually neglected, and phased-down during the consecutive military rule.[19] Military analysts Sanjeeb Kumar Mohanty and Jinendra Nath Mahanty (04 October 2011) in their research paper on the nexus of sectarian takfiri organizations and Pakistan army highlighted the evolution of ISI during the Zia military regime:

"The 1980s were the years when the CIA-ISI relationship blossomed, and during this period the ISI grew in strength and reach. Further, the realization the nuclear neighbours cannot fight a war without the possibility of it slipping out of control led General Zia to tap the mullahs and madrassas to wage a new covert war in India and Afghanistan". Religious movements, such as Jamaat-e-Islami and Tablighi Jammat were allowed by Zia to operate inside army barracks. In fact, the imposition of martial law in Pakistan for the first time in 1958 under General Ayub Khan brought the ISI into political realm. Moreover, Ayub gave the ISI primacy amongst the other intelligence agencies in Pakistan, like the MI (Military Intelligence) and the IB (Intelligence Bureau) because it combined in the one agency the dual roles of internal and external intelligence. The ISI however, concentrated more on internal rather than external intelligence for the first three decades...Under Zia the ISI grew in size and strength in the power structure due to the dependence of the regime on intelligence and the Afghan operation. From being an implementor of policy, the ISI became the policy maker. In fact, the imposition of martial law in Pakistan for the first time in 1958 under General Ayub Khan brought the ISI into political realm. Moreover, Ayub gave the ISI primacy amongst the other intelligence agencies in Pakistan, like the MI (Military Intelligence) and the IB (Intelligence Bureau) because it combined in the one agency the dual roles of internal and external intelligence. The ISI however, concentrated more on internal rather than external intelligence for the first three decades. Till the seventies, the organisation had a limited external agenda which was largely India-centric. This was because Pakistan had fought three wars with India and remained preoccupied with an Indian military threat to her national security".[20]

The military rulers acted like warlords and never thought about security sector reforms to make law enforcement agencies fit to the fight against anti-state elements, extremism and radicalization.

They acted for the interests of the United States-criminalized trade and agriculture, supported Talibanization in society, and introduced culture of soldiers for sale in Middle East. The state fostering of surrogate militants to serve Pakistan's strategic interests in Kashmir and Afghanistan played a crucial role in the rise of transnational jihadism. Sanjeeb Kumar Mohanty and Jinendra Nath Mahanty in their paper noted all weather relationship between the ISI and extremist organizations in South Asia and Central Asia:

"During the 1990s, several Kashmir-specific militant outfits were sponsored by Pakistan. The ISI helped create, mentor, finance and train outfits like Jaish-e-Muhammed (JeM), Harkat-ul-Mujahideen (HuM), Lashkar-e-Taiba (LeT) and several other shadowy extremist groups to fight a proxy war against Indian forces in Jammu and Kashmir, admittedly part of the larger Pakistani strategy to bleed India with thousand cuts. The Lashkar-e-Taiba and Jaish-e-Muhammad came into existence because of sympathy for Muslims in India and in Kashmir in particular. These two groups (JeM and LeT) along with Harkat-ul-Mujahideen (HuM) are involved in India-specific struggle. From 1989, indigenous Kashmiri militant outfits like the Jammu and Kashmir Liberation Front (JKLF) and pro-Pakistan Hizbul-ul-Mujahidden were used by Pakistani military. Since local militancy was on the wane by 1995 and disappointed with the performance of the local (Kashmiri) militant groups, Islamabad took direct control of the insurgency. At the end of 1995, it was reported that the ISI in collaboration with the Jamaat-e-Islami (Pakistan's oldest religio-political party), was raising a Taliban type force consisting of young students from Pakistan with the sole purpose of fighting Indian forces in Jammu and Kashmir. From the 1990s, the LeT became the ISI's favourite terrorist outfit operating in Kashmir and in the rest of India. The nineties were difficult years for India as jihadi violence aimed at splitting Indian Territory as a revenge for 1971 defeat continued. In 1971, "the Pakistani military saw the bifurcation of the country as the result of collaboration between secular nationalists and India. This led to the belief that Islamists were the most dependable political allies of the Pakistani state, especially in resisting Indian ascendancy in South Asia". Later, General Musharraf emulated Zia in supping with the Islamic elements and encouraged the ISI to foment terrorism in India using jihadis. Musharraf has been equally reluctant to crack down on groups that are fighting Indian sovereignty in Kashmir because they are serving Pakistan's national interests. His refusal to abandon the extremist assets that the Pakistani military had built up during the long years of officially sponsored jihad always remained a latent concern. During Musharraf's time, the infamous mullah-military alliance was strengthened even in the face of his growing unpopularity after joining the US-led war on terror. Since 9/11, the Pakistani military has tried to distance itself from militancy in Jammu and Kashmir under intense US and international pressure. The militant groups that had long depended on ISI support described Musharraf's U-turn on Kashmir as a betrayal of their struggle for independence. The changing nature and interpretation of the military establishment's national interests compelled Musharraf to rein in the ISI by transforming the agency from one that abetted militancy to one that combatted it"[21]

Under Muhammad Zia-ul-Haq's leadership, the Inter Services Intelligence (ISI) grew in strength and resources. The agency received further training from the Unites States in intelligence collection and technology use to effectively counter Russian intelligence in Pakistan. In 1950s, Ayub Khan also tried to fit the agency into the fight against the war of Indian spy agency RAW. The agency concentrated more on internal rather than external intelligence for the first three decades-discouraged political forces and fostered sectarian mafia groups to protect its own interests abroad. In 1980s, during the Soviet presence in Afghanistan, the ISI's strength became more important for both Pakistan and the United States. The fact is they were on great mission to disintegrate union of the Soviet. Pakistan's army encouraged jihad to throw Russian forces out of Afghanistan, and promoted the interests of the United States and its NATO allies.[22] The ISI got a chance to support its favourite guerrilla groups and co-ordinate the flow of foreign aid, including the recruitment of volunteers and graduates of local madrassas. Researchers and analysts Grant Holt and David

H. Gray in their paper (Winter-2011) highlighted the role of ISI during the Zia regime:

"The Afghan war created a leviathan and powerful intelligence agency in the ISI while Zia mandated Islamic fundamentalism and Deobandism (a strict interpretation of the Hanafi school of Sunni Islam) into their shadowy ranks. With aid from the U.S. and a pivotal and violent struggle against the Soviets in Afghanistan, the ISI cultivated a relationship with extremists from across the globe, including al-Qaeda. While being forced to adhere to fundamental Islam from the Pakistani state, the ISI itself became recognized in the international system and feared within domestic society. Throughout the 1990s, the ISI maintained its relationship with extremist networks and militants that it had established during the Afghan war to utilize in its campaign against Indian forces in Kashmir. ...Many high-profile terrorist incidents, ranging from the September 11, 2001 attacks on New York and Washington to the July 7, 2004 subway bombings in London to the November 2008 assault on Mumbai, have had direct connections to individuals and groups operating in Pakistan (Ganguly and Kapur 47). The sponsorship and recruitment of terrorist and guerilla movements against the Soviets in Afghanistan is paramount when examining historic ties between terrorism and the ISI. However, the agency also took part in, and was responsible for, numerous international operations and violent acts across the globe. The instilled radicalization from Zia and the campaigns in Afghanistan and Kashmir vetted and emboldened the ISI. Yet the agency's clandestine operations and sponsorship for violence and Islamic extremism abroad generated the attention of the international community".[23]

The involvement of military in operational mechanism and function of ISI adversely affected the agency's civilian reach. The agency was later unable to assess the importance of civilian stratification and intelligence strength of neighbouring states. Normally, civilian intelligence is stronger than the military agency as its civilian roots enable it to manage its operational capabilities. Pakistan corrupt political culture forced the agencies to look at civilian population and government with scorn. They were inculcated that the job of national security is beyond the reach of civilian governments.

Rajesh Bhushan (12 January 2019) has assessed the strength of ISI in his well-written analysis:

"Until 2018, Pakistan's Inter Service Intelligence (ISI) had around 6,000 people, which includes its handlers, agents and sources. According to German scholar Hein Kiessling, who represented the Hanns-Seidel-Foundation (Munich) in Pakistan from 1989 to 2002 said, "The (real) ISI budget is top secret, only a few people know the figure," he says. "In fact, officially the ISI budget today is between $300 and 400 million." According to Kiessling, the personnel strength of ISI is also considered as top secret. "During Zia-ul Haq's tenure it was estimated to be 20,000 men. In the 1990s and in the new millennium there were drastic reductions in personnel. "Therefore, it is now assumed that ISI's base strength is approximately 4,000. Higher estimates often encountered in literature and the press is grossly exaggerated." Hein Kiessling said changes in personnel policies came out in 2009 under the command of Pakistan Army Chief General Ashfaq Parvez Kayani. "Today with the exception of six-seven two-star generals, the military personnel in ISI come from the Intelligence Corps of the army —a move that serves towards the professionalism of the service. "A military-ISI staff member starts his career as a cadet in combat arms, not in the medical or engineering services. "After completing basic training comes an intelligence exam. The successful candidate goes on to become an officer in the Intelligence Corps, where he goes through additional courses," Kiessling said. It may be mentioned here that Pakistani ISI actually became financially strong during the Afghan war against Soviet Union as during that time, it was receiving hundreds of millions of dollars from the US and Saudi Arabia".[24]

Miltablishment used agencies against politicians and its critics to punish them for criticizing corruption of Generals and their cronies. They punished those who wrote stories of forced disappearances, and torture of innocent writers. The ISI professional approach of intelligence mechanism never improved due to its prolixit involvement in politics. Its internal security approach revolves around the military way of governance. Dr Bidanda M Chengappa noted some aspects of ISI relationship with Afghan Mujahideen:

"Thereafter from the early 1980s the ISI provided strong support to the Afghan mujahideen against Soviet occupation forces there and ultimately proved successful due to the material resources provided by the US. It is aptly stated that the victory was possible on account of "American weaponry and Afghan bravery". The import of the ISI involvement in Afghanistan is that the ISI developed close working relations with the CIA and Saudi intelligence organisations. More significantly the ISI developed enormous hands-on expertise to wage a proxy war in terms of handling logistics on an international scale, training Afghan guerillas in low intensity conflict operations (LICO) and intelligence-gathering activities under hostile conditions. The ISI has developed close linkages with various Islamic fundamentalist organisations like the Lashkar-e-Taiba and Harkat-ul-Mujahideen. The ISI funds their activities like para-military training and procurement of arms to wage are against the Indian State. This ISI nexus with fundamentalist parties provides the agency with manpower which can be mobilised as 'street power' to agitate against or support a political party which has taken a decision with national, regional, political, social or economic ramifications. To that extent, the ISI has some leverage to influence decision making owing to its ability to operate through fundamentalist parties".[25]

The ISI is no doubt a competent intelligence agency, and is an asset of the nation, but military and political leadership used it against political opponents. This policy of both political and military establishments destroyed the professional capabilities of the agency. The ISI was used against politicians, writers, critics, and journalists who criticized weak and incompetent security approach. In fact, this is the point in which prompted cleft between the ISI and IB. Ergo, cold war between the IB and ISI badly affected their domestic security mechanism[26]. In his research paper, Dr Bidanda M Chengappa has argued that ISI was mainly controlled and used by military against democratic government in Pakistan:

"Apparently the ISI is controlled either by the military or the political leadership depending on whichever is in power. The DG-I, as the head of the ISI is known, is an appointment made by the Prime Minister in consultation with the Chief of Army Staff (COAS). The DG-I reports to the Prime Minister considering the ISI has a political section to handle internal intelligence duties. However, the army appears to dictate the policy towards India even when the country has an elected leader. To that extent it would be appropriate to state that the PM has a degree of control over the ISI's involvement in internal affairs which the Chief of Army Staff oversees the external role of the agency. The rationale for the evolution of the intelligence service into an extra-constitutional power centre is multi-faceted and encompasses military strategy, martial law, involvement in the clandestine nuclear programme, covert support to para-military operations in the Afghan jehad and linkages with fundamental parties. While some of these causes have internal dimensions, some are completely external".[27]

In books and newspapers, there are stories about the failure of intelligence agencies in Pakistan to undermine terrorism and extremism. Recruitment from business community, wealthy and landlord societies, generals and political families for intelligence agencies prompted bureaucratic culture. Intelligentsia and political circles have often pointed to the fact that involvement of the agency in political confrontations badly affected its professional credibility. Some circles are trying to radicalize agencies, but the big concern is that all military, civilian and policing agencies have already 'purified' their souls in Tablighi congregations in Raiwand. Sectarian elements within the IB and ISI ranks are purveying secret information about the planning of political parties and military leadership, to their favourite religious and political leaders. Secondly, military intelligence agencies do not cooperate with civilian intelligence agencies on national security issues.[28] The ISI never extended a hand of cooperation to civilian intelligence agencies, or even considered IB as an older civilian brother, over the past five decades. General Musharraf removed some sectarian and radicalized element from the ISI in 2003. Analyst Taha Siddiqui (06 May 2019) noted some aspect of the ISI involvement in politics:

"Domestically, he is known to have manipulated Pakistani politics both covertly and overtly, and was instrumental in doing so in his last stint during the era of General Pervez Musharraf who ruled Pakistan from 1999 to 2008. Internationally, he is known to have linkages with jihadist organisations, including al-Qaeda, the Afghan Taliban as well as Kashmir and India-focused groups.......When Musharraf imposed martial law on October 12, 1999, Brigadier Shah was the director of the Inter-Services Intelligence (ISI) in Punjab, Pakistan's largest and politically dominant province. Thus, he became an important ally in the general's attempt at reshaping the politics of the region. Under Shah, the Intelligence Bureau became Musharraf's eyes and ears. It reported directly to the military dictator and helped him continue a countrywide 'political engineering' project. But it's not just political manipulation under General Musharraf that Brigadier Shah is known for. He was also the key to the rapid Talibanisation of the tribal belt next to the Pak-Afghan border, when Pakistan joined the so-called War on Terror in Afghanistan, led by the United States of America and its ally's post 9/11. The most incriminating allegation against Shah yet is by the assassinated former Prime Minister Benazir Bhutto, who first named him as one of the suspects behind the suicide bombing targeting her on arrival in October 2007 in the city of Karachi. Bhutto survived the attack that left at least 180 people dead. She named him again in a letter made public after her death, saying Brigadier Shah should be investigated if she were assassinated. Bhutto had alleged that Shah was conspiring with terrorists to carry out her assassination. On December 27, Bhutto met the fate she had already predicted, and the-then Musharraf government blamed Pakistani terrorist groups. At this time, Brigadier Shah was still heading the Intelligence Bureau (IB) of Pakistan, but retired soon after, in March 2008".[29]

The CIA influence on the ISI operational mechanism and domestic policy making causing misunderstanding between civilian and military stakeholders. The agency's reluctant cooperation with law enforcement agencies, and its grudging intelligence sharing with naval and air agencies, also caused disappointment among different stakeholders.[30] Involvement of high ranking officers of the agencies in corruption and land-grabbing cases is matter of great concern for policy makers. They misuse secret funds, and even purchased houses in Europe and the UK. On 01 August 2001, Indian analyst B. Raman in his research paper (No-287) noted some aspects of the evaluation of ISI during the Zia-ul-Haq regime:

"Zia-ul-Haq expanded the internal intelligence responsibilities of the ISI by making it responsible not only for the collection of intelligence about the activities of the Sindhi nationalist elements in Sindh and for monitoring the activities of Shia organisations all over the country after the success of the Iranian Revolution in 1979, but also for keeping surveillance on the leaders of the Pakistan People's Party (PPP) of Mrs. Benazir Bhutto and its allies which had started the Movement for the Restoration of Democracy (MRD) in the early 1980s.The ISI's Internal Political Division had Shah Nawaz Bhutto, one of the two brothers of Mrs. Benazir Bhutto, assassinated through poisoning in the French Riviera in the middle of 1985, in an attempt to intimidate her into not returning to Pakistan for directing the movement against Zia, but she refused to be intimidated and returned to Pakistan. The Afghan war of the 1980s saw the enhancement of the covert action capabilities of the ISI by the CIA. A number of officers from the ISI's Covert Action Division received training in the US and many covert action experts of the CIA were attached to the ISI to guide it in its operations against the Soviet troops by using the Afghan Mujahideen, Islamic fundamentalists of Pakistan and Arab volunteers. Osama bin Laden, Mir Aimal Kansi, who assassinated two CIA officers outside their office in Langley, US, in 1993, Ramzi Yousef and his accomplices involved in the New York World Trade Centre explosion in February, 1993, the leaders of the Muslim separatist movement in the southern Philippines and even many of the narcotics smugglers of Pakistan were the products of the ISI-CIA collaboration in Afghanistan".[31]

Since the departure of Pervez Musharraf in 2008, the military pledged its commitment to protect democracy, but it is a strong hyperbole, the army continues to humiliate elected Prime Ministers, and consistently undermining civilian governments to maintain military prerogatives. The army never allowed ISI to help democratic governments in the process of economic and political stabilization. The IB is under resources, while its leadership has retrieved policing training, and acts like a police officer. There is an opposition between law enforcement and intelligence, because the two entities are very different.[32] In his research paper, Dr Bidanda M Chengappa has argued that ISI is mainly controlled and used by military against democratic government in Pakistan:

"Apparently the ISI is controlled either by the military or the political leadership depending on whichever is in power. The DG-I, as the head of the ISI is known, is an appointment made by the Prime Minister in consultation with the Chief of Army Staff (COAS). The DG-I reports to the Prime Minister considering the ISI has a political section to handle internal intelligence duties. However, the army appears to dictate the policy towards India even when the country has an elected leader. To that extent it would be appropriate to state that the PM has a degree of control over the ISI's involvement in internal affairs which the Chief of Army Staff oversees the external role of the agency. The rationale for the evolution of the intelligence service into an extra-constitutional power centre is multi-faceted and encompasses military strategy, martial law, involvement in the clandestine nuclear program, covert support to para-military operations in the Afghan jehad and linkages with fundamental parties. While some of these causes have internal dimensions, some are completely external"[33]

The unending resultant tussle between civilian and military intelligence agencies forced former Prime Minister Nawaz Sharif to restructure the IB and make it more effective to counter ISI's influence in political institutions. The Prime Minister allocated huge funds to the IB to recruit and employ more agents to meet the country's internal and external challenges.[34] The greatest challenge Nawaz Sharif faced was on the national security front. The miltablishment was not happy with his national security approach.[35] The Intelligence Bureau is the country's main civilian intelligence agency, and functions under the direct control of the Prime Minister, tackling terrorism, insurgency and extremism. Over the last four decades, the ISI operated in changing security environment, but it mostly targeted democracy and political parties, strengthened miltablishment and its illegal business.[36] The ISI, the MI and the IB assumed more controversial proportions than ever before. Journalist and expert Abbas Nasir (Herald, January 1991) describes the way intelligence targets politician in many ways to retrieve information:

"On a freezing December day in Islamabad, MNA Dr. Imran Farooq, ordered the maintenance staff of the MNA hostel to service his room heater. The staff took down the gas heater, only to discover a device that didn't belong there taped to its back. Noticing that there were batteries attached to it, they immediately became alarmed and summoned the bomb disposal squad. Being experts at their job, the members of the bomb squad soon allayed the perturbed MNA's fears that the device was not a bomb of any sort. Instead, they said, they had discovered a powerful transmitter that was being used to bug the MQM MNA's room. While the federal interior minister was quick to order an inquiry into the affair, the MQM blamed the former PPP government for bugging Dr. Farooq's room. The real culprit, however, is still to be identified. A few days earlier, a heated debate in parliament had focused on the activities of our intelligence agencies as being "rather over-extended". As the range of intelligence operations came under discussion, the fact that their agencies were maintaining files and tapes – not only on all politicians in the country, but many non-political civilians as well – drew the wrath of many MNAs of all political shades. Finally, Speaker Gohar Ayub tried to round up the debate, not only by ordering a select committee to look into the matter, but also admitting that "we have all been the target of intelligence agencies."[37]

Abbas Nasir is a senior journalist who knows how Pakistani intelligence agencies are spying on citizens and politician, and how they violate their right of privacy. The evolution of ISI through different states made the agency capable to spy on civilian population. Former Prime Minister Zulfiqar Ali Bhutto was the only person who realized the importance of a strong and competent intelligence agency in enhancing the goal of foreign policy. He created the political desk of ISI, and dragged it into national political game. The agency supported Bhutto, and he also used ISI it for recuperation of nuclear materials. Bhutto was a committed leader as he had promised the nation a nuclear Pakistan, but unfortunately, military dictator dematerialized his dream. Abbas Nasir noted the zeal of Mr. Bhutto to make professionalize:

"According to him, Bhutto chose the ISI to be the premier agency because he could accomplish two tasks with it. The first related to the country's foreign policy and the second to self-preservation, as only a services intelligence agency could look into the army itself and keep Bhutto abreast with the mood and the sentiment in the forces. This part of history also had its ironical twists. It is widely believed that Bhutto promoted General Zia as the army chief, superseding several far more senior and well-reputed lieutenant generals, because the DG of the ISI had recommended him as the most "reliable and loyal" choice for the coveted post. It was no coincidence then, that when Bhutto was overthrown, Lt General Ghulam Jilani was retained as the DG of the ISI. Jilani remained one of the most trusted Zia lieutenants for a number of years, both as DG and later as the governor of Punjab. While Jilani was the governor of Punjab, he made a decision that would create obstacles in the path of the PPP for years to come. He plucked a young industrialist from relative obscurity and nurtured him as a civilian alternative to the PPP leadership. The young man would be prime minister one day. To this day, Jilani remains Nawaz Sharif's key mentor".[38]

Prime Minister Benazir Bhutto strengthened the role of the Intelligence Bureau (IB) to collect intelligence information for her government, and used it against opposition parties and ISI as well. There has been a clash of interest between the ISI and the IB management in 1990s. Some investigative reports were prepared by the IB management against the ISI interference in its internal affairs. Both the ISI and IB were trying to get the favour of Prime Minister. Prime Minister Benazir created 20 senior positions at the joint director level to strengthen the management structure in the organisation.[39] Dr. Bidanda M. Chengappa explains the role of ISI and IB against civilian government in Pakistan:

"In post–Zia Pakistan, intelligence agencies were effectively used to topple governments. One such case pertains to how an intelligence agency was used to remove then Prime Minister Benazir Bhutto from office. It has been reported that on July 17, 1989 an intelligence agency clandestinely recorded the conversation between then Prime Ministers Benazir and Rajiv Gandhi while the latter was on a state visit to Pakistan. The room was bugged by the intelligence agency and the two leaders in the course of their private meeting at Islamabad discussed, among other issues, the possibility of mutual troop reduction. Apparently, Benazir was supposed to have agreed in principle to the proposal. Soon thereafter the Chief of Army Staff (COAS) General Mirza Aslam Beg and President Ghulam Ishaq Khan met each other on July 24, 1989 and decided to topple the Benazir government. In order to convince the Opposition and obtain their backing for the need to destabilise the government these tapes were reportedly played to them. It essentially had the desired effect and successfully influenced the Opposition parties to side with the COAS and the President against Benazir Bhutto".[40]

In 2008, President Asif Ali Zardari decided to curtail the influence of military establishment in politics and ordered the Interior Ministry to bring ISI under the Interior Ministry, but within 24 hours, the President had to withdraw his orders. The ISI's primary aim (Shuja Nawaz-2011) has been 'counterintelligence and espionage, especially aimed at India, where it has been fairly successful, but the IB was countering political parties. Prominent analyst B. Raman in his paper highlighted political confrontation, and the role of army in overthrowing democratic government. Prime Minister Nawaz Sharif warned Mullah Omer to stop supporting Sepah Sahaba and cooperate with the United States.[41] The army didn't like this way of treating their proxies by the Prime Minister. B. Raman has noted aspects of the whole saga:

"The third instance was during the second tenure of Nawaz Sharif (1997-99) when his action in appointing Lt. Gen. Ziauddin, an engineer, as the DG ISI, over-riding the objection of Gen. Musharraf led to the first friction between the two. Gen. Musharraf transferred Lt. Gen. Mohammad Aziz, the then DDG ISI on his promotion as Lt. Gen to the GHQ as the CGS and transferred the entire Joint Intelligence North (JIN), responsible for covert actions in India and Afghanistan to the Directorate-General of Military Intelligence (DGMI) to be supervised by Lt. Gen. Aziz.

It is believed that the JIN continues to function under the DGMI even after the appointment of Lt. Gen. Mahmood Ahmed as the DG, ISI, after the overthrow of Sharif on October 12, 1999. Gen. Musharraf, as the COAS, stopped inviting Lt. Gen Ziauddin to the Corps Commanders conferences. He kept Lt. Gen Ziauddin totally out of the picture in the planning and implementation of the Kargil operations. After the Kargil war, Nawaz Sharif had sent Lt. Gen. Ziauddin to Washington on a secret visit to inform the Clinton Administration officials of his concerns over the continued loyalty of Gen. Musharraf. After his return from the US, Lt. Gen Ziauddin went to Kandahar, as ordered by Sharif, to pressurise Mullah Mohammad Omar, the Amir of the Taliban, to stop assisting the anti-Shia Sipah Sahaba Pakistan and to co-operate with the US in the arrest and deportation of bin Laden. On coming to know of this, Gen. Musharraf sent Lt. Gen. Aziz to Kandahar to tell the Amir that he should not carry out the instructions of Lt. Gen. Ziauddin and that he should follow only his (Lt. Gen. Aziz's) instructions".[42]

Prime Minister Nawaz Sharif experienced the same challenges as a head of the IJI-led government which also resorted to using intelligence agencies to gain unfair advantage in domestic politics. The IB spied on MQM leaders and installed intelligence monitors devices in their rooms and houses. However, Army Chief General Asif Nawaz Janjua was killed, and FIR was filed against Brigadier Imtiaz, the Director of Intelligence Bureau (DIB). The General's wife Nuzhat Janjua's formal complaint to the then President Ghulam Ishaq Khan about the unnatural death of her husband raised several important questions.[43] Dr. Bidanda M. Chengappa has noted some important aspects of General Asif Nawaz Janjua murder:

"Nuzhat Janjua suspected that her late husband had been poisoned with arsenic administered in a cup of tea served to him at a meeting of the Joint Chiefs of Staff Committee meeting. Some political commentators have also pointed out that his widow must have made the formal complaint on the basis of some strong grounds and that the bereaved lady would not make such an attempt for political purposes. Interestingly the government posted a police picket at the general's grave in order to ensure that the body was not exhumed for medical inspection. There were rumours that the general's stomach was removed prior to the burial to avoid detection of foul play. The issue snowballed in April 1993 as the Army adopted an open-minded approach to the possibility of foul play behind the general's death. The rationale for discussing General Asif Nawaz Janjua's death in such great detail is only because if the conspiracy theory is valid then the tacit role of intelligence agencies is bound to assume relevance. To that extent this could well be one more instance of intelligence agencies interfering in internal politics. The incident illustrates how even an Army chief was vulnerable to the machinations of the intelligence agencies despite the power that is associated with his office".[44]

Chapter 2

Militarisation of Intelligence, Dematerialization of Civilian Intelligence and a War of Strength between the Military and Civilian Spy Agencies

The challenges of democratic consolidation and security sector reform lies in the fact that in Pakistan, there is little public awareness about the function and operation of intelligence agencies. Books on intelligence and its operational mechanism are not recommended in colleges and universities syllabuses. Major political and religious parties have no basic knowledge of the organization of intelligence. For this reason, this book will be the prime source of knowledge for politicians and civil society. The book contains basic knowledge of the manner of intelligence operation and its role in politics.[1] Thus, ignorance about intelligence communities is combined with fear, which perpetuates inadequate dissemination of information.[2] In modern states, security and intelligence agencies play a vital role in support of government in its domestic, defence and foreign policies by supplying and analysing relevant intelligence and countering specified threats.[3]

Pakistani intelligence agencies have been shaping governments, parliaments, and dissolve it while the interests of military establishment are not served. This is a catchphrase, and a verbalism appearing in newspapers and intellectual debates since 1980s.[4] International media have also published numerous articles that highlight the role of intelligence agencies in politics and judicial matter in Pakistan. I am not going to discredit ISI or criticise the

40

IB to make my debate engrossing, because ISI is a professional intelligence agency of the country, and the IB is a policing agency. Stakeholders of both the agencies need to fix some cleft in the wall.[5] On 22 October 2019, Dr. Niaz Murtaza in his article sternly criticised military rulers and their involvement in politics. Dr. Murtaza also argued that policies of dictators caused extremism and social alienation:

> "Zia ruled for 11 years with absolute powers, guided by security-phobic lenses and with little regard for public welfare. Obviously, it would take highly capable rulers with a concern for public welfare, long tenures and full powers to undo this harm. No civilian has had the longevity or full powers to do so. His army successor Musharraf had these luxuries. But despite his enlightened moderation mantra, his policies turned Zia-era extremism into huge terrorism as he too was guided by security-phobic rather than public welfare lenses. Today, Pakistan has a sullied global reputation. The economy is industrially stagnant and suffers large deficits and debt. Politics suffers from instability, corruption, incompetence and agencies' control. Society is bigoted and intolerant with little space for freedom of thought and speech. All these reflect the corrosion of basic societal structures and the undermining of social, political, economic and national capacities primarily under Zia".[6]

Criticism is not resentment. Criticism builds societies and improves the capacity of state institutions. Not only Pakistan, intelligence in every South Asian state has weaknesses and lack of professional approach to national security challenges, but it doesn't mean they are unable to protect the interests of their own states.[7] On 25 September 2017, New Delhi Times-Pakistan Bureau noted elements of state within the state in Pakistan, and argued that IB and ISI spy on all parliamentarian, politicians, and opposition parties.[8] The newspaper also elucidated that their way of business has caused consternation among social and political stratifications:

"Over decades the role and scale of Pakistan's intelligence agencies have mutated beyond prescribed functions to major foreign and domestic policy areas, earning them dubious sobriquet of a 'State within a State'. The three key agencies- the ISI, the MI and the IB – have assumed more controversial, undercover roles invariably at odds with even each other. The parliament hotly debated their 'rather over-extended' activities like maintaining files and tapes on all politicians and many non-political civilians. Politicians either ordered spying on the opposition or were themselves the target of such 'special attention'. Speaker admitted 'we have all been the target of intelligence agencies' before ordering a select committee to look into the matter. The intelligence set up is a well-oiled, super-efficient machine, and one of the best organised befitting strategic geo-political situation of Pakistan whose very creation and the consequent sub continental environment generated hostility. Its security and survival depended on their efficiency, but civilian psyche now detests their role in foreign and domestic policies as secretive agencies are anathema to the open, consultative or accountable nature of democratic systems. The concession to intelligence agencies enhanced the size and scope of their activities. The Inter-services Intelligence Directorate existed before but evolved and grew tremendously during Bhutto's regime after the humiliating 1971 war leading to Bangladesh separation. Bhutto utilised the ISI for two tasks- the foreign policy and self preservation by constantly monitoring the pulse of the army and keeping abreast of their sentiments. Nuclear programme facilitated more funds and leeway for ISI. The irony is, Bhutto promoted General Zia as the army chief, superseding several far more senior, reputed generals, based on ISI recommendation that Zia is the most 'reliable and loyal' choice. Jilani, DG of ISI, as trusted Zia lieutenant, survived Bhutto's ouster. Made governor of Punjab, he created obstacles for the PPP by nurturing Nawaz Sharif as a civilian alternative; he still remains Nawaz's key mentor to date".[9]

The political role of Pakistan's intelligence agencies has become even more crucial for the military domination. On 22 July, 2018, Mr. Justice Shaukat Aziz Siddiqui levelled serious allegations against the ISI that the agency's interference in judicial affairs that badly affected the independence of judiciary. Addressing the Rawalpindi Bar Association, Mr. Justice Siddiqui professed that the Inter-Services Intelligence (ISI) "manipulating judicial proceedings as its officials manage to constitute benches at its will and mark cases to selected judges".[10] "The ISI approached the Chief Justice of the Islamabad High Court (IHC) and told him that the agency doesn't want release of Nawaz Sharif and his daughter before elections." He said. Mr. Justice Siddiqui divulged: "I know how messages have been conveyed to the Supreme Court; I know where the record of proceedings of the accountability court was dispatched every day and why the statutory provisions allowing the IHC to exercise administrative control of the accountability court was ceased. This was to stop the IHC judges to monitor the trial proceedings."[11]

The Secretary of the Supreme Judicial Council (SJC), and the registrar of the Supreme Court of Pakistan, submitted a note to the SJC to consider the allegations levied by Justice Shaukat Aziz, in particular the manipulation of the judiciary by the ISI. This was accepted by the Chairman of the SJC as a matter requiring attention and he directed the Chief Justice of the Islamabad High Court to respond to the allegations made against him by Justice Shaukat Aziz.[12] The judge said that officials of the secret agency were expecting a favourable response from him over their offer "but he flatly refused and replied that he would prefer to die than sell his conscience." "I don't care about my job. I even know the consequences of sharing the truth with you but I am not afraid even if I am assassinated," Justice Siddiqui said.[13] He also said that the bar and the bench were from the same family "but our home has been invaded by armed men and independence of the judiciary has been usurped". Consequently, after two months, President Dr. Arif Alvi removed Justice Shaukat Aziz Siddiqui on the recommendations of the Supreme Judicial Council (SJC).[14]

The SJC headed by Chief Justice of Pakistan Mian Saqib Nisar. Mr. Nisar ruled: "This council is unanimously of the opinion that in the matter of making his speech before the District Bar Association, Rawalpindi, on July 21, 2018, Mr. Justice Shaukat Aziz Siddiqui, Judge of Islamabad High Court, had displayed conduct unbecoming of Judge of a High Court and was, thus, guilty of misconduct and he is, therefore, liable to be removed from his office under Article 209(6) of the Constitution of the Islamic Republic of Pakistan, 1973.[15]" Mr. Justice Siddiqui said that SJC took up 'baseless reference' against him about renovation of his official residence. Dawn reported.[16] On 30 April 2019, Dr. Faqir Hussain (Pakistan Today) in his article noted some aspects of Mr. Justice Siddiqui's allegations against the Inter-Service Intelligence (ISI):

> "The Supreme Court admitted for hearing the petition of Mr. Justice Shaukat Aziz Siddiqui, former Judge of Islamabad High Court, who had challenged his removal by the Supreme Judicial Council (SJC). It is somewhat unprecedented because of the prohibition, imposed by Article 211 of the Constitution, which debars the jurisdiction of "any court" in the matter. Further, the Karachi Bar Council decided to become a party to the case and deputed two of its eminent members to argue the matter. Mr. Justice Siddiqui was a vocal critic of the government and establishment, often making remarks against them for exceeding authority and committing excesses, which came to light during the hearing of cases. Such criticism was not well received. As a judge, he possessed some unique qualities. He could stand pressure from the high and mighty, and reprimanded lawyers for coming unprepared, spurning their demands for strikes or requests for undue adjournments. Certainly, he was not amongst the special breed of judges who only "speak through their judgments". Giving a media-savvy appearance, he often expressed himself during hearings, and had the knack to drag religion into sociopolitical matters, which attracted public rebuke/criticism.[17]

Moreover, social media and newspapers criticised the removal of Justice Siddiqui. All political circles and opposition parties regretted and warned that these traditions must not prevail in Pakistan. If we look at the structure and policies of Prime Minister Imran Khan's government, we can easily guess and calculate the interests of establishment. Global Village (21 October, 2018) in its news analysis also highlighted details of the removal of Mr. Justice Siddiqui by President Dr. Alvi:

"According to details, the decision was taken under Article 209(5) on the SJC's recommendation under Article 209(6) read with Article 48(1) of the Constitution, read a notification issued by the Ministry of Law and Justice. "Consequent upon proceedings under Article 209(5) and recommendations of the Supreme Judicial Council of Pakistan under Article 209(6) read with Article 48(1) of the Constitution of the Islamic Republic of Pakistan, 1973...... The President of Pakistan has been pleased to remove Justice Shaukat Aziz Siddiqui, Judge, Islamabad High Court, Islamabad, from his office with immediate effect," reads the notification issued by the Ministry of Law and Justice..............A few months ago, Mr. Siddiqui lambasted at spy agencies of the country and held them accountable for many upsetting political and security challenges in Pakistan. Hearing the case of missing persons, the high court judge appealed to Chief of Army Staff General Qamar Javed Bajwa for "barring his persons from intervention in the matters of other institutions," adding that the army chief should take notice of the alarming situation. He claimed, "Judges' lives are in danger as their telephones are being tapped by the officials of the security agencies". Addressing a representative of the Inter-Services Intelligence (ISI), who appeared in the court, Mr. Siddiqui said: "Your personnel try to form a court bench of their own wish and the army chief should be aware of the misdeeds committed by them". Mr. Siddiqui warned the spy agencies not to cross their constitutional limits and perform their duties according to the constitution of the country. Just a day before Mr. Siddiqui made these comments, the CEO of Dawn Hameed Haroon was jolted by BBC's Stephen Sackur when he leveled some allegations against the security agencies of Pakistan.[18]

Civilian control over intelligence agencies and parliamentary oversight in Pakistan is impossible without the consent of miltablishment. The fact is, they are an asset of military establishment that use them against politicians. Every agency in the country is above the law and they are free to detain, kidnap and harass civilians in many ways. General Musharraf not only sold his countrymen to the CIA, but also killed tortured and humiliated thousands of children and women. General Shahid Aziz, who worked with Gen Musharraf unveiled secrets of his government in an interview with journalist Hamid Mir. Musharraf was passionate to make ISI a strong arm of his government.[19] He was mentioning the support of ISI to his illegal military government in every forum, interview and statement, but he also knew that he illegally expelled more than 100 competent, educated, and religious officers of ISI from 2002-2005.

In September 2001, Pervez Musharraf appointed a new Director-General for ISI, Lieutenant General Ehsanul Haq who was later on replaced by Lieutenant General Shuja Pasha, because he was close to China. On 3 November 2007, Musharraf declared emergency rule across Pakistan and suspended the Constitution, imposed a state of emergency, and fired the Chief Justice of the Supreme Court again. In Islamabad, troops entered the Supreme Court building, arrested the judges and kept them detained in their homes. Independent and international television channels went off air. Public protests were mounted against Musharraf.[20] Research scholar Frederic Grare (18 December 2015) highlights political developments after the departure of General Musharraf in 2008:

> "Since the departure of Pervez Musharraf in 2008, the military has pledged its commitment to protecting democracy. Yet it has consistently undermined the civilian government to maintain military prerogatives and, if not establish direct control of the state. It has also attempted to secure a power-sharing arrangement guarantying military authority over key sectors such as defense, foreign affairs, or internal security. As a result, most analysts regard the Pakistani army as the true center of power in those matters. Following the 2008 elections, the Pakistani military has successfully inserted itself into the political sphere during the post-Musharraf administrations. This is evident in military's consolidation of power during the civilian regimes of Asif Ali Zardari and Nawaz Sharif. Pervez Kayani, Chief of Army Staff (COAS) during the presidency of Asif Zardari, "was very much part of Pakistan's political machinery even while cultivating meticulously the impression at home and abroad that he [was] a professional officer waiting for the civilian to lead" (Fair 2011: 580). He never ceased

to manipulate the system, shrewdly using the judiciary to pressure the president and make him more amenable to the army's desires. A similar game is currently in play against the administration of Nawaz Sharif. In both cases, the military's resentment of the mainstream political establishment stems from the attempts of the civilian government to assert its control over foreign policy and, more specifically, over Pakistan's policy vis-à-vis India and Afghanistan. Relations with India in particular are viewed as an existential issue by the security establishment, and constitute a clear divide between the civilian and military authorities. The military has previously taken dramatic action to establish its autonomy over Pakistan's policy toward India".[21]

On 13 February 2015, Dawn newspaper reported former military ruler Gen (retd) Pervez Musharraf's yell for an end to militant proxies in Afghanistan. In his exclusive interview with Guardian newspaper (2015), Musharraf admitted that he had ordered ISI to train suicide bombers and send them back to Afghanistan to weaken the Karzai government in Kabul. "In President Karzai's times, yes, indeed, he was damaging Pakistan and therefore we were working against his interest. Obviously, we had to protect our own interest," Musharraf said. He also admitted that: "Pakistan had its own proxies; India had its proxies, which is unhealthy. I do admit this, it is most unhealthy. It is not in favour of Afghanistan, or Pakistan or India. It must stop," he said. Former army chief asserted that ISI trained Taliban: "Obviously we were looking for some groups to counter this Indian action against Pakistan," he said. "That is where the intelligence work comes in. Intelligence was in contact with Taliban groups. Definitely, they were in contact, and they should be."[22]

Musharraf first used ISI against politicians and then discredited the agency in his interview with the British newspaper. He, however, purportedly involved ISI in training suicide bomber, and gave the impression that the agency was directly involved in acts of terrorism in Afghanistan. After Musharraf, the role of agencies in decision-making process remained strong; while President Zardari ordered the control of ISI under Interior Ministry, but his dream vanished due to a stern reaction of military establishment.[23]The military was making alliances through ISI's social and political contacts. This untraditional way of making alliances affected the popularity of the agency.[24] However; Dr. Suba Chandran (2008) has further highlighted the issue of civilian control over the ISI. He also elucidated weakness and fear of civilian government to bring ISI under Interior Ministry, because the Zardari regime was threatened of dire consequences before the implementation of the plan he designed:

> "On 26 July 2008, the Pakistan People's Party (PPP) led government surprised everyone by bringing the ISI under civilian control, through a memorandum. The memorandum placed the administrative, operational and financial control of both the ISI and the IB under the Interior Ministry. The stated objective of this change was to improve coordination among various intelligence organisations and the need to work with the civilian authorities; to avoid the army acquiring a bad name (by associating with the ISI). However, in reality, the notification was born out of fear, pressure and an anxiety to control the ISI. The PPP has always been uncomfortable with the ISI. Its role in assembling an anti-PPP coalition–the Islamic Jamhoori Ittehad (IJI)–in the 1980s to prevent Benazir from assuming power after the death of Zia is well known. Ever since the ISI has worked against the interests of the PPP, it played an important role in her removal from the post of Prime Minister–both in 1990 and in 1996. In turn, the PPP also attempted to curb the role and influence of the ISI. During her first tenure as prime minister, Benazir Bhutto attempted to bring the ISI under control. From Benazir's forced exile to Zardari's arrest and the attempts to split the party, the PPP considers the ISI as the main force behind all anti-PPP activities.[25]

Dr. Nasreen Akhtar in her dissertation to The School of Politics and International Relations of Quaid-i-Azam University Islamabad, described civil-military relations during the Zardari government in Pakistan with different perspectives. President Zardari strived to establish good relationship with the army, but due to his government's massive corruption and his personal resentment against the ISI clefts further opened up, and his government experienced irksome situation while military establishment threatened him of dire consequences. Dr. Nasreen also argued that President Zardari had pushed military establishment to the wall:

"In the background of four military interventions in Pakistan's politics and the emergence of security establishment as a centre of power within the structure of the state, this study explores civil-military relation in the post-military regime (2008-2012). Unlike in the past, we witness that a weak and unpopular civilian government of Zardari, despite facing many challenges, survived and completed its tenure for the first time in the history of the country. The central question we address is how it became possible? Was it due to the structural changes in the society or on account of self-assessment of the military leadership of its role essentially as professional soldiers to provide security to the country? Actually, it is an expansive definition of national security that has brought the military into politics besides imbalance in the power of the military and the civilian sectors. For that reason, the self-reassessment is not what it seems would chart a new course for the military rather it provided the post-Musharraf civilian government led by Zardari, a space to flourish, watched its performance, orientations and handling of national security. What is evident in this case study is that while the military watched its interests carefully, protected its influence over national security and critical foreign relations, at the same time it allowed the Zardari regime to complete its tenure."[26]

In September 2008, Zardari became the President, and entered an agreement with Nawaz Sharif under the Murree declaration in 9 March 2008, and decided to reinstate 60 judges sacked by Musharraf. In December 2009, the Supreme Court ruled that the National Reconciliation Ordinance amnesty was unconstitutional, and President Zardari had immunity from prosecution. The removal of NRO challenged the legality of his Presidency due to his massive corruption cases.[27] Dr. Nasreen Akhtar highlighted his political journey and challenges:

"While combating the internal and external challenges and efforts to complete its tenure, the Zardari-led regime made a history in two important aspects. First, as indicated earlier, it completed its tenure of full five years, the term of the Parliament. Second, it transferred power to its rival party, the PML-N when the later won majority in the 2013 elections.......On the other hand, we see the military spreading out on several fronts in the country due to many internal security challenges with terrorism on the top of list along with insurgency in Balochistan and the proliferation of sectarian and Jihadi organisation connected with transnational radical Islamic movements. There was an image problem for the military as well. Musharraf's decision to align Pakistan with the US in War on Terror and use of the military power to eradicate groups that were once the allies of the state in Afghanistan was not popular, at least with the religious sections of the society. The overthrow of a popular political government of Nawaz Sharif when his party enjoyed two-third majority, humiliating treatment of the judiciary and unnecessary use of force in Balochistan had badly tarnished the image of the armed forces. However, the post-Musharraf military institution developed its consensus to restore their positive image by not overthrowing civilian government".[28]

According to Muhammad Hassan, Pakistan represents an example of how military could be slowly drawn into the political field due to the failure of political institutions and politicians, low political mobilization, as well as external factors. The real extent of the military's control over foreign policy and, by contrast, the degree of freedom of elected governments in conducting foreign policy cannot be determined without assessing the impact of public opinion on foreign policy matters.[29] The agencies and miltablishment have been hurting political leadership time and again to make a peace in state institutions, but President Zardari never genuflected. Consequentially, he was openly threatened of murder and humiliation by military agencies and the GHQ. Major Pakistani newspapers published military intransigencies on their front pages.[30]

Involvement of civilian intelligence agencies in politics raised important questions that this way of business can affect professional mechanism of the IB and CID. Mr. Nawaz Sharif once released a secret tape to make the Benazir government controversial, and the ISI distributed money among loyal candidates.[31] According to Dr. Bidanda argument, on 16 June 1997, Mirza Aslam Beg said that General Durrani had received the money and spent Rs 60 million for funding certain candidates and other operations. With the US intervention in Afghanistan, under heavy pressure from the Bush regime, General Pervez Musharraf, moved to bring the ISI into line. Those who resisted, including Mahmud Ahmed, were forced out. Gen. Musharraf shamelessly admitted that some retired officers of ISI were helping Taliban groups against the Karzai government in Afghanistan. Thus, he again discredited the agency.[32]

The nexus of Mullah and miltablishment was making the situation even worse. The deep state was expanding its sphere of influence to all state institutions to gradually undermine democracy, and enrich its private enterprise. The nexus of jihadists, wealthy individuals and serving and retired bureaucrats, as well as opportunistic politicians, had lent support to the invisible forces of disorder so that the deep state could be able to preserve and continue a lucrative business enterprise. Pakistani intelligence agencies were undergoing a deep crisis of confidence, professional credibility, lack of modern intelligence collection technology, and national security management.[33] A contest of strength between the Inter-Services Intelligence (ISI) and the Intelligence Bureau (IB), and their joint fight against the policing agencies, a misplaced sense of patriotism, poor, politicised, and sectarian management; and an inefficient approach to national security and national integration, prompted tug-of-war, scorns and regional alienation.[34]

Pakistan's military leaders most often used the ISI's political wing against the civilian leadership of political parties. Indeed, within Pakistan, the implications of the move were seen as being almost entirely domestic. But President Asif Ali Zardari's civilian government claims that taking the military spy agency out of domestic politics will also allow it to focus more on counterterrorism operations. The Zardari's government has acknowledged publicly that elements within the ISI were sympathetic to Islamists in Pakistan and the insurgency in Afghanistan. Those agents have been portrayed by Islamabad as "rogue" operators pursuing their own private agendas. In October 2008, President Zardari received stern domestic criticism for repeatedly calling Kashmiri Mujahideen terrorists, which gave more pain to the military establishment. In November 2008, the President proposed no-first-use nuclear policy between Pakistan and India. It was a good proposal to normalize relationship between the two states, but the army didn't support his plan. The relationship between the two nations was damaged by the Mumbai attacks in November 2008.[35]

The News International newspaper analysis (2012) noted aspects of the involvement of ISI in politics: "That the ISI had been deeply involved in politics under Lt Gen Pasha's command ever since the 2008 general elections can be further gauged from a US diplomatic cable which was made public in December 2010. In that cable, the WikiLeaks had quoted Interior Minister Rehman Malik as telling then US ambassador Anne Patterson that it was not General Ashfaq Kayani but Ahmed Shuja Pasha who was hatching conspiracies against President Asif Zardari. The US Embassy cables revealed that Rehman Malik had sought an urgent appointment with Ms Patterson in November 2009, saying that Ahmed Shuja Pasha was hatching plots to dislodge President Asif Ali Zardari, and adding that the president needed political security at this stage. However, Patterson was certain that the ISI chief could not do it alone". However, Dr. Nasreen Akhtar (2017) in her PhD thesis highlighted some aspects of relationship between President Zardari and the ISI. President Zardari and his party didn't like role of ISI in politics, while Prime Minister Bhutto used ISI for his political purpose. Dr Nasreen Akhtar highlights relationship between President Zardari and the armed forces:

"Despite the fact that relations between Zardari, ISI, and the military were pernicious but Zardari as president completed his term and compromised with the military establishment. However, political cost was paid by his 'nominated' Prime Minister Gilani who wanted to protect his party leader and the president Zardari. Zardari was considered 'master' to bargain and facilitate his opponents. However, the army and ISI both remained dominant factors in Zardari regime and played fundamental role in internal and external policies because democracy under Zardari's leadership was fragile, ineffective, and dysfunctional, which promoted corruption, lawlessness, and personal interests of the party leaders in power. Zardari appointed his close aides and trusted friends to important positions, both home and abroad, and made a few attempts to curtail military's power in the domain of national security. For this reason, civil-military relations during Zardari regime remained highly problematic. A number of events like Memogate, American attack on Salala check post, and killing of Osama bin Laden in Abbottabad in a military raid complicated these relations"[36]

Pakistan's armed forces are among the most modern and well-funded in the world and the only ones in the Muslim world, while most analysts have tended to view Pakistan's political system as authoritarian and label it as a dictatorship. In every democratic government, the army retained a final say on sensitive issues such as regional policies, defence expenditures, and the nuclear sector, and refuses any interference in internal postings, transfers, and promotions.[37] The return to a civilian government in 1988 did not mark a reversal of the situation; in fact, Benazir Bhutto and Nawaz Sharif provided the military with even greater economic opportunities in order to appease it while trying to reduce its political role. Dr. Nitin Prasad (20 February 2016) highlights political and democratic development in Pakistan:

"Pakistan has exercised different forms of Political systems like Presidential, Parliamentary, Federation and One Unit. Local Bodies system has also been influenced by these experiences. It has been facing Political, non-political, dictators and bureaucratic influence. Pakistan has poor facts of democracy. It has been ruled by the military, while the Military governments always generated mistakes with the politicians. Pakistan's capacity to protract the low cost conflict in Kashmir is beyond any doubt. Although the likely spillover effects of this on Pakistan's polity are obvious, they will be, to a great degree, manageable. The Islamist organisations, in spite of their opposition to elements of the state and its armed forces, are in favour of maintaining the unity of the country that is, for them, "the fortress of Islam" and "the only Islamic nuclear power". And though the US wants to tame the Pakistan army, and especially ISI its intelligence agency, it knows it will not benefit from the disintegration of the country. Nevertheless, the pressures that imperialism and neoliberalism are putting on the country are creating a complex mesh of ethnic and nationalist tensions that could lead to a spiraling war. Only by fighting for a unified working-class response to the pressures of globalisation and war can we hope to be able to offer an alternative".[38]

The lack of security sector reforms in Pakistan prompted the surge of extremism and jihadism within the ranks of the agencies. In different political and intellectual forums, critics raised the question on the credibility of the country's intelligence and security infrastructure that they have been unable to maintain security and stability of the country's violence affected provinces. Pakistan's Supreme Court in 2012 remarked that the entire state machinery, including Frontier Corp and agencies failed in stabilizing Baluchistan province.[39] As we all know capabilities of Pakistan intelligence agencies and their access to remote parts of the country, we are witnessed to the fact that they have been unable to even collect intelligence information from these regions. The fact is, they are mostly militarised and their operational mechanism is also militarised, their informers and officers have been unable to establish networks within civilian population, because intelligence information collection in remote regions needs friendly environment.[40]

However, on 18 July 2012, the Daily Nation reported: "Chief Justice Iftikhar Muhammad Chaudhry, who was heading the three-member bench, told Attorney General Irfan Qadir that since the ISI was under the Prime Minister he should be informed about it and if any such cell was still operating, it must be closed. As the activities of the cell amounted to undermining the political process in the country, the Chief Justice warned that the court would not allow the strengthening of one institution at the cost of another, though no doubt would very much like to see Pakistan Army as a robust organisation. As if recalling the government's obstinate defiance of judicial verdicts, Justice Chaudhry maintained that it would also not be possible to strengthen Parliament by weakening the judiciary. "There will be supremacy of the Constitution alone in the country" and nothing that was not legitimate under the Constitution would be tolerated, he asserted. Nor would any sort of Bangladesh model be tolerated".

On 21 May 2018, Journalist Zahid Gishkori in his article reviewed the Asghar Khan case and its important players. Zahid has also highlighted other important aspects of the case: "Before this, Gen Mirza Aslam Beg claimed that he had vehemently claimed the-then spy chief Gen Durrani against dragging the military into "political engineering" ahead of the 1990 polls. "I warned Durrani to be careful in handling of those [ISI] funds. After this, I never again discussed this matter with him [Durrani]. I gave him no names of politicians or the money to be distributed, because this was entirely his domain, and he was responsible to report to the president," Gen Beg revealed in his written statement submitted to the FIA and the apex court.

Zahid Gishkori (21 May 2018) also documented names of other players who were deeply involved in the case of public money distribution: "About other individuals who were accused of operating for that political cell, former DG ISI revealed that "I know Brig (R) Amanullah. He was in Quetta MI. I also know Lt Col (R) Eqbal Saeed Khan. He was in Rawalpindi GHQ. I do not now Lt Col (R) Ejaz. I know Lt Gol (R) Mir Akbar Ali Khan who was posted in MI Directorate. I also know Brig (R) Kamal Alam Khan who was posted in ISI when I was leaving ISI and I do not know much about him. I meet President [Ishaq Khan] once a month or after two months or as and when required". Samson Simon Sharaf, (The Nation 03 August, 2012) in his analysis of Pakistan's intelligence agencies noted some underwhelming aspect of intelligence and law enforcement operations that with relation to militancy inside Pakistan, separatist sentiments in Balochistan and undercover efforts to spread ethno-nationalism are a nightmarish function of the intelligence and enforcement arms:

Pakistan's intelligence operations can be categorised as, first, intelligence and information relating to the capabilities, intentions, or activities of foreign governments or elements, foreign organisations, foreign persons and their trail inside Pakistan. These are conducted and coordinated at the highest levels of the government, involving the Foreign Office, Ministry of Interior, Provincial Home Departments and the intelligence community under parliamentary oversight. This leads to the second, i.e. counterintelligence and information collected and collated to protect against espionage, hostile intelligence activities, sabotage, assassinations conducted by or on behalf of foreign governments or elements, foreign organisations like security services, foreign funded NGO's, and terrorist activities through local militias influenced as such. With relation to militancy inside Pakistan, separatist sentiments in Balochistan and undercover efforts to spread ethno-nationalism are a nightmarish function of the intelligence and enforcement arms. The manifestation of this war in public eye is missing persons, extra-judicial killings, body bags, corpses with torture marks, abductions, shooting sprees, ethnic and sectarian cleansing and selective/targeted assassinations of leadership. Gone unnoticed are hundreds of national, provincial and nationalist leaders, who have been assassinated, including Mohtarma Benazir Bhutto. Many times, despite compelling circumstantial evidence, the inability of the investigators to make a credible case allows these criminals to go scot-free and resume anti-state activities". [41]

The Abbottabad Operation remained controversial. Although, it was welcomed in the US and many European countries, and gave them an opportunity to cheer up, but many in Pakistan were of the opinion that it was an attack on their sovereignty and integrity. It divided and embarrassed Pakistan institutions. On 11 July 2011, in reaction to series of events and actions of agencies against journalists and human rights activists in Pakistan, Mr. John R. Schmidt repudiated the extrajudicial killing of journalists by the Inter Services Intelligence. He noted in his analysis the brutal murder of Salim Shahzad in Islamabad:

"But now there are accusations, publicly embraced by U.S. officials (including Joint Chiefs chairman Admiral Mike Mullen), that ISI ordered the murder of Pakistani journalist Saleem Shahzad, whose tortured and severely beaten body was found outside Islamabad on May 31. Shahzad had recently written a piece for the Asia Times alleging that the Pakistani Navy had arrested several naval personnel for helping al-Qaeda attack the Pakistani naval base in Karachi on May 22. Suspicion that ISI may have been responsible for his death surfaced after it was revealed he had earlier told colleagues he had received death threats from the intelligence agency. These threats had allegedly come in the wake of a previous article he had written accusing Pakistani authorities of releasing Afghan Taliban deputy leader Mullah Baradar in October 2010 after eight months in custody. According to Shahzad, senior flag rank ISI officials had pressed him to reveal the source of his information and, when he refused, had made a point of telling him they had recently gotten a hold of an Islamic terrorist hit list and would let him know if his name was on it. Shahzad interpreted this as a threat. The speculation following his death was that the Karachi-naval-base story was the last straw and that ISI had ordered his murder, not just in retaliation, but as a warning to the entire Pakistani journalist community, whose criticisms it believed had gotten out of hand..............If ISI was responsible for murdering Shahzad, it may well have been a first. The Committee to Protect Journalists reports that fifteen journalists have lost their lives in intentionally targeted killings in Pakistan since the murder of Daniel Pearl in early 2002, all of them Pakistani. Almost all were killed by radical Islamists affiliated with al-Qaeda or the Pakistani Taliban. The remainders were murdered for investigating regional ethnic conflicts or local corruption".[42]

For decades, (Dhruva Jaishankar, Foreign Policy, 15 February 2019) Islamist terrorists belonging to groups like Jaish-e-Mohammed and Lashkar-e-Taiba benefited from recruitment, financing, training, and other forms of support provided by Pakistan's security establishment. Groups targeting India and Afghanistan continued to operate with relative impunity inside Pakistan, which has only cracked down on militancy against the Pakistani state.[43] The killing of Osama Bin Laden near Islamabad painted an ugly face of Pakistani intelligence for their involvement with al Qaeda and its leader. Mr. Salim Shahzad's Karachi Naval Base story also occurred irksome, but Salim didn't accused ISI for its improper action. Mr. Davis was protecting a CIA cell that was trying to collect information on the terrorist group Lashkar-e-Taiba, one of the ISI's chief assets in its proxy war with India. The two men that Davis killed were alleged by Pakistani sources to have been tied to the ISI, likely as contractors. Mr. John R. Schmidt (2011) noted some aspects of the love and hate relationships between the two countries:

"Just two days after Admiral Mullen made his accusations on the Shahzad murder, the New York Times revealed the United States was suspending military assistance to Pakistan. Washington has been increasingly frustrated at Islamabad's unwillingness to go after those Afghan Taliban forces using the North Waziristan tribal area as a safe haven for conducting operations in eastern Afghanistan. The Pakistanis have refused to do so because they see the Afghan Taliban as a hedge against the emergence of a hostile government in Kabul allied to India after U.S. forces depart the region. Although little publicized in the West, the Indians have developed close ties to the Karzai government, flooded the country with aid workers and provided the Afghans with over a billion dollars in aid. Although the Pakistanis have no particular love for the Afghan Taliban—whose support for Osama bin Laden got them into their current fix—they fear the Indian presence in Afghanistan even more. Not only has the United States shown little sympathy for these Pakistani concerns, it has grown increasingly angry at Pakistani reluctance to do what it wants. Seen in this context, the U.S. decision to publicly accuse ISI of complicity in the Shahzad murder can be viewed as just another manifestation of American displeasure".[44]

Relationship between the two states remained strained, but after the killing of Osama Bin Laden, their relationship further complicated. "The death of bin Laden (Amir Hamza Marwan October 2015, PP-25) provided a reason to US to celebrate, and set a platform to claim that "Justice has been done" but the operation was perceived very differently in Pakistan, where the media outlets, politicians and several opinion leaders started questioning the one-sided US operation (considering it as violation of the sovereignty of

Pakistan); expressing doubts about the role played by the Pakistani military and its intelligence agencies in helping the US to conduct the successful operation; the failure of the Air Force department of Pakistan to trace the US helicopters, which reportedly flew from Jalalabad (Afghanistan); and the inability of the Pakistani forces to counter the US forces, which remained in Pakistan for almost 40 minutes".[45] Whatever the ISI has done against al-Qaeda—and even the deepest skeptics about Pakistani motives do not deny that the ISI has at times been very helpful. On 12 May 2011, in his National interests' article, Mr. John R. Schindler argued that weak democratic control on intelligence agencies in Pakistan, jihad in Kashmir and war on terror in Afghanistan, and Pakistan's reluctant support to the US and NATO campaign caused funny feeling between the two states:

"The lack of Pakistani civilian control of the military generally, and the ISI specifically, should no longer constitute a pass for dubious conduct. The unspoken quid pro quo—that the U.S. and other Western partners would look the other way on certain ISI misdeeds, especially its support for "liberation movements" in Kashmir and Afghanistan as long as it worked with us against al-Qaeda—has been overtaken by events in Abbottabad and elsewhere. This alleged wall between acceptable and unacceptable jihads has existed only in the Western mind anyway. The ramifications of the Headley case have been one of the causes of the fraying of ties between Islamabad and Washington. Even more provocative, from the Pakistani viewpoint, has been the increasing number of U.S. intelligence operations run without coordination with the ISI, known as "unilaterals" in the trade. While it is hardly unknown for the CIA and other agencies to run unilaterals, especially against high-value targets, even in friendly countries, this has grated on Islamabad, which appears fearful of what our personnel might find if they start digging too deeply. Pushback culminated in early 2011 with the arrest of Ray Davis, a CIA contractor, who shot two armed Pakistanis—suspected intelligence operatives—whom Davis believed threatened him. Davis was released after payment of blood money to the families, but this public spectacle brought the always-touchy relationship between Islamabad and Washington to a new low. They have descended further still with the outrage in Pakistan over the Abbottabad raid, the ultimate unilateral. The embarrassment of the Zardari government, which has had trouble knowing quite what to say to the global media, has been matched by the fury of the ISI, now that it is obvious to all that they were either sheltering bin Laden or were so incompetent as to have had no idea the world's most wanted man was living, barely concealed, practically in a Pakistani Army base".[46]

Chapter 3

The Challenges of Civilian Control over Intelligence Agencies, Democratic Governments, Military Establishment and a War of Strength

President Asif Ali Zardari (Financial Times - 12 January 2012) was locked in an interminable battle with the army, ISI and judges. His conflict with judges and generals intensified on both fronts- precipitating a session of puffing speculation by television channels that his government was on the verge of collapse.[1] Intelligence agencies had controlled print and electronic media. There were different perceptions about the performance of Pakistan's intelligence agencies in war and peace, but one couldn't deny the fact that the agencies were deeply politicised and their loyalties were with their private and bureaucratic stakeholders.[2] They were shamelessly protecting their masters and kept sharp-eyed about the political developments in the country. Political leadership had serious apprehensions about the working style of the intelligence agencies. According to Brigadier (r) Shaukat Qadir, the ISI, under Gen Mehmood from 2000-2001, completely went out of control until he was sacked. It was more of an ego problem, where Gen Mehmood, the ISI Director General, considered him unaccountable. Ali K Chishti, Pakistan's security analyst highlights the whole story of distrust, tug-of-war and mismanagement with the intelligence agencies:"

"The civilian-military distrust could also be witnessed in the intelligence community where it is part of the book by the

61

uniformed intelligence agencies, the Military Intelligence and the ISI to seals off the K-Block or the IB's Headquarters as a routine whenever there's a coup which shows a thread of animosity and mistrust between the civilian and military institutions. The politicisation of the intelligence agencies could be judged with the fact that at least 4,000-5,000 sacked Intelligence Bureau officials, who were previously profiled to be "unfit for service" due to political connections, were reinstated by the Pakistan People's Party (PPP) government with back pays and benefits only recently. The IB often accuses other intelligence agencies of interfering in its affairs remember only in recent years more IB operatives have gone down than anyone else. So, how do our intelligence agencies work? They send out a daily report to the president and the prime minister via COAS, titled "eyes only" mostly "googled stuff" and constantly play up threat levels apart from nagging for more funds. While the three big intelligence agencies have received all the latest tech and surveillance equipment from the United States, including serious investments in a new field, quantum computing to break terrorist codes, it is the human intelligence which the Pakistani intelligence agencies normally rely upon but lacks training in. They work like sub-inspectors and mostly tap phones and chase people, confirmed a former intelligence operative".[3]

In 2013 and 2015, Prime Minister Nawaz Sharif faced challenges when he criticised the involvement of military generals in politics. Mr. Nawaz Sharif extended hands of friendship to India and invited Prime Minister Modi to Lahore to further strengthen relationship between the two states, but miltablishment and its political cronies launched a dirty campaign against his government in the pretext that he might possibly wanted to establish the RAW networks in Punjab.[4] Moreover, intelligence agencies requested Dr. Thahirul Qadri to help them in undermining the MLN government. The Intelligence Bureau was consecutively receiving instructions from the Prime Minister office to keep tightrope around the ISI and GHQ. Research scholar Frederic Grare (18 December 2015) highlights the role of Qadri in humiliating the Nawaz government:

"The so-called "Qadri episodes" are viewed by many in Pakistan as illustrative of the relationship between the army and the intelligence services. Tahirul Qadri is a Canadian cleric of Pakistani origin who, in December 2012, returned to Pakistan and initiated a political campaign "calling for a democratic revolution through electoral reforms aimed at preventing corrupt candidates from participating in the forthcoming elections" (Grare 2013: 989). Qadri, who also had apparently unlimited access to resources of vague and unclear origin, called for the resignation of Asif Zardari, the dissolution of the parliament, and the participation of the military in the caretaker government. Many Pakistani observers interpreted Qadri's anti-corruption campaign as an attempt by the security establishment to create the conditions of an indefinite postponement of the elections, thereby facilitating the replacement of the existing government by a body composed of technocrats and military leaders. Such was the case in the 1990s, when the army repeatedly felt the need to get rid of the Prime Minister of the moment, alternately Benazir Bhutto and Nawaz Sharif. The 2013 Qadri plot ultimately proved to be a failure. The government made no concession, and although Tahirul Qadri was allowed to save face, he had to back off, only to consequently reemerge with Imran Khan, leader of the Pakistan Tehreek-e-Insaf (PTI) and a favorite of the security establishment. The two initiated a campaign against the Nawaz Sharif government, which began in the summer of 2014. Starting in August 2014, Islamabad, Pakistan's capital city was paralyzed by tens of thousands of protesters led by Imran Khan and Qadri, who not only called for the resignation of the Prime Minister on the allegation that he had rigged the May 2013 general elections, but also repeatedly threatened him and his ministers with violence (Siddiqi 2014). Soon the military intervened, playing the role of mediator between the government and opposition figures (Hashim 2014). Pakistani observers, not without evidence, privately pointed out the role of the intelligence agencies in the political turmoil as well".[5]

On 07 February 2019, Agence-France-Presse reported Pakistan's Supreme Court call on intelligence agencies for upholding free speech and staying out of politics. This strong criticism was issued in a judgment criticising the role of the intelligence agencies in anti-blasphemy protests which paralysed the capital Islamabad for several weeks in 2017.[6] "If any personnel of the Armed Forces indulges in any form of politicking or tries to manipulate the media he undermines the integrity and professionalism of the Armed Forces," stated the judgment.[7] The 2017 protests were led by a then little-known Islamist group called the Tehreek-e-Labaik Pakistan (TLP), and were only dispersed after violent clashes led to a military-brokered deal which forced the resignation of the country's law Minister. France Presse reported.[8]

On 26 January 2020, daily Dawn quoted the report of a local think tank which noted challenges of Pakistan's external environment throughout 2020. The Islamabad Policy Institute warned that the country's tense relations with neighbouring states might consume much of Pakistan's strategic and diplomatic interaction.[9] The report (Pakistan Outlook 2020: Politics, Economy & Security) highlighted persisting trends in external environment, economy, political stability, and security and on the basis of that made short-term projections in these areas. Pakistani state has been weak and fragile since 1947.[10] Since 1990s the state has been trying to showcase its divergent approach to religion and religious institutions from its previous position. The United States and European Union have already pressed successive Pakistani governments to reform the country's intelligence agencies to counter their influence on civil society and politics, but agencies further intensified their watchdog campaign against civilian population.[11] Privacy International (July 2015) in its research paper has highlighted the role of agencies in changing surveillance mechanism in Pakistan:

> "The Pakistani government is engaged in a protracted conflict against armed militant groups within its borders and outside its borders, it is a key player in the global 'war on terror'. Communications surveillance - of phone and internet protocol (IP) traffic, domestically and internationally-and other forms such as biometric or device registration, is justified by the government as necessary to counter these internal and external threats, even as it becomes less and less targeted and more widespread against ordinary civilians. The military's defence budget has ballooned in recent years as result of significant levels of international assistance, with the military's

access to sophisticated technologies having increased in turn. Attacks against civilian targets in Pakistan's cities have also fed popular support for communications surveillance and other efforts to register and monitor the civilian population, including national databases and mandatory SIM card registration. Pakistan's intelligence agencies have abused their communications surveillance powers, including by spying on opposition politicians and Supreme Court judges. Widespread internet monitoring and censorship has also been used to target journalists, lawyers and activists. This report outlines the state of communications surveillance in Pakistan. It compares the vague and imprecise laws that govern it against international human rights law standards. The report also gives an overview of the international intelligence operations that Pakistan has participated in and been subject to, including programs operated by the US National Security Agency (NSA) and the UK Government Communications Headquarters (GCHQ)".[12]

Pakistan's intelligence agencies have long faced accusations of meddling in the privacy affairs of its civilian population. Intellectual forums and newspapers have often stepped up suggestions that this way of watchdog might alienate citizens from the state. In June 2013, the Inter-Services Intelligence (ISI) developed a mass surveillance system by directly tapping the main fiber optic cables entering Pakistan that carried most of the nation's network communication data.[13] These and other intransigencies of the agencies in 2008, forced the PPP government to bring ISI under democratic control, but faced tenacious resistance from the armed forces. Privacy International (July 2015) in its report noted the import of surveillance technology by Pakistani government to intensify incarceration of civilian population, political and religious leaders in their house:

"Mobile monitoring equipment for identification and/or interception is particularly widely used by law enforcement agencies across Pakistan. The Pakistani government has imported many of these tactical communications surveillance technologies from Europe. In 2010, Germany granted German companies export licenses valued at € 3.9 million to export "monitoring technology and spyware software" to Pakistan. Between 2012 and 2014, Swiss companies were granted licenses to export dual-use communications surveillance technology to Pakistan. The total value of the three exports based on the category provided was over CHF 1 million according to records obtained by Privacy International. Finland, too, granted licenses to companies based in Finland, exporting surveillance technologies to Pakistan. For instance, the Finnish export authority authorized four export licenses to ABB, a Finnish automation technology company, to provide "waveform digitisers and transient recorders" in Pakistan, which are used to analyse audio and remote sensing data. The Pakistani government is also a confirmed user of intrusion technologies which enable the remote hacking of targeted devices. Intrusion technologies are capable of collecting, modifying and extracting all data communicated and stored on a device. To do this, malware, short for malicious software, must be installed on the device. Installation often occurs when the user inadvertently installs a Trojan, which is a disguised or concealed programme. Once the Trojan is installed it embeds itself in all system functions, collecting and transmitting data to the operator of the Trojan as the infected device operates normally from the user's perspective. Malware provides its operator with extraordinary access to an individual target's computer. They can view an individual's actions in real-time on their computer, enabling the user to records passwords, and even impersonate the target; sending out e-mails and Facebook messages as the target, for example. The user can also use the Trojan to turn on the camera and microphone on a target's computer, thereby seeing and hearing everything in the vicinity of the target's computer, without the target ever being aware. Due to their staggering monitoring capabilities, intrusion technologies are eagerly sought, bought and used by repressive regimes worldwide".[14]

On 25 July 2019, Prime Minister Imran Khan on his official visit to the United States claimed the presence of 30000-40000 armed terrorists in the country. This interaction also allowed the

Islamic fundamentalist parties in Pakistan to extend influence over armed forces personnel.[15] The U.S. Country Reports on Terrorism described Pakistan as a "Terrorist safe haven" where terrorists are able to organize, plan, raise funds, communicate, and recruit fighters, while the ISI, has often been accused of playing a role in major terrorist attacks across India including terrorism in Kashmir. President Hamid Karzai was regularly reiterating allegations that militants operating training camps in Pakistan have used it as a launch platform to attack targets in Afghanistan.[16] Alexandra Gilliard (18 December 2018) noted important aspects of the role of Pakistani intelligence agencies in using terrorists against Afghanistan:

"The ISI Directorate in Pakistan has enjoyed unparalleled power since its creation in 1948. As the ISI Director-General is selected by the Military Branch, the agency has remained steeped in army and military affairs for seventy years. From its outset, the ISI has backed terrorist organizations that provide strategic depth within India and greater influence in Afghanistan. These efforts are designed to promote Pakistan's regional hegemony—all while wreaking havoc on the national security interests of both India and Afghanistan. ISI support and aid for several terrorist organizations, including the Afghan Taliban and the Haqqani network, have resulted in international condemnation of the ISI's failures to prevent "systematic and persistent human rights violations," albeit with little effect. Within Pakistan, terrorist attacks have declined in recent years following legislation and ISI counter-terrorism policies enacted between 2013 and 2016. However, the ISI's continued covert support for extremists has fostered a growing radical community and new splinter groups that have spread throughout the region. After former President Musharraf's pledge to join the War on Terror, the ISI vacillated between continued sponsorship of extremist groups in support of its interests and cracking down on radical anti-ISI groups within Pakistan. Ultimately, due to inconsistencies in its counter-terrorism campaign, Pakistan's intelligence agency was quietly listed as a terrorist organization in U.S. military documents, instructing that ISI officers be treated the same as terrorists".[17]

On 06 October 2016, Dawn newspaper reported an unprecedented warning of civilian government to the military leadership of a growing international isolation of Pakistan and sought consensus on several key actions by the state. First, Director General of ISI Gen Rizwan Akhtar, accompanied by National Security Adviser General Nasser Janjua, was instructed to travel the four provinces with a message for provincial apex committees and ISI sector commanders.[18] However, Dawn newspaper reported former Prime Minister Nawaz Sharif directions for fresh attempts to conclude the Pathankot investigation and restart the stalled Mumbai attacks-related trials in a Rawalpindi anti-terrorism court.[19]

Those decisions, taken after an extraordinary verbal confrontation between Punjab Chief Minister Shahbaz Sharif and the DG ISI, appeared to indicate a high-stakes new approach by the PML-N government. However, during the meeting, Gen Akhtar offered that the government should arrest whomever it deems necessary, but Shahbaz Sharif told Gen Akhtar that whenever action has been taken against certain groups by civilian authorities, the security establishment has worked behind the scenes to set the arrested free. Dawn reported.[20]

The uninterrupted militarisation of society and the enfeebled operational mechanism of civilian intelligence in the country resulted in a popular mindset where every movement, action and way of thinking of Pakistan's political leadership, as well as a common man, have become militarised, and accordingly, seeks a military solution for every major or minor issue.[21] Expanding the spectrum of their illegal business of forced-disappearance to cover major foreign and domestic policy areas, the agencies assumed a more controversial position than ever before. Normally, the prime task of intelligence agencies is to lead policymakers in the right direction, based on detailed and reality-based intelligence, but the case in Pakistan is different.[22]

The agencies were misleading political leadership and policy-makers, driving them into the wrong direction, and making alliances with radicalised elements in support of the miltablishment's business of forced disappearances and torture.[23] In all previous democratic governments of the country, even Ministers of Cabinet rank never dared to question the secret agencies about their illegal prisons, and kidnapping for ransom.[24] Nevertheless, civilian and military intelligence agencies in Pakistan faced numerous challenges, including widespread lack of civilian support, faith in themselves, sectarian and political affiliations, as well as the war in Waziristan and Balochistan, where the circle of intelligence information collection has contracted drastically.[25]

Over the last two decades, the role and scale of Pakistan's intelligence agencies was grown over and above their prescribed functions, to the degree that their operations, often undercover and at odds even with each other, have earned them the repute of being a "State within a State".[26] In most parts of the country, intelligence information collection faced numerous difficulties since the Taliban and other militant groups returned to important strategic locations. Having faced serious difficulties in dealing with insurgent forces in Balochistan and Waziristan, the agencies started translating their anger into the killing and kidnapping of innocent civilians with impunity. The real journey of the ISI and IB began in the 1980s, when they tightened their belts to challenge the Soviet KGB (Komitet Gosudarstvennoy Bezopasnosti) and other European intelligence networks in Afghanistan.[27] A secret war goes on between the ISI, and the IB which painted a murky picture of concordance and cooperation. It is known that the officials from the military's ISI agency had their phone calls eavesdropped at the height of civil-military tension in 2014.[28]

The rivalry between the IB and ISI boiled over in June 2017, when a Joint Investigation Team (JIT) probing alleged money-laundering by the Sharif family made a written complaint to the Supreme Court that the IB was wiretapping JIT members, including ISI and military intelligence personnel. The JIT further reported that the IB was hampering its inquiries, adding that military-led intelligence agencies were not on "good terms" with the IB. It said that IB had collected intelligence on members of the JIT from the National Database and Registration Authority (NADRA) and presented it to Prime Minister Nawaz Sharif for use against them.[29.]

The Intelligence Bureau (IB) was established by the British Army's Major General Sir Charles MacGregor who, at that time, was Quartermaster General and head of the Intelligence Department for the British Indian Army at Shimla, in 1885. Appointment for IB's Director-General is made by the Prime Minister and confirmed by the President. The IB, which was patterned after the IB of British India, used to be a largely police organisation, but the post of Director-General (DG), IB, is no longer tenable only by police officers as it was in the past. Serving and retired military officers are being appointed in increasing numbers to senior posts in the IB, including to the post of DG. In the 1990s, the IB remained actively involved to curb sectarianism and the fundamentalism in the country. Many of its operations were directed towards infiltration, conducting espionage, counterespionage, and providing key information on terrorist organizations.[30]

The IB has been using against political opponents by successive governments in Pakistan since 1970s, while former Prime Minister Benazir Bhutto and Nawaz Sharif painted a controversial picture of its operational mechanism. In 2017, a list of 37 law makers was issued by the IB that the law makers had established secret relationship with terrorist organizations. The list first came to light when a private television channel (ARY News) aired a report claiming that former Prime Minister Nawaz Sharif had directed the IB on July 10 to keep watch on the listed legislators, mostly belonging to the PML-N.[31] On 26 September 2017, Director General of IB Aftab Sultan came under scathing criticism from PTI Chief Imran Khan for visiting London for a meeting with former PM Nawaz Sharif. In October 2017, more than 37 parliamentarians staged walkout from National Assembly after the report of Intelligence Bureau (IB) accused them of having links with terrorist organizations. While addressing the participants in the assembly, Federal Minister Riaz Peerzada said that the government should launch an investigation into the matter and unveil the name of the person who prepared the report.[32]

The intelligence community of Pakistan was once described by the daily Frontier Post (May 18, 1994) as an invisible government[33] and by the daily Dawn (April 25, 1994)[34] as secret godfathers consists of the Intelligence Bureau (IB) and the ISI. After PTI Chief Imran Khan became Prime Minister, the IB started dancing to his tango. Analyst Azaz Syed (28 September 2018) noted some developments within the intelligence infrastructure, and the IB loyalties to Imran Khan who used the agency against the deposed Prime Minister Nawaz Sharif:

"Amid a major reshuffle within the premier civilian intelligence outfit, the Intelligence Bureau (IB) has been directed to concentrate on fighting corruption instead of countering terrorism, The Friday Times has learnt. Although IB chief Dr Suleman Khan denied this development while talking to TFT, sources within the agency insist that they have been tasked to bring forward corruption cases against prominent political figures and pay attention to these areas. "There are other agencies and organisations which were trained for anti-corruption efforts. IB should not do this. Its expertise is in countering terrorism and its focus should not be redirected towards corruption," said Ehsan Ghani, a recently retired former chief of the IB while talking to TFT. Dr. Suleman, who has also served the agency in Khyber Pakhtunkhwa, is counted among those who played a vital role in countering terrorism in the province with the help of the police and the Counter-Terrorism Department (CTD). Now, sources say, he has agreed to shelve counterterrorism as a subject of the agency, as another agency has been tasked to deal with it. Dr Suleman was appointed chief of the agency by former Prime Minister Shahid Khaqan Abbasi on the recommendation of Aftab Sultan, the then IB chief. But in a conversation with TFT, Dr. Suleman denied this. "I come from a background of counter-terrorism; how can I abandon something I have worked on for years?"[35]

The third most important and powerful agency was Federal Investigation Agency (FIA). FIA has also been playing political role for different governments in Pakistan since 70s. Mr. Nawaz Sharif, Benazir and Choudhry Shujaat Husain deeply politicized the agency and used it against their opponents. The FIA was also involved in human trafficking by the PMLQ government in 1990s. The FIA's main objective is to protect the nation's interests and defend Pakistan, to uphold and enforce criminal law, and law enforcement in the country, even so, the agency has now completely politicised as its management has launched a humiliating campaign against political forces. The Federal Investigation Agency (FIA) was established on 13 January 1975, after being codified in the Constitution with the passing of the FIA Act, 1974. The FIA is headed by Director-General who is appointed by the Prime Minister, and confirmed by the President. Appointment for the Director of FIA either comes from the high-ranking officials of police or the civil bureaucracy. The DG FIA reports to the Interior Secretary of Pakistan.

All civilian and military agencies have adopted a specific mindset[36]. Their sectarian affiliation and dearth of electronically trained manpower, lack of professional surveillance approach, and the absence of a proper intelligence sharing culture raised serious questions about their credibility, and weak national security approach.[37] These and other things also caused the failure of the National Counter Terrorism Authority (NACTA) to effectively counter the exponential growth of radicalisation and extremism within Pakistan.[38] Military and civilian intelligence agencies did not cooperate with NACTA in its war against radicalised forces. As a matter of fact, NACTA established a Joint Intelligence Directorate (JID) with officers from ISI, MI, IB, and Law Enforcement Agencies (LEAs) to fight terrorism and extremism in close cooperation of these agencies, but could not succeed in winning their loyalties.

The NACTA Act 2013, Section 4 (a) mandates the Authority to receive, collate and disseminate intelligence and coordinate between all relevant stakeholders to formulate threat assessments. Section 47 of the National Internal Security Policy 2014-2018 spelled out the need for establishment of Directorate of Internal Security (DIS) under NACTA where thirty three civilian and military intelligence and operational agencies are represented, having clear articulation of command and control by integrating all grids of tactical, operational and strategic intelligence, civil and military, under one roof. In this context, a Joint Intelligence Directorate (JID) was established under the National Coordinator, NACTA, at it's headquarters.[39]

The JID's goal was to manage and pool effective intelligence works undertaken by both civilian and military intelligence agencies of the country, and to increase intelligence sharing with Police Departments, Provincial and Federal LEAs. The JID was to help the democratic government in dealing with extremism and Talibanisation in four provinces, but the government didn't pay long-term attention, nor did it receive sufficient financial support. The military establishment, moreover, failed to help train its operational managers. Under the NACTA Act, the agency was entrusted to the Board of Governors (BOG).

The Prime Minister was the Chairman, and its members included defense, finance, foreign and law ministers, members of the Senate and National Assembly, Chief Ministers of the four provinces, the Prime Minister of Kashmir, the Interior Secretary, Director General of Federal Investigation Agency (FIA), all chiefs of intelligence agencies, and chiefs of Police department from all provinces. On September 25, 2018, Prime Minister Imran Khan chaired the first meeting of the BOG. Expressing dissatisfaction over the NACTA's performance, he ordered the establishment of a special committee to oversee its performance and make it competent.

The intelligence war across Pakistan was making headlines in newspapers. Several disgruntled officers and double-crossers raised their voices against the illegal business of their intelligence management. on 26 September 2017, Dawn newspaper reported a serving Assistant Sub-Inspector of Intelligence Bureau (IB), Malik Mukhtar Ahmed Shahzad's accusation against his senior officers of not taking action against terrorism suspects and filed a petition before the Islamabad High Court (IHC) requesting it to refer the matter to the Inter-Services Intelligence (ISI) for a thorough probe.[40] The newspaper reported. Dawn also reported Islamabad High Court Registrar's Office fixation of the petition before Justice Aamer Farooq who referred the case to IHC Chief Justice Mohammad Anwar Khan Kasi, with a note that the matter could be transferred to Justice Shaukat Aziz Siddiqui since an identical matter was pending in his court.[41] In a petition filed through his counsel Masroor Shah, Mr. Shahzad said he joined the IB in 2007, and that he "reported against various terrorist groups having roots in Uzbekistan, Iran, Afghanistan, Syria and India". The ASI told court he reported against terrorist groups from various countries, but no action was taken:

> "However, to the petitioner's utter dismay, no action was ever been taken by IB in this respect despite concrete evidence provided to it in the form of the intelligence reports", the petition said.[42] "Upon thorough intelligence gathering process, it transpired that certain high officials of the IB themselves are directly involved with the terrorist organizations having linkages with hostile enemy intelligence agencies" the petition reads. It goes on to say that the matter was even reported to the IB director-general, who also did not take any steps.[43] It says some IB officials travelled to Israel and had direct links with Afghan intelligence which, it was found later, had links with another terrorist group from Kazakhstan. "These terrorists used to disguise themselves as citrus dealers in Kot-Momin and Bhalwal, Sargodha. The business was a mere camouflage," the petition said.[44]

Moreover, the petition revealed that the son of Joint Director IB (Punjab) had established links with these terror groups. The petition uncovered that some officials of Afghan and Iranian intelligence used to take refuge in the places of the citrus dealers. The petition named certain IB's officials who were on the payroll of foreign intelligence agencies which included a Joint Director General, Directors and Deputy Directors. The petitioner said: "Senior IB officials also facilitate Afghan nationals in getting Pakistani nationality.[45] Mr. Shahzad said he "has been running from pillar to post including approaching the Prime Minister of Pakistan to raise this issue of national security and protection of lives of the citizen of this country but in vain." The petitioner requested the court that the issue of connivance, complacency and involvement of official of IB and other senior bureaucrats raised in the petition may graciously be entrusted to ISI for investigation.[46] There were speculations within intellectual circles in Pakistan that ISI was behind the petition to discredit the Intelligence Bureau (IB) Dawn reported that the Intelligence Bureau (IB) also came under attack by a Joint Investigation Team (JIT) consisting of officials from

ISI, Military Intelligence and officials from other departments for 'hampering the investigation' into the assets of former Prime Minister Nawaz Sharif's family. The Intelligence Bureau (IB) has been accused by one of its own spies of "protecting" terrorists.[47]

On 30 September 2017, Abhinandan Mishra documented revelations of the IB Inspector Malik Akhtar Ahmad Shehzad, in which he accused senior intelligence officers for their direct involvement with terrorist organisations functioning within that country: "The Sunday Guardian has accessed a copy of the petition that was filed by advocate Masroor Shah in the Islamabad High Court on behalf of Malik Mukhtar Ahmad Shahzad, an assistant sub-inspector rank officer with the Pakistan's Intelligence Bureau, who is currently posted at the organisation's headquarters in Islamabad. Shahzad has been working with the agency since 2007 and, as per the petition, which has been admitted by the Islamabad High court, he has been described as an officer who has received many commendation certificates during his 10-years long service. According to Shahzad, he prepared and submitted "reports against various terrorist groups having roots in Uzbekistan, Iran, Afghanistan, Syria and India". His petition states: "However, to the Petitioner's utter dismay, no action was ever taken by (Pakistan) Intelligence Bureau in this respect despite concrete evidence provided to it in the form of the Petitioner's intelligence reports. The inaction on part of (the) Intelligence Bureau alarmed the Petitioner where-after the Petitioner endeavored to unearth the actual cause thereof. Upon thorough intelligence gathering process, it transpired that certain high officials of the Intelligence Bureau themselves are directly involved with the terrorist organisations having linkages with hostile enemy intelligence agencies".[48]

Malik Shahzad said that during his operation days, he uncovered links of terrorists with the son of one Joint Director level officer: "Arslan Ahmad Shah Bokhari, the son of Joint Director, Intelligence Bureau (Punjab) Khursheed Alam Shah Bukhari, was involved in dealings with the said terrorist groups, which were apparently running Shah Taj Kinnow Factory, Sultan-Pur Turn, Haweli Qureshianwali, Bhabra Road, Kot-Momin and Habib Sahreef Kinno Factory, Chak No. 27/NB Sargodha.[49] It is averred that to the

Petitioner's utter dismay, the higher authorities in the (Pakistan) Intelligence Bureau, despite in full knowledge gained by reason of the Petitioner's reports and even otherwise, did not take any action", alleges the petition. These revelations were encouraging for ISI who successfully planted Malik Shehzad Ahmad against his own organization. The fact is that the ISI wanted to settle the dust in its own favour, and teach a lesson to the IB management. In October 2016, the Intelligence Bureau trapped ISI in a new case.[50]

Dawn newspaper published an article of journalist Almeida, which said that some in the Pakistan's civilian government confronted military officials at a top-secret national security Committee meeting. They said that they were being asked to do more to crack down on armed groups, yet, whenever law-enforcement agencies took action, "the security establishment ... worked behind the scenes to set the arrested free". He reported that the civilians warned that Pakistan risked international isolation if the security establishment didn't crack down on terrorist groups operating from Pakistan. Dawn said that the Cyril Almeida report was "verified, cross-checked and fact-checked" and it stood by the story. The Editor-in-Chief of Dawn urged the government to refrain from "scapegoating" the newspaper in a "malicious campaign".[51]

On April 29, Major General Asif Ghafoor, the spokesman of Pakistan army's Inter-Services Public Relations (ISPR) department expressed his institution's dissatisfaction over the government's probe into the leak that put military and the civilian government on a collision course. "Notification on Dawn Leak is incomplete and not in line with recommendations by the Inquiry Board. Notification is rejected," Ghafoor said on Twitter.[52] When Ghafoor was writing this tweet; he probably had no idea it would anger a large number of people in Pakistan. Journalist Almeida's story came out at a particularly sensitive time for Islamabad, as its ties with New Delhi deteriorated following tensions on the Kashmir border. Indian Prime Minister Narendra Modi vowed in a speech that he would work to isolate Pakistan internationally due to its alleged support for Islamic militants in Kashmir.[53]

Pakistani establishment never allowed controlling the hydra of intelligence agencies to introduce security sector reforms, and make them fit to the fight against radicalization, terrorism and jihadism. Consequentially, the agencies became militarised and a tool of miltablishment to harass political leaders and those who write against the corruption of military Generals. Scholar Frederic Grare (18 December 2015) has painted a nice picture of the business of military establishment in his well-written paper: "Despite more than eight years of continued civilian power, Pakistan can be labeled as a transitional democracy at best. True, the country has experienced two successive and relatively democratic elections in February 2008 and May 2013, and the mainstream political parties--essentially the Pakistan Muslim League Nawaz faction (PML-N) and the Pakistan People's Party (PPP)--are no longer willing to let themselves be played off the other by the military, thereby limiting the margin of maneuver of the security establishment...Today, as much as in the past, "operations against dissenting politicians, objective intellectuals, and other activists, are still carried out through systematic harassment, disinformation campaigns, fictitious trials, kidnap, torture, and assassinations", as demonstrated by the de facto genocide in Balochistan."[54]

In 2017, the then Prime Minister Nawaz Sharif tried to take control of foreign and internal policy of the country, but was disqualified from his post by the Supreme Court. He sought to lead Pakistan's India and Afghan policy in the right direction; but was intercepted, humiliated, and his movements were salami-sliced. However, when former President Asif Ali Zardari tried to bring the ISI under democratic control, he faced the same fate. He was pushed around, and his crippled and tortured body would be shifted to hospital in an army ambulance.

On November 27, 2013, the then Prime Minister Nawaz Sharif appointed General Raheel Sharif as Chief of the Pakistan Army, but Sharif later resisted his governments pressure to introduce security and intelligence sector reforms.[55] This change of face ensured that any action against the Taliban would be ineffective, even as General Sharif's mission of killing Pashtuns in Waziristan failed to eradicate domestic militancy. Moreover, a large number of General Sharif's Army officers and soldiers refused to fight against the civilian population.[56] The Army Chief declined to negotiate with tribal leaders, and refused to respect Parliament and democratic norms. Instead, he designed the policy of shoot to kill in Waziristan, causing death of large numbers of innocents, including women and children, with impunity, and the kidnapping of tribal elders[57].

On 15 July 2016, New York Times reported a poster regarding General Raheel Sharif to take over the country in a military coup. The posters immediately sparked all-too-familiar speculation. Was the military planning a coup? Were the generals tired of prodding the civilian government, saddled by one crisis or another? However, journalist Imad Zafar recently reviewed Mr. Shuja Nawaz new book, which appeared in US market:

> "The downfall of military dictator General Pervez Musharraf, General Ashfaq Parvez Kayani's role in restoring the judiciary is a well-known fact, but Nawaz summarizes this with details. Nawaz' most startling revelation about politics in Pakistan is the reference to former US ambassador to Pakistan Richard Olsen.[58] According to Nawaz, Olson had information that General Zaheer-ul-Islam, then the director general of ISI, was planning to stage a coup against Nawaz Sharif's government during the 2014 sit-in organized by Imran Khan. However, General Raheel Sharif stopped him from doing that.[59] This revelation was first made public by Pakistan Muslim League-Nawaz (PML-N) stalwart Senator Mushaid Ullah Khan, who in an interview to the British Broadcasting Corporation claimed that Zaheer-ul-Islam was the main architect of Khan's sit-in. Mushaid Ullah Khan had to resign from his ministry after the interview, as the military establishment did not like it".[60]

The consecutive militarisation and Talibanisation of society, and instability led to the catastrophe of disintegration and failure of the state, which was further inflamed by the US war on terrorism, and involvement of NATO forces in Afghanistan.[61] Pakistan's weak and unprofessional diplomatic approach towards Afghanistan prompted a deep crisis, including the closure of trade routes and a diplomatic impasse.[62] One can easily focus on the Army's political and bureaucratic role in state institutions. According to the Constitution of Pakistan, every democratic government is answerable to the people of Pakistan. But in reality, they are actually answerable to the Army headquarters in Rawalpindi. Every single Prime Minister in Pakistan can only do his or her job smoothly if they completely surrender defense, interior, strategic decisions and foreign policy to the Army.[63]

It means the rules for civilian governments are pre-planned and they have been told to go by the book and not cross the red lines defined by the military establishment. This makes it a "State within a State" that, instead of ruling the country from the front, prefers that the politicians and civilian governments implement its decision and exercise power.[64] To punish Afghanistan's National Army, the US government provided sophisticated weapons to the Taliban and other extremist organisations to make the war in Afghanistan disastrous and unfavorable to Kabul since 2001. Pakistan's military establishment continues to train, arm, and transport terrorist groups inside Afghanistan to target civilian and military installations, and make the lives of civilians, including women and children hell. The ISI has often been accused by the Afghan Army and Government of playing a role in major terrorist attacks. Scholar Frederic Grare (18 December 2015) has reviewed the power and operational mechanism of Pakistani intelligence agencies. Their relationship with journalists and their newspapers is irksome for politicians and civil society:

"Pakistan's three most powerful intelligence outfits–the Inter-Services Intelligence (ISI), the Military Intelligence (MI), and the Intelligence Bureau (IB)—are known to recruit informants among journalists (Grare 2008: 24). But the link between journalists and the intelligence agencies is a complex one, and cannot be reduced to a simple power dynamic in which the journalists are merely the victim. Journalists need information, and thus have an interest in maintaining a good relationship with intelligence agencies. In return, journalists are often asked to provide information themselves to intelligence agencies. This connivance sometimes results in a collusion that extends beyond appropriate journalistic conduct. Pakistani journalists are a diverse lot with a vast range of opinions-some of which are closer to the security establishment than others-but in Pakistan, like everywhere else in the world, proximity to power is an efficient way to climb the social ladder.[65]

Military Courts, Fair Trials Violations, Confessions without Adequate Safeguards against Torture, Rough-Handling of Prisoners, and Denial of Public Hearing

In 2014, the killing of innocent school children in Peshawar fashioned a good opportunity and an iron in the fire for the army to attack North Waziristan and kill the children of poor Pashtuns. The army established their own courts to execute innocent Pashtuns. Prime Minister Nawaz Sharif and General Raheel forged a consensus 'to come down hard on Pashtuns through a concerted national effort, and later on, it was changed into a so called twenty-point National Action Plan (NAP) approved by Parliament on 24 December 2014. Pakistan's military courts challenged the authority of the country's judicial system, and awarded death sentences to people in their custody.[1] Former DG ISPR Major General Asif Ghafoor favoured the continuance of military courts in Pakistan as a matter of "national requirement. Journalist Mohsin Raza Malik (22 January, 2019) in his article highlighted the controversial function of military courts:

> "It was an important point in the National Action Plan (NAP) to establish some military courts in the country for the period of 2 years. After the unfortunate 2014 APS Peshawar incident, the Parliament passed the 21st Constitutional Amendment in January 2015, paving the way for establishing a number of military courts in Pakistan primarily "for speedy trial of certain offences relative to terrorism, waging of war or insurrection

against Pakistan and prevention of acts threatening the security of Pakistan". Consequently, some 11 military courts were set up in the four provinces in Pakistan for 2 years. In March 2017, the Parliament extended the tenure of these courts for another 2 years. Meanwhile, the Supreme Court of Pakistan also formally validated the establishment of these military courts through a landmark verdict. According to ISPR, military courts have taken up 717 cases, and 345 terrorists have given death sentences in four years. So, the conviction rate in these courts has been pretty high compared to civilian criminal courts in the country. The military courts established in Pakistan have constantly been criticized by various quarters for some reasons. Essentially rejecting the extraordinary-circumstances-warrant-extraordinary-measures   reasoning, the critics find it hard to accord this 'parallel judicial system' with the tenets of human rights and due process of law. To them, the procedure adopted by the military courts is not strictly in accordance with the Article 10-A of the Constitution of Pakistan, which ensures the due process and fair trial to an accused person".[2]

On 24 November 2015, President amended the army act, and allowed intelligence agencies to detain civilians even before the passing of the 21st Amendment. The army was authorised to detain, kill, and torture Pashtuns, and try them in military courts where no human rights organization, or journalist forum were allowed to cover the court proceeding. Dr. Muhammad Zubair, (28 January 2019) in his article highlighted the changing shape of the army act:

"It also authorized military courts to hold in-camera proceedings and keep identities of individuals associated with the cases secret. Moreover, it gave protection and indemnity to court officers for any act done in 'good faith' in pursuance of the military trials. Contents of the presidential ordinance came to public knowledge only nine months later when it was placed before Parliament for approval, which was granted on 11 November 2015 through the Pakistan Army (Amendment) Act, 2015. The constitutional amendment included a sunset clause of two years, with the possibility of extension. The first two-year term of the military courts ended on 7 January 2017. In March 2017, under the watchful eyes of the military leadership, and after three months of negotiations, the government and opposition parties agreed to a two-year extension. It was claimed that the 'extraordinary situation and circumstances' continued to exist and that the extraordinary measures 'have yielded positive results in combating terrorism'. Thus, Parliament passed the Constitution (Twenty-Third Amendment) Act, 2017 and the Pakistan Army (Amendment) Act, 2017. However, this time Parliament provided four basic rights to accused persons facing military trials: informing them of charges at the time of arrest, their production before courts within 24 hours, allowing them to engage private defense counsel and application of the regular law of evidence in the court proceedings".[3]

Pakistan's human rights commission was in hot water when the army tightens the rope around the neck of civilian government. The HRCP only expressed concerns over the planned extension of military courts. However, International Commission of Jurists (ICJ) also criticized the military trial of civilians as a 'disaster for human rights' in Pakistan. An Indian analyst and research scholar, D. Suba Chandran (NIAS, 11, December 2017) in his research paper on Pakistan's Military courts highlighted procedure of courts, and the involvement of military establishment in judicial matter:

The military courts were established through the 21st constitutional amendment (Pakistan Army (Amendment) Bill, 2015) passed with huge support following the tragic terrorist attack on an Army Public School in December 2014 in Peshawar. The TTP led massacre witnessed the killing of nearly 140 persons in a School in Peshawar, most of them children. In January 2015, both houses of the Parliament passed the bill unanimously thereby establishing military courts for speedy trials of terrorists. The bill had a clause providing for the closure of military courts by 7 January 2017. The military courts also became a part of the Pakistan's National Action Plan (NAP); along with the Zarb-e-Azb, these three were seen as Pakistan's primary counter terrorism strategy. While the Army is still continuing with the Zarb-e-Azb, the achievements and failure of the NAP have become a political issue during the recent months, whereas the military courts technically came to an end on 7 January 2017. According to media reports, close to 270 cases were tried by the military courts; of which majority of them (around 160) were sentenced to death (though a small number were actually executed) and the rest to prison. Despite a 90 percent conviction, civil society does complain about lack of transparency in the above trials. Though, there were discussions in the media during the late 2016 itself on the impending deadline, there were no political debates within the Parliament on providing an extension to the military courts. With no action, the tenure of the military courts automatically came to an end in early January.[4]

Some political circles supported the idea of military courts that high courts couldn't prosecute militants. The matter was not that simple. On a number of instances, civilian courts' judges were openly threatened by Islamic militant groups such as the Taliban and the Lashkar-e-Taiba. A number of lawyers were killed for prosecuting extremists. Many judges fled the country after receiving death threats. Military courts in Pakistan never convicted a single corrupt military official. These courts received tenacious criticism from civil society and international human rights organizations. Protection of Pakistan Act 2014 can easily deal with judicial matter, and can settle terror-related cases. Ayaz Gul (January 16, 2019) in his analytical article has reviewed operational mechanism of these courts and criticism of International commission of jurists:

The military tribunals have been in operation since January 2015. At that time, the Pakistani parliament authorized them for two years to conduct trials of suspected terrorists in a bid to deter growing terrorism in the country. The ICJ denunciation comes as Prime Minister Imran Khan's government consults with opposition parties on legislation to extend the tenure of the courts. The ICJ cited "serious fair trials violations in the operation of military courts, including: denial of the right to counsel of choice; failure to disclose the charges against the accused; denial of a public hearing; a very high number of convictions – more than 97 percent – based on "confessions" without adequate safeguards against torture and ill treatment.".........The Pakistani army and civilian officials reject the charges and maintain the legislation allowing the trials binds the special tribunals to conduct "fair and transparent" hearings. Political parties have backed the military courts, noting Pakistan's regular judicial system does not offer protection to witnesses. Moreover, judges and attorneys prosecuting suspected hardcore militants have complained of receiving death threats, or have come under attack. In January 2015, Prime Minister Nawaz Sharif's government promised to reform the civilian criminal justice system and presented the military courts as a temporary solution. Since then, the government has not taken any significant measures to reform the judiciary. From January 7, 2015 to January 6, 2017, military courts convicted 274 individuals and handed down 161 death sentences. At least 17 people have been executed after being convicted by a military court.[5]

Lawyer Kamaran Murtaza expressed deep concern over the apex court judgment and said: "Article 10 of the Pakistani constitution gives every citizen the right to an open trial, and this is not possible in the military courts. Forget about the fair trial, nobody even knows the names of the convicts the military courts have thus far sentenced, and he would appeal against the Supreme Court's decision as it violates fundamental constitutional rights of the people." The HRCP chairperson hammered political parties for not taking advantage of the consensus against Islamist militancy and surrendering their powers to the army. "It is unfortunate that the nationwide resolve against the Taliban and other extremist groups did not translate into political action. It remained a military affair. International human rights forums have deeply criticised the confession by torture in military dark cells and demanded the removal of this cruel justice system". On 16 January 2019, International commission of jurists deeply criticised the illegal function of military courts in Pakistan. In its briefing paper, the ICJ documented serious fair trials violations in the operation of military courts, and warned that high number of convictions–more than 97 percent–based on "confessions without adequate safeguards against torture and ill treatment:

"The trial of civilians by military courts is a glaring surrender of human rights and fundamental freedoms, found the ICJ in its

Briefing Paper Military Injustice in Pakistan released today. The Pakistani Government must not extend the tenure of military courts to try civilians for terrorism-related offences, the ICJ said. "Military trials of civilians have been a disaster for human rights in Pakistan," said Frederick Rawski, ICJ's Asia Director. "As a recent judgment of the Peshawar High Court has confirmed, proceedings in these tribunals are secret, opaque, and violate the right to a fair trial before an independent and impartial tribunal," he added. In the briefing paper, the ICJ has documented serious fair trials violations in the operation of military courts, including: denial of the right to counsel of choice; failure to disclose the charges against the accused; denial of a public hearing; failure to give convicts copies of a judgment with evidence and reasons for the verdict; and a very high number of convictions – more than 97 percent – based on "confessions" without adequate safeguards against torture and ill treatment. The ICJ has also demonstrated how military courts are being used to give legal cover to the practice of enforced disappearances. The use of military courts to try civilians is inconsistent with international standards, the ICJ recalled. According to the military, in the four years since military courts were empowered to try terrorism-related offences, they have convicted at least 641 people. Some 345 people have been sentenced to death and 296 people have been given prison sentences. Only five people have been acquitted. At least 56 people have been hanged."[6]

On 12 January 2019, Dr. Mehdi Hasan, Chairperson of the Human Rights Commission of Pakistan (HRCP) expressed grave concern at the government's decision to table a bill in favour of extending the tenure of military courts, which were otherwise due to end their term. In a statement issued the HRCP categorically stated that 'the institution of military courts was an anomaly in any democratic order that claims to uphold the fundamental rights and freedoms of its citizens: "It is the state's duty to uphold the rule of law in a manner that ensures that every citizen is entitled to due process and a fair trial. Equally, it is the state's duty to uphold the rule of law to ensure the security of its citizens. These are not mutually exclusive obligations. Moreover, there is little evidence to show that military courts have succeeded in increasing respect for the rule of law. The perception of 'speedy justice' is no substitute for rooting out the militant extremism that led to the institution of these courts in the first instance or indeed for taking the time to train and equip domestic judicial and police mechanisms that are, and ought to remain, responsible for maintaining civilian law and order under a civilian mandate".[7]

In the aftermath of the December 16 school attack, Pakistan also lifted a seven-year-long moratorium on death penalties. The military, responding to public anger over the Peshawar killings, was moving fast. The military promised that it will not abuse its new powers by prosecuting politicians, journalists or rights activists, as happened in the 1980s. The mandate of the new courts was set to expire after two years, and the trials were subject to civilian oversight. Journalist Imad Zafar once argued that political system had been the target of milablishment propaganda machine. The hatred between the two political camps, Imad Zafar viewed it reaching boiling point and no one liked to be contradicted or criticized for his political affiliations or ideologies. The military establishment's power and control over state resources and institutions is immense. This means creating a counter-narrative has always been the toughest of jobs for the many political parties that have tried. Daily Dawn in its 06 March 2017 analysis of military courts highlighted consecutive conviction of military courts:

"Since February 2015, a total of 274 individuals have been convicted in military courts. So far, the army has sentenced 161 individuals to death, 12 of whom have been executed and 113 have been given jail terms (mostly life sentences). There are roughly 11 military courts that have been set up across Pakistan; three in KP, three in Punjab, two in Sindh and one in Balochistan. With the sun today having set on Pakistan's military courts, Dawn.com recaps this paper's position against military courts with excerpts of past articles. In April 2015, Sabir Shah disappeared from Lahore's central jail. His family and lawyers did not know where he had gone. Five months later, the family was informed via an ISPR press release, that Sabir had been awarded a death sentence by the military courts. Sabir's lawyer claims he is unaware of the evidence that may have been used to convict his client. Sabir was originally indicted on murder charges. The trial was underway at the civilian courts when he was mysteriously moved to a military internment centre. In August 2016, families of 16 civilians found guilty by the military courts filed a review petition at the Supreme Court of Pakistan in what turned out to be an iconic hearing. "These trials before the military courts need to be proceeded again after sharing complete evidence and the case record with the accused and also ensuring complete freedom to the accused to engage a counsel of his choice," argued Asma Jahangir before a five-judge Supreme Court bench, headed by Chief Justice Anwar Zaheer Jamali. At first the 21st Amendment, as it is popularly known, was met with much debate, but over time, military courts weaved themselves in to the fabric of Pakistan's criminal justice system".1- Pakistan's military courts-here's why it should never rise again: Murky procedures, no transparency or right to appeal in civilian courts-a snapshot of Pakistan's military courts.[8]

However, ISPR in 2016 issued a press statement in which its chairman indicated that 135 out of 144 people convicted in military courts had "confessed" to their crimes. That the confession rate was higher than 90 percent points towards a disturbing possibility; that confessions might be elicited using questionable interrogation methods. This statement was rejected by International Commission of Jurists and noted: "suspects tried by military courts remain in military custody at all times, even after the magistrate records their "confessions". However, Amnesty International in its report (27 March 2019) noted some statements of victim families and the illegal disappearances of Pakistani intelligence agencies:

"We are repeatedly given advice that if we stop protesting, end our activism against enforced disappearances and sit at home, our Baba will come back." Sasui Lohar, daughter of Hidayatullah Lohar, forcibly disappeared since April 17, 2017 from Nasirabad, Sindh, Pakistan. In April 2017, Hidayatullah Lohar, schoolteacher (headmaster), blacksmith and political Sindhi activist was forcibly disappeared from the school where he taught. He was taken away in a "double-cabin grey coloured" vehicle by men in police uniform and civilian clothes. Since then the authorities have refused to disclose his whereabouts. Despite the presence of eye-witnesses, his family had to petition the Larkana High Court to order the area police station to register the First Information Report. Hidayatullah Lohar is one of Sindh's "missing persons". His family has been patiently seeking truth and justice through the courts and on the streets of Pakistan since his disappearance. His daughters, Sasui and Sorath Lohar are at the forefront of the campaign against enforced disappearance in the southern province of Sindh. Lohar's case was also registered in the Commission for Inquiry of Enforced Disappearances of Pakistan (COIED) and a number of Joint Investigation Team (JIT) (appointed by the COIED) hearings have taken place in the province on the commission's order but to no effect. The JITs comprise of government stakeholders, including the interior ministry, police officials, federal investigation agency officials and intelligence agencies.[9] Moreover, Amnesty International on 27 March 2019, in its reports warned:

 The issue of disappearances has been occasionally raised in public and parliament by political parties, including PPP, PML (N), MQM, BNP (M), and NP (when on Opposition benches). Initially, the media and courts were vocal on the issue. When Iftikhar Muhammad Chaudhry was Chief Justice of the Supreme Court of Pakistan, the apex court entertained a petition of the Balochistan Bar Council. Although, in Pakistan's power structure, law courts are not empowered to punish the Army personnel guilty of enforced disappearance of Baloch people, the Chaudhry-headed bench exerted pressure on the Pakistan Army, FC and intelligence agencies to release missing persons and stop inhuman practice of enforced disappearances. The said petition led to a tussle between the apex court and the Pakistan Army, which resulted in the dismissal and arrest of judges by General Pervez Musharraf. The Pakistan Army and intelligence agencies have been using enforced disappearances as a covert policy to bear down on the Baloch freedom movement and have been vociferously disputing the reports of enforced disappearances of people".[10]

However, General Ghafoor admitted in a Press conference on 29 April, 2019: "We know you have a great attachment to missing persons (issue). We too have. We don't want any person to go missing but where there is a war, you have to do a number of (undesirable) works. It's said that everything is fair in love and war. War occurs to be ruthless."[11] The DG ISPR justified the enforced disappearances with his comments "everything is fair in love and war".[12] Moreover, Sayed Irfan Raza in his Dawn (30 January 2019) analysis noted standpoint of military courts about the missing persons. In 2019, Pakistani human rights defender Idris Khattak was forcibly disappeared, activist Muhammad Ismail was arbitrarily detained on trumped up charges, while his daughter and women rights activist Gulalai Ismail fled the country. The authorities also denied entry to a representative from the Committee to Protect Journalists' (CPJ), warned news anchors not to express their opinions, while journalists from the Dawn newspaper faced threats for their reporting. Student protesters including Alamgir Wazir were arrested and charged for their activism. In his Asia Times, (17 September 2019) article, Imad Zafar argued:

"Pakistani establishment is not simply powerful in its own right, with the controlled media and hegemony over state resources, but the current engineered discourse has been backed by Riyadh and Washington. Not a single analyst could have predicted that a regime backed by these superpowers could be defeated. However, all that changed when the establishment proved incapable of pre-empting India's annexation of Kashmir. That proved to be the last nail in the coffin of the current political discourse. According to whistleblowers in the power corridors who do not wish to be named, there is a rift within the security establishment, with many high-ranking officials wanting not only an end to military involvement in political matters but for certain heads to roll. The announcement by Fazal-ur-Rehman, president of the Jamait Ulema-e-Islam (F) party, of a planned "long march" to Islamabad in October and to hold a sit-in there is not a coincidence by any means. It is believed by many whistleblowers that Fazal has the backing of certain quarters within the establishment who do not want the current dispensation to continue. These people are angry over the Kashmir fiasco and the political engineering that resulted in the current political and economic turmoil in Pakistan".[13]

In January 2018, Human Right Watch in its report warned that notwithstanding the establishment of military courts, and a elected government of Prime Minister Imran Khan, cases of human right violation, rape, enforced disappearance, torture in dark prisons exacerbated:

"In March, parliament reinstated secret military courts empowered to try civilians after the term for military courts ended in January 2017. Pakistan human rights groups said that many defendants facing military courts were secretly detained and tortured to coerce confessions. Several remain forcibly disappeared. Authorities do not allow independent monitoring of military court trials. The Pakistan government failed to sufficiently investigate and prosecute allegations of human rights violations by security forces. Security forces remained unaccountable for human rights violations and exercised disproportionate political influence over civilian authorities, especially in matters of national security and counterterrorism. In March, parliament passed a constitutional amendment reinstating secret military courts to try terrorism suspects for another two years. Security forces were implicated in enforced disappearances and extrajudicial killings throughout the country. The government muzzled dissenting voices in nongovernmental organizations (NGOs) and media on the pretext of national security. Militants and interest groups also threatened freedom of expression. Women, religious minorities, and transgender people faced violent attacks, discrimination, and government persecution, with authorities failing to provide adequate protection or hold perpetrators accountable. The inclusion of the transgender population in the 2017 census and the first-ever proposed transgender law were positive developments. The human rights crisis in Balochistan continued with reports of enforced disappearances and extrajudicial killings of suspected Baloch militants. Baloch nationalists and other militant groups continued attacking non-Baloch civilians".[14]

The Pakistani Godfather: The Inter-Services Intelligence and the Afghan Taliban 1994-2010

Adrian Hanni and Lukas Hegi

In the decade following the attacks of September 11, 2001, Pakistan ostensibly played a key role alongside the United States in the "war against terrorism" and the counterinsurgency in Afghanistan. The country received almost 90 percent of Coalition Support Funding (CSF) and altogether was allotted around 20 billion dollars in military and economic aid. But Pakistan played a double game. Behind the scenes, its powerful intelligence service ISI continued to provide large-scale support to the Taliban. Using the Taliban as a proxy force to pursue strategic objectives in Afghanistan, the ISI aggravated the instability in its neighbouring state and has undermined initiatives for a peaceful solution to the conflict.

This article aims to outline the history of the relationship between Pakistani intelligence and the Taliban from the sudden emergence of the armed Islamist group in southern Afghanistan in 1994 until 2010. Besides a review of the literature, the analysis is based primarily on a large number of declassified or leaked U.S. intelligence and diplomatic documents. The historical account is structured in three distinct phases: (1) the two years from 1994 to 1996, when the Taliban was one of several warring factions in the Afghan civil war; (2) the period from 1996 to 2001, when the Taliban ruled Afghanistan; and (3) the decade after the US-led invasion, when the Taliban lead an insurgency against the government of Hamid Karzai and the U.S. and NATO troops in Afghanistan from their sanctuary in Pakistan. After outlining the nature and evolution of ISI support for the Taliban in the first three sections, we examine the arrest of the influential Taliban leader Mullah Baradar in 2010 to further illustrate the Pakistani double game. The article concludes with a discussion of Pakistan's main motives to support the Taliban: the rivalry with its neighbour India and the objective to control the Pashtun tribal areas, which were divided by colonial border drawing in the late 19th century.

The Taliban: From Their Emergence to Their Coming into Power in Kabul (1994-1996)

When the Taliban first appeared in southern Afghanistan in November 1994, their ideology fell on fertile soil. More than 15 years of war had left their mark on the country. The constant interference of foreign powers proved to be particularly fatal. Specifically, the unequal treatment during the resistance against the Soviet occupation (1979-1989) had increased the mistrust among the tribes and ethnic groups. The United States and Saudi Arabia, amongst others, had given around ten billion dollars of subsidies to the Mujahideen in Afghanistan during the Soviet occupation. These funds were distributed with the help of Pakistan's Inter-Services Intelligence (ISI).

The ISI systematical preferred the Pashtun tribes around Peshawar in the distribution of weapons and money provided by the Americans. Conversely, Pakistan regarded the south of Afghanistan around Kandahar as backward and the Durrani Pashtuns dominating the area at the time as untrustworthy.[1] Founded in 1948, ISI is the largest intelligence service of Pakistan. The exact number of employees is not known but it is estimated to be at least 25,000. There are a further 30,000 serving as informants or performing similar tasks. De jure, the ISI is subordinate to the Prime Minister, but de facto it is the Chief of Staff of the Army that the ISI reports to and from whom it receives its orders. The ISI, which is often referred to as a state within a state partially going about its own foreign policy, is undoubtedly the most powerful and most politicised of the Pakistani intelligence agencies.[2]

The clashes between various factions and warlords in late 1994 led to the disappearance of the old and more moderate leadership, and thus left room for the Taliban extremists. The whole country was divided among various warlords, forming and dissolving alliances as they pleased. In order to finance their war, the warlords exploited the population, cut down almost all forests and sold anything that was not nailed down. The on-going insecurity in turn called the truck mafia into action, which was operating from the Pakistani city of Quetta and from Kandahar. The fragmentation of the southern Afghan territory by many local warlords had been seriously restricting their activities.[3]

Although the exact origin of the Taliban is controversial and shrouded in myth, the lawlessness and lack of leadership have certainly paved the way for this radical movement. The Taliban initially had to manage without the support of the ISI, which at that time was backing Hekmatyar's Hizb-i-Islami. However, in 1994, the defeat and the loss of prestige of Hekmatyar were becoming apparent, and Pakistan began to look for a new proxy. Then there was the desire of the new Pakistani Prime Minister, Benazir Bhutto, to open a trade route to Central Asia as quickly as possible. Because of the fighting around the capital, the northern route via Kabul to Mazar-i-Sharif and on to Uzbekistan was impassable. Therefore, the idea formed to open the route via the southern part of the ring road from Quetta via Kandahar to Heart and on to Ashqabat.[4]

The first battle between Taliban and Hekmatyar fighters took place in mid-October 1994. At Spin Baldakon the Afghan-Pakistani border, the Taliban overran a garrison of Hekmatyar. With the consent of Pakistan they then conquered a vast weapons and ammunition depot built by the ISI.[5] The seizure of the weapons allowed the Taliban to continue fighting for quite some time and gave the Pakistanis the opportunity to hide their support for the Taliban.[6] This action can still be viewed as merely tolerated by Pakistan, but anything that happened after November 3rd must be considered active help. On this day, Taliban marched out at the request of the Pakistani to free a convoy detained by southern Afghan warlords. Shortly thereafter, they went on to take Kandahar. Already at that time, foreign diplomats were speculating that the Taliban were operating with the covert support of Pakistan.[7] At the same time, the Pakistani Interior Minister Nasrullah Babar boasted the success of "his boys".[8] However, the Taliban continued trying to demonstrate their independence and to resist the Pakistani influence.

While the origins of the Taliban still appeared mysterious to many, by the end of year, some sources were "concerned that the GOP [Government of Pakistan] (ISI) is deeply involved in the Taliban takeover in Kandahar and Qalat."[9] The same source also expressed concern that the influence of the unpopular Pakistani in the south could further destabilise the country and sooner or later lead to an Afghan-Pakistani conflict. Meanwhile, the Taliban continued their conquest of Afghanistan and marched north.

Pakistan was still putting its eggs into two baskets: On the one hand there were the Taliban, who had contributed to the opening of smuggling routes in the south, and on the other hand there was Hekmatyar and his Hizb-i-Islami, who were exerting pressure on the government in Kabul. Whether it was a double game of the ISI, or whether the simultaneous support of both Afghan factions rather represented a power struggle between the civilian government of Benazir Bhutto and the ISI is unclear. According to Jason Burke, a confrontation between the civilian and military leadership of the country was at the origin of the support for the Taliban.[10]

The same assessment was given in a report by Human Rights Watch in 2001: "The subsequent shift to the Taliban also reflected changes in Pakistan's domestic politics. Newly elected in 1993 Prime Minister Benazir Bhutto sought to move away from Hikmatyar and the ISI and find new ways to open trade routes in Central Asia.[11]" This would imply that the support for the Taliban came first from the Home Office and its director Nasrullah Babar, while the ISI and the army still supported Hekmatyar, who was, however, involved in a grueling two-front war. In mid-February the Taliban coming from the south had taken over his headquarters. They opened the roads to Kabul and enabled the supply of the city that had been under a long siege. Thus, the Taliban gained great sympathy among the population, but also satisfied a key demand of the transport mafia.[12]

After Hekmatyar had been the crown prince of the ISI for a long time and had enjoyed generous support, the Pakistani intelligence service appears to have radically shifted to the Taliban in early 1995: "[a]t around this time the weight of opinion within the upper echelons of the ISI – (...)–now began to swing towards the Taliban. While in late 1994 Babar appears to have been the leading voice in the Islamabad establishment propounding the student's cause, by January the ISI was taking a growing interest.[13]" During that time, Taliban warfare also changed dramatically. This may reflect the fact that the former Afghan Defence Minister Lieutenant General Shahnawaz Tanai was reactivating his still existing network of connections to other officers of the communist regime for the cause of the Taliban. According to Anthony Davis, "none of this could have been done without permission, if not active encouragement, from the ISI itself."[14]

After their rapid initial successes, the Taliban suffered some heavy defeats in the first half of 1995. Ahmed Shah Massoud and his fighters drove them from the area in front of Kabul and in the West they had to desist from their attacks on Herat, after Ismael Khan had received support from Massoud, who had been bombarding the Taliban for several days. However, a poorly planned offensive of Khan against the weakened Taliban ended in a disastrous defeat and the final loss of Herat. However, it seems that this defeat resulted not only from poor planning. Western intelligence services suspected "infusions of well-trained reinforcement and new weapons – now supported by a functioning logistics machine".[15] Thereafter, riots broke out in Kabul. A mob attacked the Pakistani embassy and killed an employee. The relations between the two countries hit rock bottom. Afghan President Burhanuddin Rabbani accused Pakistan openly of trying to oust him with help of the Taliban.[16] The Pakistanis were not very cautious and openly admitted to supporting the Taliban in front of the Americans. The Pakistani ambassador defended himself saying "that in the wake of last months' sacking of the Pak embassy in Kabul, GOP Afghan policy has been increasingly driven by intense domestic opposition towards Afghanistan."[17]

In March 1996, Pashtun scholars came together for a large gathering. The discussions on the future of Afghanistan "were conducted in strictest secrecy, and all foreigners were expelled from Kandahar for this time. Pakistani officials, however, were present to monitor the Shura, including Qazi Humayun, Pakistan's ambassador in Kabul, and several ISI officials, including Colonel Imam, Pakistan's consul general in Herat."[19] The meeting had been convened as a result of the stalemate between the Afghan factions. Rabbani's position had been consolidated and his prestige abroad increased. Consequently, Pakistan tried to forge an alliance against Rabbani with Hekmatyar, the warlord Rashid Dostum and the leaders of the Jalalabad Shura, but this was categorically rejected by the Taliban.[20] The regional powers feared the consequences of Afghanistan dominated by the Islamist Taliban and gave massive support to Rabbani and Massoud. In return, Pakistan and Saudi Arabia increased their support for the Taliban.[21]

True to the motto "the enemy of my enemy is my friend", Bhutto even tried to convince the U.S., which had an interest in curbing Iran, to support the Taliban. The United States declined, but also the Taliban refused to continue cooperating with other warlords.[22] Yet the Taliban managed to convince Pakistan and Saudi Arabia to support them again. Riyadh and Islamabad had reached an agreement with them. In late September, the Taliban led a surprise attack on Jalalabad and overran it. At the same time, Pakistan let hundreds of gunmen enter unmolested across the borders into Afghanistan. The Taliban lost no time and continued their advance towards the capital from an easterly direction. A month after the attack on Jalalabad the first pickups with Taliban had already reached the streets of Kabul.

The pro-government troops fled and Massoud also ordered a retreat for his troops. One of the first acts of the Taliban in Kabul was the execution of former President Najibullah, whose battered body they then put on display in the streets of Kabul. Taking Kabul didn't mean the end of the war. The formerly warring warlords pulled together to form a new Alliance to defend Afghanistan against the Taliban. Massoud decided to make a full-scale attack on the scattered Taliban forces and advanced as far as Bagram. The success of the Taliban seemed seriously threatened. As a consequence, Pakistan again let thousands of 'volunteers' cross the border area of Pakistan into Afghanistan to fight for the Taliban. This enabled the militia of Mullah Omar to launch a new offensive and recover the lost territories.[23]

The way was paved for the Taliban, and the prevailing lawlessness and lack of leadership since the departure of the Soviets have certainly increased their acceptance in parts of the population. However, their success is down to more than just this. In addition to these pull factors a number of push factors have played their part. This includes logistics, enabling the Taliban to carry out their operations equipped with enough weapons and ammunition. They also had enough fighters as new religious students from the Pakistani madrassas could enter the country unimpeded at all times.[24] Furthermore, indoctrination and training played a crucial role. The Taliban broke up the deadlock with mobile warfare and relatively quickly caused large shifts in territorial ownership. Mobile warfare was made possible because the Taliban had large numbers of vehicles and sufficient communication infrastructure available.

This included a mobile communications network and a wireless network for the Taliban leaders, both of which had been set up by Pakistan. Moreover, Pakistan had roads, the Kandahar Airfield and fighter jets for the Taliban repaired.[25] They could also benefit from the experience of former officers of the communist army. These had been reactivated through the network of former Defence Minister Tanai, who had found refuge in Pakistan after a failed coup against Najibullah, which had most likely been supported by Pakistan in the first place. But corruption and the effects of money are also not to be underestimated. Many field commanders quite simply let themselves be bought. In any case, the substantial backing from

Pakistan has significantly promoted the rapid advance and the takeover of Kabul by the Taliban.

The Taliban in Power in Kabul (1996-2001)

The support of the Taliban by the Pakistani government and the ISI continued after the gang around Mullah Omar took Kabul in September 1996 and overthrew the Tajik-dominated government of Rabbani and Massoud. Abdul Salam Saif, the Taliban ambassador in Pakistan, wrote what previously was the only detailed inside account of the movement, in which he describes in detail how he was inundated with offers from the Pakistani intelligence officials.[26] The ISI continued pumping money, weapons and advisers into Afghanistan to help the Taliban win against the Northern Alliance.[27] In addition, Pakistan provided diplomatic support, organised training for Taliban fighters, some of whom it had itself recruited, planned and commanded offensives, delivered ammunition and fuel and on several occasions apparently got directly involved in combat support.[28]

Undoubtedly, the Pakistani army and intelligence agencies, with the ISI at the forefront, made a vital contribution to the Taliban becoming a highly effective military force.[29] The covert support of the Taliban by the ISI came from the corps headquarters in Peshawar.[30] To give an example: a contact person deemed trustworthy by the U.S. consulate in Peshawar in October 1996 reported the border crossing from Pakistan into Afghanistan of an ISI convoy, consisting of 30-35 ISI trucks and 15-20 fuel trucks, at Torkham.[31] The ISI itself in late 1996 estimated the total Pakistani aid to the Taliban to be as high as 20 million rupees.[32] A number that may well be set too low. Two years later, a Pakistani source of the U.S. State Department put the support of the Pakistani government for the Taliban at "about a million dollars every few months".[33]

According to a 2001 report by Human Rights Watch, the first direct military contacts between the Afghanistan office of the ISI and the Taliban after they seized power was established by sending a small team of Pakistani military advisers to the former stronghold of the Afghan army in Rishikor.[34] The base in Rishikor, southwest of Kabul, was subsequently used as the main training centre for Pakistani volunteers, who had been carted off to fight for the Taliban in Afghanistan. No later than 1999, the accommodation of the Pakistani military and intelligence personnel were in a guarded area within the camp.[35] According to a DIA[36]-report, Pakistani religious students also received military training at Kandahar and Herat.

There, a combination of members of Pakistan's Frontier Corps (FC), staff of the Najibullah era, as well as former supporters of the Wahhabi warlord, Abdul Rasul Sayyaf, and the long-standing ISI protégé Hekmatyar provided training.[37] This use of Pakistan's Frontier Corps was apparently not an isolated case. In addition to the training of fighters, company-size FC elements in Afghanistan were also used for command and control tasks and, if necessary, for fighting action itself. The reason for the use of the FC was that its units, as opposed to those of the Punjabi-dominated army, were completely or at least predominantly composed of Pashtuns. This represents the Taliban and the people in the South of Afghanistan.[38]

The ISI used supplies of fuel and ammunition to consolidate its influence on the Taliban operations. Its actions were based on the system that the intelligence service had set up to control the military operations of its Afghan proxies during the Soviet occupation. In accord with this system, large amounts of ammunition and fuel were made available to the Taliban commanders only when an operation had been approved by the ISI and the Pakistani military. The Taliban were not happy with this system and hence began looking for alternative arms suppliers. That is why private actors soon got involved in arms trading with the Taliban. Private offers were available particularly because the Bhutto government had fired dozens of ISI officers in 1994, some of which with ties to the Taliban. Some of these officers had then founded their own import-export firms or participated in existing companies organising large private security and import-export operations.

After General Pervez Musharraf came to power by an army coup in 1999, he increased the Pakistani support for the Taliban.[39]

Musharraf publicly declared that Pakistan's strategic interests lie in supporting the Afghan Pashtuns, whom he associated solely with the Taliban. The new ruler then went on to say that: "This is our national interest [...] the Taliban cannot be alienated by Pakistan. We have a national security interest here [...]".[40] Apart from army chief Musharraf, the power within the military junta lay in particular with three hard-line generals who had made the decisive coup of 1999: Mahmoud Ahmad, Mohammed Aziz and Muzaffar Usmani.[41] All three were passionate supporters of Islamic fundamentalist parties and the Taliban. Aziz, Director of Covert Operations in the ISI in the late 1990s served as the main organiser behind the military victories of the Taliban against the Northern Alliance.

Ahmad has been one of the most vocal supporters of the Taliban within the regime - in his function as ISI chief practically made the foreign policy of Pakistan. Thus, the U.S. State Department concluded in September 2000: "While Pakistani support for the Taliban has been long-standing; the magnitude of recent support is unprecedented."[42] The Clinton Administration at that time also appeared increasingly concerned that the direct participation of Pakistan in Taliban military operations had become more and more frequent in recent months, and that Pakistani military personnel had taken a more active role in the fighting.[43] Towards the end of the year 2000, Pakistani aircraft helped Taliban forces with troop rotations during combat operations and staff of the ISI as well as of the army were involved directly in the planning of major military operations of the Taliban.[44] In November 2000, UN General Secretary Kofi Annan Pakistan accused them at least implicitly of providing such support.[45]

Thus, the UN Security Council in January 2001 finally imposed sanctions against the regime in Kabul, which were aimed directly at getting it to stop the Pakistani weapons deliveries to the Taliban.[46] But apparently, the sanctions missed their effect, for an intelligence dossier stating that Pakistan was circumventing the UN sanctions by continuing to deliver fuel and other goods to the Taliban was presented to the Security Council by both Russia and France.[47] In April and May 2001, a few months before September the 11th, 30

ISI trucks were still crossing the Pakistani border into Afghanistan every day - the same number that the U.S. consulate in Peshawar in October 1996 had reported immediately after the coming into power of the Taliban. Some of these convoys were equipped with artillery shells, tank ammunition and anti-tank missiles.[48]

The intentions and actions of Pakistan regarding the Taliban immediately after the terrorist attacks of September the 11th 2001 cannot yet be conclusively assessed due to the few and contradictory sources. What is certain, however, is that the Pakistani military regime in accordance with its longstanding Taliban policy tried to persuade the U.S. to refrain from a military campaign against the Taliban, or at least limit it to air strikes, and to negotiate with the government in Kabul to find a solution.[49] ISI director and de facto Foreign Minister Mahmoud Ahmad tried to convince U.S. Ambassador Wendy Chamberlin that the aim of the United States of eliminating Osama bin Laden and al-Qaeda could best be achieved by forcing the Taliban to do it themselves: "[…]it is better for the Afghans to do it. We could avoid the fallout. If the Taliban are eliminated […] Afghanistan will revert to warlordism."[50]

In September 2001, Ahmad not only met with many members of the Bush administration, but also twice with Mullah Omar in Kandahar. The question of whether or not at that time he made a last-minute attempt to get the Taliban to extradite Osama bin Laden after all, whether, as the U.S. State Department believed, this was merely a delay tactic, as claimed by Ahmed Rashid, or whether, quite to the contrary, Ahmad Mullah Omar encouraged them to brave an American attack rather than turn in Bin Laden, as is claimed by leaks to the CIA, must be left unanswered due to contradictory source material.[51] In any case, during the ensuing Operation Enduring Freedom, the attack by the US-led coalition on the Taliban government, the ISI played a great double game. On the one hand, Pakistan officially made a U-turn, presenting itself as a close U.S. ally in the "war against terrorism" and accepting the "seven points" of the U.S. government, pledging to stop supporting the Taliban and, explicitly, promising to stop all supplies of fuel as well as any other goods and to cancel the transport of weapons and fighters into Afghanistan.[52]

On the other hand, and with the consent of Musharraf the ISI continued providing the Taliban with weapons, ammunition and fuel. As before, ISI trucks were rolling into Afghanistan on a daily basis. In addition, dozens of members of the Frontier Corps and ISI officers remained in Afghanistan to assist the Taliban in their defence. CIA agent Gary Berntsen realised "from the beginning of the conflict that ISI advisers were supporting the Taliban with expertise and material [...]".[53] This double game was to shape and Pakistan's Taliban policy after the expulsion of Mullah Omar's gang from Afghanistan and continues to do so to this day.

The Taliban Insurgency (2002-2010)

Although Pakistan officially became coalition partner of the United States in the Global War on Terror after the overthrow of the Taliban regime by the Northern Alliance and the American Operation Enduring Freedom in late 2001, it simultaneously continued supporting and directing the Taliban as a deputy government in Afghanistan. As opposed to how it is usually being represented in the Western media, the uprising against the US- and NATO-backed Afghan government of Hamid Karzai is not a monolithic, centrally run movement, but highly fragmented.[54] The three main groups are the Taliban of Mullah Omar, the Hizb-i-Islami of Gulbuddin Hekmatyar and the Haqqani network. These three militant groups have all been protected by the ISI since their expulsion from Afghanistan.[55]

In Balochistan, the Taliban were left undisturbed and allowed to settle. Just as they did with the Taliban leaders, the ISI granted refuge to Hekmatyar who, after secret talks with the ISI in Dubai, moved from his exile in Iran to Peshawar in the North Western Frontier Province (NWFP), and was able to operate freely under the protection of the ISI. Thus, the ISI let Hekmatyar set up a base in a refugee camp outside Peshawar, where many of his former combatants were living. Jalaluddin Haqqani was eventually granted refuge in North Waziristan, where he rebuilt his network on both sides of the border. Thereby, the Pakistani military and the ISI played a central and active role, which included urging the Haqqani group take up the fight again and promising them money, weapons and other kinds of support.[56] The ISI didn't only apply pressure to Haqqani fighters, but also warned Taliban families from returning to Afghanistan. Otherwise, the ISI would extradite them to the Americans.[57]

In order to pull off the balancing act as a U.S. ally and supporter of the Taliban, the ISI developed a dual policy. While Pakistan was extraditing al-Qaeda fighters to the U.S, the Taliban were protected.[58] In the first five years after their flight from Kabul not a single Taliban commander was extradited to the Americans. A year after 9/11, as Ahmed Rashid concludes, it was therefore clear that Musharraf's support for the war fought by the U.S. and its allies in Afghanistan did not mean the promised strategic U-turn (which would end the traditional support of the army for Islamic extremists) but only a short-term tactical move to appease the United States and to prevent an Indian hegemony in the region.[59] For Pakistan, the Taliban remained a deputy, through whom it believed to be able to regain control in Afghanistan in the future.

According to a prominent former commander of various militant groups, who, as a fighter, leader and trainer of insurgents in Kashmir, Bosnia, Chechnya and Afghanistan has been in the pay of the ISI since the nineties, it had been as early as the end of 2001, shortly after the fall of the Taliban government, that in the NWFP a meeting between Taliban leaders and several former ISI agents had been held, during which strategies for opposition against the U.S. military were being planned and Afghanistan was divided into individual areas of operation.[60] Among the approximately 60 attendees were the Ambassador of the Taliban government in Pakistan, Abdul Salam Saif, Mohammed Haqqani, one of the sons of Jalaluddin Haqqani, the former ISI agent Colonel Imam, (who, in the course of his illustrious career had been officer in the Special Service Group (SSG) of the Pakistan Army, Consul General in Herat, Afghanistan, as well as trainer and mentor of militant groups like for example the Taliban), but also Major General Zahirul Islam Abbasi, also a former ISI Chief, (who, as commander of the Pakistani army in Kashmir had planned and executed attacks on positions of the Indian army, and who had been convicted of involvement in an attempted coup against the government of Benazir Bhutto in 1995). Abbasi was said to have been one of the most active supporters of the insurgents in Afghanistan in the years after September 11.

The involvement of the ISI in the early stages of the revolt against the Karzai government and international troops (2003-2005) has been widely documented.[61] After the Taliban attacks in Afghanistan had increased in 2003, the ISI provided support again.[62] U.S. and NATO intelligence shows a systematic and pervasive system of ISI collusion. The ISI held training camp for Taliban recruits north of Quetta, handing out money and weapons from the Gulf States and organized shopping tours in Quetta and Karachi, where the Taliban were able to stock up on material, buying hundreds of motorcycles, pickup trucks and satellite phones.

Pakistani army trucks drove Taliban fighters to the border at night in order to infiltrate Afghanistan and were there to receive them when they returned several days later. In doing so, the Pakistani artillery provided fire protection as well as medical care near the border to the Taliban. Moreover, the Pakistani army officers upheld communications from the border with Taliban commanders in Afghanistan via mobile phone. Just like in the early days of the Mullah Omar gang, the Taliban, the ISI and the madrassas of Jamiat Ulema-e-Islam (JUI) were holding in place a well-organized system.[63] Young militants in the madrassas first underwent "religious training" for several weeks before being recruited by Taliban recruiters - who often appeared in the company of ISI officers - and sent to the front. Every month, the heads of all JUI madrasas met with an ISI officer in Quetta to discuss the operational procedures and funding.

The great double game soon proved to be an institutional difficulty for the ISI.[63] Under the watchful eyes of Western intelligence agencies, it was almost impossible for Pakistani intelligence to help the CIA on the one hand and to support the Taliban on the other hand. This challenge was met through privatization. A new secret organization was set up that was to operate outside the military and intelligence apparatus. Former ISI coaches of the Taliban as well as retired Pashtun officers of the army and especially the Frontier

Corps were re-hired on a contractual basis. Logistics and funding no longer went directly via the ISI but the less closely observed Frontier Corps. Diplomatic representatives of the U.S. in Pakistan often complained about the inefficiency and poor provisioning of the Frontier Corps.

However, the available source material invites the conclusion that not (only) incompetence and corruption, but rather Pakistan's double game is at the bottom of it. For example, the Pakistani military received 100 million dollars from the U.S. to fund military assistance to the Frontier Corps in 2007 alone. However, by the end of the year the FC had not even received basic medical assistance.[64] It is quite possible that the extensive medical assistance that the U.S. had agreed to make available to the Frontier Corps instead arrived in the medical supply station for the Taliban that the Pakistani military had built at the border with Afghanistan.

By the end of 2005, even retentive analysts of the U.S. State Department stated in a report to Vice President Cheney: "Some Taliban leaders operate with relative impunity in some Pakistani cities, and may still enjoy support from the lower echelons of Pakistan's ISI."[66] In 2006, the Taliban intensified their offensives in the south and east of Afghanistan. The battles in Helmand provided clear evidence to the NATO of Pakistan's support of the Taliban.[67] A joint intelligence report of the U.S., NATO and the Afghan executive of June 2006 describes the role of Pakistan unequivocally: "ISI operatives reportedly pay a significant number of Taliban living/operating in both Pakistan and Afghanistan to fight. [...]

A large number of those fighting are doing so under duress as a result of pressure from ISI [...] The insurgency cannot survive without its sanctuary in Pakistan, which provides freedom of movement, safe havens, logistic and training facilities, a base for recruitment, communications for command and control, and a secure environment for collaboration with foreign extremist groups. The sanctuary of Pakistan provides a seemingly endless supply of potential new recruits for the insurgency [...]".[68] The interface between the ISI and the Taliban was in Quetta - the lair of the Rabari-Shura - in whose vicinity the ISI had training camps and where the Pakistani gave logistical assistance to the Taliban.[69] There are clear indications that in the capital of Balochistan the ISI went as far as to give direct help to organise Taliban offensives. For example, according to a report published by WikiLeaks from the "Afghan War Diary", ISI agents met with the Taliban leaders in Quetta in June 2006.

At this meeting they are supposed to have urged the Taliban to attack Maruf, a district of Kandahar.[70] In fact, the Taliban soon after launched an offensive to regain control of Maruf. Apart from the two sources cited here, there is further evidence that the ISI continued putting fighters and commanders of the Taliban under pressure. An example is the case of the local commander Lal Din, who was killed in an attack of the coalition forces in January 2007. Shortly afterwards, members of a Provincial Reconstruction Team (PRT) in eastern Afghanistan gave evidence of what Lal Din's younger brother, Fakir, had told them: namely, that Lal Din had confided to Fakir that he had been urged by the ISI to continue his fight in Afghanistan.[71] If we cast our minds back to the fact that as early as 2002 the ISI had put pressure on the Haqqani group to resume the armed fight and had threatened fugitive Taliban families with extradition to the U.S. unless they remained in the Pakistani cities to which they had fled, it becomes evident that Pakistani intelligence plays the role not only of supporting the Taliban, but rather as the driving force behind the insurgency in Afghanistan.

The support of the ISI for the insurgents in Afghanistan continued over the following years and reached a bloody climax with the suicide attack on the Indian Embassy in Kabul on July 7, 2008. This attack, in which 40 people, including the Indian military attaché, were killed, was most likely the act of the Haqqani network and the ISI.[72] Five days after the attack, the Chairman of the Joint Chiefs of Staff, Admiral Mullen and the Deputy Director of the CIA, Stephen Kappes, travelled to Islamabad and showed General Kayani and the political leaders their evidence of the complicity of the ISI and the fighters of Haqqani. Musharraf and Kayani confirmed "that elements of ISI may be out of control" and the

Pakistani government responded to the visit during which Mullen and Kappes had put them under pressure by making concrete demands by arresting several members of the Taliban Shura in Quetta.[73] However, the Haqqani network was never addressed - although army and intelligence service would have been in a position to do so. The U.S. diplomats in Pakistan recognised: "The Army/ISI can do the job, but they cling to 'old think'[…]"[74]

Another reaction of the Pakistani government was the proposal that the United States and the International Security Assistance Force (ISAF) expand their border patrols to curb the drug trade in Afghanistan, whose proceeds the insurgents had been using to buy weapons and fund military operations. However, it is likely that Pakistani leaders continued their brazen duplicity with this initiative. On the one hand, they could appease the U.S. after the attack in Kabul; on the other hand they could increase their control over the Taliban by letting the international troops dry up alternative funding sources of the insurgents and thereby increase their dependence on the Pakistani supporters.

A variety of independent sources indicate that the extensive, comprehensive and systematic support for the Taliban has been maintained by the ISI after 2008. The U.S. State Department clearly stated in a secret background analysis of December 30, 2009: "Pakistan's intermittent support to terrorist groups and militant organizations threatens to undermine regional security and endanger U.S. national security objectives in Afghanistan and Pakistan. Although Pakistani senior officials have publicly disavowed support for these groups some officials from the Pakistan's Inter-Services Intelligence Directorate (ISI) continue to maintain ties with a wide array of extremist organizations, in particular the Taliban, LeT [Lashkar-e-Taiba] and other extremist organizations. These extremist organizations continue to find refuge in Pakistan and exploit Pakistan's extensive network of charities, NGOs, and madrassas. This network of social service institutions readily provides extremist organizations with recruits, funding and infrastructure for planning new attacks.[75]

Even the Saudi General Intelligence Presidency (GIP), which has traditionally played an important role in the region, considered the Afghan Taliban to be largely under the control of Pakistan.[76] Some Taliban were said to be against such a strong influence of Pakistan and would have preferred to pursue their own goals without outside interference, General Massoudi, the Director General of Internal Affairs of the GIP, told Barnett Rubin, the Special Advisor to the Special Representative to Afghanistan and Pakistan of the U.S. government, during a meeting in January 2010. However, this was but a weak group. The vast majority of the Taliban, he continued, were exploited by foreign powers, and only used as "fuel for the fight".

These powers like Iran and Pakistan made the uneducated Afghans believe that the U.S. was working against the Afghan people. The Saudi intelligence service identified two reasons for Pakistan's Afghanistan policy. Firstly, Pakistan was very concerned about losing influence in Afghanistan to India and Iran. "The Pakistanis felt that they deserved to have a big part in Afghanistan [...]. They wanted to be 'the closest friend' and were offended when they thought Iran or India was taking this role." Secondly, the Pakistani-Afghan border was an important factor, "even if the Pakistanis didn't say it. This single issue was a very important factor in the 1980's when Pakistan was deciding which mujahidin groups to support. [...] Pakistan would support only those leaders who promised to recognize the Durand Line as an international border. This was why Pakistan did not support Ahmad Shah Massoud". Incidentally, when General Massoudi worked for GIP chief Prince Turki al-Faisalat the time of the Soviet occupation, Afghanistan was his area of responsibility.

Interviews with several commanders of the Taliban and the Haqqani network in Afghanistan, carried out by Matt Waldman of the Carr Center for Human Rights Policy at Harvard, illustrate the kinds of assistance that the ISI provided the insurgents with and the considerable influence of Pakistan on the resistance in Afghanistan.[78] Even if with a critical analysis of the source these statements have to be taken with some caution, they seem to be credible in their central points, on the one hand through the corresponding testimony of the commanders of various resistance groups and the other by the fact that they are confirmed by documents from the U.S. State Department, countless front reports of the American military in Afghanistan, testimony of former Pakistani generals as well as statements of Afghan government officials.

In 2010, for example, Talat Masood, a retired Pakistani general and one of the leading experts of the Pakistani military, claimed that the ISI has maintained its traditional links to the Taliban.[78] And according to Afghanistan's national security adviser, Dr. Rangin Spanta, Pakistani influence on Afghanistan is still huge. When for example his government wanted to talk with the Haqqani group, it was only possible to do so via the ISI, which operates as the true power factor behind the insurgency.[79] Furthermore, the relationship with the ISI outlined by the commanders of the Taliban to Waldman essentially corresponds to the status quo since the emergence of the Taliban in the mid-nineties: The Pakistani intelligence provided shelter to the Taliban and protects them with supplies, ammunition and money on a grand scale. In addition, the ISI provided the Taliban with tactical, operational and strategic intelligence.[80] The interviews even suggest the conclusion that the ISI supported the most violent and brutal commanders and units within the movement.[81] The ISI continues to tolerate and support military training camps for insurgents and participates in their recruitment in a large number of madrassas that encourage their students to actively fight in Afghanistan.[82]

The interviews, however, strongly suggest that the ISI not only supports the Taliban, but also exerts a strong influence on the group around Mullah Omar - both at the strategic and the operational-tactical level. This influence appears to happen both directly - through several ISI agents in the Quetta Shura - as well as indirectly, through the arrests of unpopular commanders. More will have to be said on the subject of the arrest of Taliban commanders. The presence of several ISI agents in the Quetta Shura means that the Pakistani intelligence service is involved at the highest management levels of the Taliban. A Deputy Minister of the former Taliban regime, which is still collaborating frequently with the Taliban, said that the ISI takes responsibility for the meetings of the Quetta Shura[83] and exerts pressure on the participants prior to the meeting, especially when important decisions are to be taken.[84] The testimony of another expert Taliban commander is representative of many others: "Every commander knows about the involvement of the ISI in the leadership but we do not discuss it because we do not trust each other, and they are much stronger than us.

They are afraid that if they say anything against the Taliban or ISI it would be reported to the higher ranks – and they may be removed or assassinated … Everyone sees the sun in the sky but cannot say it is the sun." And the commander added: "The leadership of the Quetta Shura is in the hands of the ISI".[85] In the face of the powerful internal forces of the movement one political leader went as far as to say, probably exaggerating a bit: "Everything is controlled by the ISI. Without the agreement of the ISI, then the insurgency would be impossible[…]".[86]These statements by the Taliban leader are confirmed by a comprehensive study of the history and structure of the Quetta Shura, which comes to the conclusion that the ISI "maintains a hand in controlling its operations."[87]However, in accordance with the brazen duplicity of his country, the Pakistani Brigadier Sajjad in autumn 2009 told representatives of the American and Canadian troops and Afghan border police that the existence of the Quetta Shura was pure fabrication and that the Americans had been taken in by rumours.[88] The results of Waldman about the Haqqani network correspond largely with those about the Taliban: Even the commanders of Haqqani report that their group is funded by the ISI, which is also taking care of training and recruitment, and is represented in the group of leaders of the network.[89]

Based on his interviews, Waldman answered three more crucial questions that are controversial among observers: Firstly, the support of the Afghan resistance is official ISI policy, secondly it is offered by both active and former ISI officers, and thirdly it is approved at the highest level of Pakistan's civilian government under President Zardari and Prime Minister Gilani.[90] There is sufficient evidence in the source material presented here to prove that the current support of the Taliban continues to be official policy of the ISI (meaning that active ISI officers are involved in it too). The same conclusion is reached in a study by Seth Jones, who notes that the United States in mid-2008 had collected solid evidence of the complicity of the leaders of the ISI.[90]

While it is beyond reasonable doubt that the assistance of the Taliban was sanctioned by the upper echelons of the ISI, the involvement of Pakistan's civilian government that took office in 2008 cannot be conclusively evaluated yet. The thesis of Waldman is, however, supported by a study of Christine Fair, who also comes to the conclusion that the army did not operate alone.[92] In sharp contrast, the leaders of the Pakistani government presented themselves to their American colleagues as a reliable ally in the war on terror and underlined their determination to fight the Taliban.[93]

The United States seemed at first to give credence to these affirmations. The embassy in Islamabad stated in February 2009 that Zardari and Gilani had turned against the Taliban. The military and the ISI, on the other hand, had not yet taken this step and would continue to support the insurgents in Afghanistan as an instrument of foreign policy.[93]A security assessment by the U.S. Consulate in Peshawar in February 2009 also stated that"[…]there is a divided loyalty within ISI ranks which may cause inaction or assistance to Taliban and anti-US groups." The consulate staff, however, already mentioned that–contrary to official pronouncements- there were probably Taliban sympathizers "within the ranks of the Pakistani government"[94]. But apparently, the Obama administration changed its assessment. In September 2009, a review of the Afghanistan/Pakistan strategy in the State Department repeatedly stated that "the Pakistani establishment" was supporting the Taliban as a key part of its national security strategy, which was directed at India as the perceived primary threat.[95] The somewhat vague term "Pakistani establishment" probably included the civilian government of Pakistan and had been coined in order to avoid explicitly naming the latter.

The documents published on the Internet platform WikiLeaks as the "Afghan War Diary" in the summer of 2010, which portray the ISI as the main foreign supporter of the Taliban, seem to illustrate three further characteristics of the relationship between Pakistan and the insurgents in Afghanistan: the key role of the former ISI Director General Hamid Gul, conspiracies to kill Afghan leaders like Hamid Karzai and the orchestration of suicide bombings by the ISI. The sources are problematic, since the documents are mostly front reports from soldiers and employees of the intelligence services of the international forces. They don't amount to intelligence analyses or even "finished intelligence". In addition, the sources of the reports were often connected to the Afghan intelligence service (which was adversely minded towards Pakistan) or paid informants. Although plausible, the mentioned three characteristics therefore still need verification by independent sources. However, neither the Afghan government nor the government of a NATO state called the key points of the documents into question. Their representatives, such as U.S. President Barack Obama, emphasized on the contrary that they contained "nothing new".[96]

In addition, numerous reports are based on sources classified as reliable by the U.S. military, and members of the U.S. executive branch considered the portrayal of the collaboration between the ISI and the Taliban to be largely consistent with classified intelligence analyses. Despite the questionable quality of the sources, the main findings of the Afghan War Diary regarding Pakistan's support for the Taliban will, therefore, be briefly summed up. According to numerous documents, Hamid Gul, who had led the ISI in the final stages of the Soviet occupation of Afghanistan from 1987 to 1989, remained a driving force and organizing hand among the Taliban, as well as the groups of Hekmatyar and Haqqani, whom he had already supported as ISI director.[97] The front reports describe Gul as a major arms supplier of the Taliban and as a mastermind of suicide bombings. Gul is also said to have urged the Taliban commanders to put their operational focus on Afghanistan, so that Pakistan in return could accept their presence in its tribal areas. These reports are given additional plausibility by the pressure that the U.S. exerted on the United Nations to put Gul on its list of international terrorists and by testimony from senior members of the Obama administration, who described the general as a critical link between active Pakistani officers and the insurgents.

According to the Afghan War Diary, ISI agents have also hatched plans to assassinate Afghan leaders. Even President Karzai was allegedly among the target persons: in a warning in August 2008, an ISI colonel is identified who is said to have told a Talib to bring about the assassination of Karzai. The documents also record the attempts by ISI agents to manage the network of suicide bombers in Afghanistan, who have been plying their deadly trade since 2006.[98] Various documents describe how current and former ISI officials, among whom the apparently omnipresent General Gul, recruited candidates for suicide attacks in madrassas in Peshawar, who were then trained in Pakistan. American intelligence agencies realised that the Haqqani network unleashed suicide bombers to attack the representatives of the Indian government in Afghanistan, aid workers and engineers on behalf of the ISI. This evidence for the involvement of the ISI in suicide attacks corresponds to the already discussed complicity of Pakistan's intelligence service in the suicide attack on the Indian Embassy in Kabul in July 2008 and is supported by the study of Matt Waldman.[99]

The Baradar Case: A Symbol of Pakistan's Double Game

In Mid-February 2010, the New York Times reported on its front page the arrest of Mullah Abdul Ghani Baradar Akhund, the number two of the Afghan Taliban leaders, by Pakistani security forces.[100] Baradar was arrested at an Islamic school near Karachi. In the United States, this arrest was hailed as a great success. On the one hand because this appeared to deal a serious blow to the leaders of the insurgency in Afghanistan, but on the other hand also because many experts and commentators seemed to recognise this as a long-awaited change in the strategy of the Pakistani leaders. Soon, however, critical voices were increasing, not least from Pakistan itself, which considered the operation against Baradar and other cadres of Taliban and al-Qaeda to be the pursuit of Pakistan's own interests rather than cooperation in the "war on terror".

Baradar, probably born in 1968, is a Zirak-Durrani Pashtun and belongs to the Popalzai tribe. During the Soviet occupation, he fought with the mujahedeen against the Soviets. After the occupation, he is said to have founded and led an Islamic school in Maiwand together with Mullah Omar. In 1994 he was among the founders of the Taliban, who, according to their founding myth, created the new movement under the impression of the disgusting behaviour of some commanders.[101] Varying information is circulating about his function during the Taliban era. He is said to have served as governor of the provinces of Herat and Nimroz, have been deputy chief of staff and held the position of deputy defence minister of the Taliban government.[102]

After the commencement of operations of the United States and its allies to topple the Taliban in October 2001 Baradar is said to have got his fellow combatant Mullah Omar to safety in the mountains with a motorcycle.[103] He himself was imprisoned by coalition troops, but was set free after a short time following intervention by the ISI.[104] Thereafter, Baradar was increasingly considered "de-facto leader" of the Taliban. Mullah Omar appeared noticeably less frequently, and operational decisions seem to have been made more and more by Baradar. Since then, Baradar has increasingly become the real leader of the Taliban. Mullah Omar appeared increasingly less frequently, and operational decisions seem to have been increasingly made by Baradar. Meanwhile, he is considered "de-facto leader" of the Taliban. Mullah Omar appeared noticeably less frequently, and operational decisions seem to have been made more and more by Baradar.[105]

Baradar also has connections with President Karzai. When, in late 2001 he returned to Afghanistan with the help of the Americans and tried to regain control in his home region, he got into a dangerous situation during negotiations with warlords. Baradar saved him and in return got the promise that he would not be prosecuted by the government of Hamid Karzai for his time as Taliban Minister. Karzai is also said to have promised him to let the Taliban participate in a new Afghan government. This deal never materialised, and after the coalition troops attacked his home, Baradar fled to Pakistan.[106] From there, he was involved in the development of resistance against the U.S. and NATO forces. Baradar became more and more of a leader figure, even though his name and prominence were probably familiar only to a few. His rise was also helped by the elimination of colleagues and rivals, such as the notorious Mullah Dadullah.[107] Since 2007; Baradar also seems to have been the strong man in the highest military body of the Taliban, the Quetta Shura.

During the whole period, the contact between Baradar and the government in Kabul seems never to have been interrupted. According to a Newsweek article by Ron Moreau, who has communicated with Baradar also by e-mail, the Taliban leader actively supported entering into discussions with the central government of Karzai on at least two occasions, 2004 and early 2009.[108] Baradar, therefore, had a very influential position: Firstly, as a leading member of the Quetta Shura, he had a crucial role in shaping the military strategy of the Taliban in Afghanistan. Secondly, he also had ties to Pakistan's ISI, which becomes evident, if from nothing else, from the fact that the agency released him from American captivity. And thirdly, Baradar has never let the connection to the government in Kabul be interrupted and has signalled his readiness for dialogue.

On the morning of the 8th of February 2010, Pakistani security forces stormed a madrassa in Karachi.[109] They arrested several people. The ISI had allegedly become active following a tip-off, but had been unable to locate the leader of the Taliban themselves. Therefore, he had requested the assistance of American experts. When Baradar switched on his mobile phone, the trap snapped shut. The technicians of the CIA had located his position and guided the Pakistani security forces to it. It is unclear who knew how much about the person they targeted. The ISI was said to have asked the Americans for help without informing them about the purpose, and the statement of the CIA "that the ISI initially wasn't aware of the fact that they had arrested Baradar either caused hilarity in Islamabad".[110] While, after learning of the identity of the high-ranking prisoner, the arrest was celebrated as a huge blow to the Taliban in the United States, some questions arose in connection with the spectacular way in which it had been carried out. The mere fact that Baradar was arrested near the metropolis of Karachi should be cause for reflection, as the Pakistanis have been denying the fact that their country served as a refuge and abode of leaders of both the Taliban and the al-Qaeda for years. Three explanations are possible:

1. It was a fluke. The ISI really had no idea who they were arresting;

2. It was a change of strategy. Pakistan actually has made a U-turn on its Taliban policy and will deny the insurgents help in the future;

3. It was part of the double game. Pakistan is once again playing a double game and has, with Baradar, taken the most influential person who sought a dialogue and a solution through negotiation with the Government of Karzai, out of circulation, because Pakistan saw its strategic objectives endangered.

The first explanation can be excluded, because on the basis of the above-mentioned earlier contacts of ISI to Baradar it may be assumed that he was well known in Pakistan. A high NATO official confirmed this assessment: "Baradar is too high-profile for them not to have known who it was."[111] Nor is it likely that individual elements of the ISI were acting independently. This leaves the question of whether the change in thinking that has long been desired by the U.S. has actually taken place in Pakistan or whether the leaders of the country have once more betrayed their allies in favour of their own goals.

The United States, in any case, responded to the news of the arrest with pleasure. Experts and commentators spoke of a "sea change in Pakistani behavior"[112], a "turning point in Pakistan's policy towards the Taliban"[113] or a "strategic recalibration".[114] Pakistan, it seemed, finally met a key demand of the United States by beginning a crack-down on the Taliban. The arrest of Baradar was neither the first nor the last. In fact, the Pakistani authorities could present an impressive list of arrested Taliban and al-Qaeda extremists. The names included the former finance minister as well as the former police chief of the Taliban.[115]

Many indications, however, contradict this interpretation and suggest that the ISI, the military, and the Pakistani government once again played the familiar double game. Pakistan saw itself at risk of a negotiated peace between the government and the insurgents in Afghanistan without its interests being adequately considered. Precisely these fears were fueled by secret negotiations that Baradar and other Taliban leaders arrested in February 2010 had been undertaking with the Karzai government.[116] Baradar and the other high-ranking detainees such as Mullah Abdul Rauf Aliza and Mullah Ahmed Jan Akhundzada belonged to the moderate forces within the Taliban, who were ready to engage in peace negotiations. Thomas Johnson and Chris Mason thus came to the conclusion that the arrests were intended to take out Taliban leaders who had a positive attitude towards negotiations with the Afghan government. For Johnson and Mason, it is evident that "this is not cooperation against the Taliban by an allied state; it is collusion with the Taliban by an enemy state."[117]

Waldman concludes that Pakistan wanted to demonstrate that it would block negotiations until it was fully involved in the process. He quotes a diplomat claiming that the Pakistani government had all high-ranking Taliban who had signaled their readiness for peace talks arrested by February 2010.[118] Members of the Pakistani executive branch revealed their intention to stop the secret peace negotiations that Baradar had held with the Afghan government, which had excluded Pakistan. A member of the security forces confirmed: "We picked up Baradar and the others because they were trying to make a deal without us.[…]We are not going to allow them to make a deal with Karzai and the Indians.[119]" On the other side, most of the rebels interviewed by Waldman also interpreted the arrests as an attempt to block the peace negotiations.

Western observers in Pakistan shared this view. A high-ranking NATO staff officer, for example, admitted that "we have been played before. That the Pakistanis picked up Baradar to control the tempo of the negotiations is absolutely plausible."[120] A former diplomat with extensive experience in the Middle East likewise considered the wave of arrests to be a warning of the ISI directed at the Taliban. Finally, a report of the Congressional Research Service about the raid against Osama bin Laden in May 2011 also noted that the U.S. and other Western governments had seemingly been anxious for some time that Pakistan had begun to take a more aggressive and unilateralist course in 2010 to determine the progress of peace negotiations in Afghanistan. As signs of this new course the report listed the arrests of certain Taliban who had pushed negotiations with the Karzai government, as well as Pakistan's protection of the Haqqani Network in North Waziristan.[121] Therefore, there remains little doubt that Pakistan once again played the double game: On the one hand, it appeased the United States by signaling that it was now seriously cracking down on the extremists on its territory. On the other hand, it influenced the strategy of the Taliban to the effect that negotiations with the Karzai government without Pakistani permission were considered off limits. In doing so; the ISI kept the Taliban as a proxy to pursue its strategic interests in Afghanistan and strengthened its control over the insurgent group.

Conclusions

Since September 11, 2001, the subsequent acceptance of the "seven points" by President Pervez Musharraf and the start of Operation Enduring Freedom in Autumn 2001, Pakistan have been presenting itself as a reliable coalition partner of the United States and the West in the "war on terrorism"–and has been publicly acknowledged as such by NATO countries. In December 2009 President Barack Obama reiterated characteristically:"[…]we are committed to a partnership that is built on a foundation of mutual interest, mutual respect and mutual trust."[122] In April 2010, the U.S. Department of Defense called Pakistan an ally and "effective partner".[123] As a result of its apparent strategic U-turn, Pakistan received from the United States 10.7 billion US dollars in Coalition Support Funding (CSF) for its security apparatus since 9/11, and on top of that another 8,7 billion US dollars in economic aid.[124] This means that Pakistan has received almost 90 percent of the total CSF worldwide.[125]Pakistani officers even sat in the Tripartite Joint Intelligence Operations Center, located in the ISAF headquarters in Kabul.[126]

Behind this façade of a faithful ally in the "war on terrorism," Pakistan played a bold double game that has blown the outcome of the war in Afghanistan wide open. From the foundation of Mullah Omar's group in 1994 to 2010 the ISI gave the Taliban extensive, comprehensive and systematic support. The ISI supplied the Taliban with money, weapons, ammunition and intelligence, provided for their military training, organized the recruitment of new Islamist militants in the madrassas, and helped in planning military offensives. Although the organisation, the nature and also the extent of assistance varied and evolved over the 16 years covered in this article, the provision of support has been a constant feature of the relationship between the ISI and the Taliban. Moreover, since the Taliban fled from Afghanistan in the winter of 2001/2002, the ISI harboured Taliban leaders in Balochistan and also supported the other two major factions of the rebellion in Afghanistan, the Hizb-i-Islami of Gulbuddin Hekmatyar and especially the Haqqani network. Without this support and guidance from Pakistan, the insurgency in Afghanistan would have been impossible in the extent it had reached by 2010.

The ISI was not only by far the most important foreign sponsor of the Afghan insurgency but also manipulated the intentions of these groups. The Pakistani intelligence service had a significant influence on the Taliban, including at the strategic level, which it exerted both directly, through ISI agents in the Quetta Shura, and indirectly, through (threatened) arrests, as in the case of Mullah Baradar. Starting in 2002, the ISI has put its Afghan proxy under a lot of pressure to continue the armed struggle against the Kabul government and the international forces by threatening to murder or arrest them or to extradite them to the United States. The attempt of the ISI to control or at least influence Islamist proxies in Afghanistan, which goes back to the time of the Mujahedeen's fight against the Red Army, shaped the sometimes problematic relationship between the ISI and the Taliban from the beginning.

There is also some evidence that parts of the money Pakistan received from the United States as security assistance to wage the "war on terrorism" ended up reaching the Taliban. Moreover, the ISI and the Pakistani military may at times have exploited the American troops as unintentional helpers to increase their control over the Taliban and to keep the Afghan insurgency alive. This is at least what happened when Mullah Baradar and other leading Taliban were arrested in February 2010. The question remains why the ISI continued supporting the Taliban on a grand scale in spite of the U.S. carrot-and-stick policy, which consisted of both strong pressure and more than 10 billion dollars in Coalition Support Funding, and despite the growing blowback caused by the Pakistani Taliban, who developed into a serious threat for Pakistan from 2007 onwards and at times controlled large areas in the Federally Administered Tribal Areas (FATA) and KP province. Why did Pakistan play the double game? Even though Pakistan's Afghanistan policy can certainly not be explained in a strictly monocausal way, the perception of India as the largest and existential threat has constituted a guiding motive.

This perception, which is associated with deep-rooted fears, explains Pakistan's strategic objective of a stable government in Afghanistan, which, if not directly controlled by Islamabad, should at least be well-disposed towards it, and in any event free of Indian influence. Since the mid-1990s, the ISI pursued this aim almost exclusively by using the Taliban as a proxy force. Closely connected with national interests is the concept of "strategic depth". This concept stresses the importance of access to enough space west of the Indus for a regrouping of the Pakistani army, if they were to be pushed behind this river by an Indian invasion. Although the need for "strategic depth", which ostensibly requires a pro-Pakistan government in Afghanistan, had been convincingly refuted by Pakistan's civilian strategists, the concept still played a paramount role in the thinking of military leaders.[127] As recently as 2010, General Kayani, the Chief of Staff of the Pakistan Army, reduced the objective of his country to a simple denominator: "We want a strategic depth in Afghanistan."[128]

India, in turn, challenged Pakistan's strategic objective of minimising the influence and presence of India in Afghanistan. New Delhi has been taking an important role in the civilian reconstruction in Afghanistan, in which it invested between 0.5 and 1.3 billion US dollars until 2010. India financed roads, bridges, canals, schools, the training of Afghan officials, and even the reconstruction of the Afghan parliament.[129] India's reconstruction strategy, one of the best and most comprehensive ever at the Hindu Kush, was designed to gain ground in every sector of Afghan society, to give India a good reputation in the Afghan population, to derive the maximum political advantage and of course to prevent Pakistani influence.[130] In addition to increased development assistance, India has, encouraged by the U.S. government, stepped up its investments in and its trade with Afghanistan.[131]

India also maintained close relations with the Karzai administration. It established a network of four consulates in Afghanistan, reopening the consulates in Kandahar and Jalalabad, which had been closed since 1979, and the country's foreign intelligence service, the Research and Analysis Wing (RAW), also expanded its presence and increased its activities.[132] In addition, India has desired to take an important role in training the Afghan security forces. "[We] will not leave Afghanistan because we have strategic interests there", YK Sinha, secretary for Afghanistan, Pakistan and Iran in the Indian Foreign Ministry, told a representative of the U.S. government at a meeting in February 2010.[133] In short, India has been trying to profit from the lack of Pakistani influence over the Afghan government in an increasingly aggressive way. The ISI in turn attempted to counter India's, perceived or actual, influence by supporting the insurgents in Afghanistan as a proxy.

A secondary motive of Pakistan's support for the Taliban is the question of Pashtunistan and the controversial border demarcation with Afghanistan. During the Second Anglo-Afghan War, Afghanistan had to cede parts of western Balochistan, Quetta and the bulk of the FATA to Britain in the Treaty of Gandamak in 1879. In 1893, Sir Mortimer Durand determined Afghanistan's present borders with Pakistan (then British India) in accordance with this contract, permanently dividing the Pashtun tribal areas.[134]

No Afghan government has accepted the Durand Line, which has always been rejected by a large number of Pashtuns on both sides of the border.[135]

Pakistan has thus traditionally tried to gain influence among the Pashtuns to prevent the emergence of a Pashtunistan and to silence Afghan demands for territory in north west Pakistan. This objective provides a second explanation of why the ISI supported the Taliban since the mid-1990s. The Durrani Pashtuns, who occupied most government posts in Kabul, are known to decidedly support the idea of Pashtunistan and made claims to Pakistani territory – unlike the Ghilzai Pashtuns, their historical rivals who dominate the upper echelons of the Taliban.[136] Pakistan's Afghanistan policy has therefore been strongly shaped by a historical perspective. On the one hand by the fateful legacy of the colonial border between Pakistan and Afghanistan, but above all by the rivalry with India, which goes back to the foundation of the two states in the wake of the decolonization of British India in 1947 and has since then been cemented by four wars.

The Authors

Dr. AdrianHänniis a political historian teaching at Distance Learning University Switzerland and the University of Zurich. His research interests include the history of propaganda, intelligence services, and terrorism with a focus on the Cold War era. In early 2020, he edited the book Über Grenzen hinweg: Transnationale Politische Gewalt im 20. Jahrhundert ("Across Borders: Transnational Political Violence in the Twentieth Century"). His latest monograph, Terrorismus als Konstrukt ("Terrorism as a Construct"), was published in 2018. He may be contacted at adrian@adrianh.ch.

Lukas Hegi works as an expert in the field of integral risk management with specialization in crisis management. In this function he advises and supervises projects of companies in the aviation, critical infrastructure and public sector. His interests include military history and the history of intelligence services. He is also an officer of the Swiss Armed Forces in the rank of major. He may be contacted at hegi@swissint.ch.

Chapter 6

The US's Greatest Strategic Failure: Steve Coll on the CIA and the ISI

Ann Wilkens

"Directorate S" is Steve Coll's second major study of the CIA's role in recent Afghan wars. While "Ghost Wars" chronicled the years 1979-2001, "Directorate S" – referring to a subdivision of Pakistan's inter-services intelligence directorate that covers Afghanistan – takes up the story in 2001 and follows it through to 2016. AAN Advisory Board member Ann Wilkens found Coll's renderings of the lack of cohesion between the US and its Western allies, as well as between various US institutions, particularly compelling. Equally powerful were Coll's startling account of the shifting and frequently contradictory views the US held off its Pakistani ally – and the slow unraveling of the bilateral relationship.

Steve Coll has shed more light on the murky politics that govern the relations between the intelligence services of United States, Afghanistan and Pakistan than any other writer. His seminal work "Ghost Wars, The Secret History of the CIA, Afghanistan and Bin Laden, from the Soviet Invasion to September 10, 2001", first published in 2004 chronicled the role of the CIA in the defeat of the Soviet army in Afghanistan during the emergence of the Taleban movement and in the pre-9/11 hunt for Osama Bin Laden. Earlier this year, it was followed by "Directorate S, The C.I.A. and America's Secret Wars in Afghanistan and Pakistan, 2001-2016". Directorate

124

S refers to a branch within the Inter-Services Intelligence (ISI), the most powerful of Pakistan's intelligence agencies, that deals with Afghanistan. It provides a rich and detailed account of the prolonged failure of the international community to bring stability to Afghanistan, recording the minutiae of 'who-said-what-to-whom-and-when' in an accessible narrative form. This review and dispatch will concentrate on Coll's coverage of Pakistan's intelligence service.

Western incoherence

The lack of cohesion among members of the international intervention in Afghanistan has been well-documented previously, and emerges once again in "Directorate S" as a major cause of Western failures in Afghanistan. The divide between the United States and ISAF partners is richly illustrated through the book's focus on the CIA (which ran its covert war in parallel with, not inside, ISAF). Coll cites as one example the "Riedel review", compiled in 2009 by former CIA officer Bruce Riedel to help define the Obama administration's approach to Afghanistan, in which Riedel "found that the United States had only one truly 'vital' interest in the region: to defeat Al Qaeda. [...] America had other interests in the war, such as stability in South Asia and the reduction of heroin trafficking, but Al Qaeda trumped all others." (p. 366)

State-building in Afghanistan, an important goal for ISAF partners, is shown not to have been an American priority, at least not in the early stages of the intervention. When it does become more prominent, with the counterinsurgency (COIN) strategy launched by ISAF commander Stanley McChrystal in 2009, it is accompanied by a military surge emulating developments (then deemed successful) in Iraq two years earlier. Similarly, partner countries, with the exception of the United Kingdom, hardly figure in the many conversations rendered from decision-making circles in Washington. People talk about Afghanistan as if it were an American war, not the joint international effort hailed in official contexts.

Incoherence stands out as a hallmark of decision-making within the US as well. Already during the Bush administration, an "incoherent command structure [...] had grown up in Afghanistan as a result of ad hoc compromises with N.A.T.O. and within the American military." In Kandahar and Helmand, the units deployed included "American 'black' or covert Special Operations units, 'white' or Green-Beret-style American Special Forces, British forces, Dutch forces, U.S. Marines and multinational Provincial Reconstruction Teams."(p. 331-332) At the beginning of 2010, Coll writes, there were three different strategies for Afghanistan in Washington: "From ISAF headquarters, Stanley McChrystal commanded an intensifying ground war based on the clear-hold-build-transfer principles of counterinsurgency.[...]From the Global Response Center in Langley, the CIA independently ran a drone war against al Qaeda and the Taliban holed up in Waziristan. [...] Simultaneously, from the ground floor of the State Department, [the US's special representative for Afghanistan] Richard Holbrooke and his aides [...] pursued a third: trying to talk to [Taleban leader] Mullah Mohammad Omar's lieutenants about peace. [...] On paper, Obama's National Security Council supported all three policies. But it would require feats of mental gymnastics to call these lines of action synchronized."(p. 438)

Among these actors, Holbrooke –who passed away in 2010 –seems to be the only one to have focused on the wider, regional picture. Coll renders a private conversation Holbrooke had with a reporter in 2010: "There are three countries here–Pakistan, Afghanistan and India –with vastly different stages of political, social and economic development. They share a common strategic space. As has happened so many times in history, the weak state is the one that sucks in the others. That's the history of Afghanistan and now the Great Game is being played with different players. The India-Pakistan relationship is an absolutely critical driver."(p. 430-431)

His boss, Foreign Secretary Hillary Clinton, is also wary of the possibility that the US might get bogged down in contradictions: "What was the 'end-state vision' that the United States sought in

Afghanistan? Clinton asked. That was perhaps why Karzai pressed so hard for Israel-like guarantees – perhaps he sensed correctly that the Obama administration did not know the answer. 'Pakistan knows what end state they want,' Clinton said. 'They have gotten more threatening to Afghanistan recently. They are letting loose the Haqqani network. But we don't know our end-state vision because we don't have one. We don't have a Pakistan strategy or a reconciliation strategy. Just words and process.'" (p. 455-6)

In his concluding chapter, Coll comes back to the US-Pakistan-India relationship: "The rising, embittered skepticism toward Pakistan at the Pentagon, in Congress, and at the C.I.A. engendered by America's experience of the Afghan war after 2001 helped to solidify ties between the United States and India; after 2001, the two countries judged increasingly that they shared a common enemy. Yet India proved to be cautious about working too closely or explicitly with Washington in Afghanistan or the region. The country's noisy democratic politics contained a large strain of skepticism about American power. And India's security establishment remained wary of taking risks in Afghanistan–say, by providing lethal military aid and troops to bolster Afghan forces against the Taliban–that might confirm Pakistan's fears of encirclement and thereby provoke ISI to retaliate by sponsoring more terrorism inside India."

He also touches on the Pakistan-China relationship: "The fallout from the Afghan war also persuaded Pakistan's leaders, after 2011, to give up on any strategic partnership with Washington and to deepen ties to Beijing. This effectively opened Pakistani territory to Chinese companies and military planners, to construct transit corridors and bases that might improve China's regional influence and links to the Middle East. Overall, the war left China with considerable latitude in Central Asia, without having made any expenditure of blood, treasure or reputation." (p. 663)

Pakistan's consistently ambiguous stance

In contrast, Pakistan's policy stands out as consistent, i.e., as being consistently ambiguous. Coll describes Pakistan's support to the Taleban as "just enough to keep the war broiling while avoiding aid so explicit that it might provoke the international community to impose sanctions on Pakistan or withdraw military sales."(p. 679) still, while consistent, the strategy was not cohesive. While Pakistan used a variety of channels to supply the Taleban, the theory of a "rogue I.S.I." is refuted: "American intelligence reporting on individual, serving I.S.I. case officers, who managed contacts with the Quetta Shura or the Haqqanis/.../, showed that they were clearly in the Pakistan Army's chain of command."

However, the picture is complex and confusing: "Overall, it was very difficult to reach a judgment that 'Pakistan' did this or that or even that there was such a thing as 'Pakistan's policy', when there were so many actors and when Directorate S was engaging diverse militant groups for different purposes at different times. In the tribal areas, ISI sometimes made deals with violent radicals for defensive, tactical reasons – to forestall attacks on themselves or to get military supplies through to isolated bases. Other times the I.S.I made deals for strategic reasons – to encourage the groups to enlarge their influence inside Afghanistan or to attack Indian targets there. Still other times the army attacked these same groups in retaliation for attacks inside Pakistan." (p. 289)

Throughout the book, Washington deals with the Pakistani army, not its government, as its natural counterpart. The civilian government structure hardly figures, much less parliament or civil society. After the replacement of the Musharraf regime by a civilian PPP-led government, the US ambassador in Islamabad warned her government: "'let's not fool ourselves that we have a democracy' to work with in Islamabad. The United States had to work with the Pakistan army." (p. 403)

Ashfaq Parvez Kayani

The period covered throughout the book largely coincides with Ashfaq Parvez Kayani's position at the helm of, first the ISI and then of the army, for a prolonged tenure (2004-2013). Kayani, thus, is the central Pakistani character in the drama surrounding Afghanistan. He comes across as sophisticated (more so than some of his American counterparts), low-key and circumspect. And consistent–he never comes close to giving up on the idea that Pakistan needs to exert influence in Afghanistan to counter the threat from India, ie the old concept of "strategic depth". He is also better at keeping his cool when bullied by Americans than Hamid Karzai, the Afghan president who keeps irritating his US sponsors. With Kayani, there is no shouting, no show-downs, just quiet reservation and, yes, consistency in the face of a host of different American interlocutors.

One of them is CIA deputy director Steve Kappes, dispatched to Islamabad to challenge Kayani after the bombing of the Indian embassy in Kabul on 7 July 2008, which, according to "American, British and other allied intelligence services", had been carried out by "a special Haqqani unit [...] under I.S.I. orders to hit hostile targets in Afghanistan, including Indian ones." During the meeting, Kayani "was reticent, professional, a listener, but his method was to never really say yes and never really say no."(p. 308) Kayani's main counterpart as army chief, however, was Mike Mullen, the most senior military officer on the American side. Between 2008 and 2013, Mullen visited Kayani in Pakistan 27 times, in addition to many meetings elsewhere and frequent telephone conversations. Mullen's hypothesis about the ISI was a layered one:

"At the very top of its hierarchy, I.S.I. was a black-and-white organization, fully subject to discipline and accountability [...]. In the middle the organization started to go gray, fading into heavily compartmented operations that drew upon mid-level officers, civilians, contractors, and retirees. Then there were retired I.S.I. director-generals or senior brigadiers with their own followings among militants." (p. 322) Other American analysts "started to grasp that the Taliban forces operated on a formal rotation system – training in Pakistan, field deployment, and then rest and recuperation back in Pakistan. Pakistan Army and Frontier Corps troops along the Pakistani border were firing on American border posts to provide covering fire for the Taliban to infiltrate into Afghanistan and return – the same tactics Pakistani forces employed for Kashmiri militants along the Line of Control." (p. 329-330)

Providing a sign that the relationship between Kayani and Mullen went quite deep, Kayani discusses even his possible prolongation as army chief with his American counterpart: "When he met Mullen, Kayani returned to a delicate subject they had been reviewing privately for months. Should Kayani engineer and accept a three-year extension as chief of army staff and de facto head of state? Mullen wanted him to extend but talked to him gently about the pros and cons. In public, the Obama administration emphasized the importance of Pakistani democracy and civilian rule; in private, it negotiated for the continuation of favorable military control." (p. 500).

Osama Bin Laden

Ironically, while these rather intimate conversations were taking place, CIA analysts started investigating a certain compound in Abbottabad, suspected of housing Osama bin Laden and his family. On this subject, Coll writes: "Kayani had been I.S.I. director for less than a year when Bin Laden set up in Abbottabad. The Al Qaeda emir and his family enjoyed support from a sizable, complex network inside Pakistan–document manufacturers, fund-raisers, bankers, couriers, and guards. His youngest wife, Amal, gave birth to four children in Pakistani hospitals or clinics after 2002. Bin Laden limited his movements, rarely leaving his homes, but he did travel on Pakistani roads numerous times without getting caught, as did his sons and wives. Amal traveled at least once on an internal flight. In one case a man dressed as a policeman accompanied Bin

Laden, according to one of the women who traveled with him. It is entirely plausible that I.S.I. ran a highly compartmented, cautious support operation involving a small number of case officers or contractors who could maintain deniability. Yet there remains no authoritative evidence – on-the-record testimony, letters, or documents – of knowing complicity by I.S.I. or the Pakistani state. [...]

C.I.A. and other administration officials have said that they possess no evidence – no intercepts, no unreleased documents from Abbottabad – that Kayani or Pasha or any other I.S.I. officer knew where Bin Laden was hiding. Given the hostility toward Pakistan prevalent in the American national security bureaucracy by 2011, if the United States possessed such hard evidence, it almost certainly would have leaked." (p. 548-549)

If Kayani had indeed been unaware of Osama bin Laden's presence in Pakistan, the same may not have been true of Mullah Omar's presence. When US Foreign Secretary John Kerry hosted Kayani and Karzai in Brussels in 2013 to discuss the possibility of peace negotiations with the Taleban, "Kayani insisted that he did not know where Mullah Mohammed Omar was. More than two years later, the Taliban would admit that on [that] very day [...] Omar died of tuberculosis in a Karachi hospital. If Kayani knew of the Taliban emir's dire condition, he kept it to himself while working on the statement in Omar's name. None of the Americans had a clue. Kayani continued to represent to the Americans that he was carrying messages from Omar. Afghan intelligence did have a sense that Omar might be dead, but it could not prove it to the satisfaction of the Americans." (p. 637-638) (1)

No advice, please

After his appointment as commander of US and ISAF forces in 2009, General McChrystal flew to Brussels to meet Kayani, who had been invited to talk at a NATO meeting there. Together with Mullen and General David Petraeus, later to become McChrystal's successor, he met separately with Kayani to discuss the situation on the ground in Afghanistan. According to one of the meeting's participants quoted in the book, McChrystal talked of the need "to hit the center of gravity." Kayani disagreed: "'You don't identify the center of gravity for the purpose of attacking it [...]. You find ways to unbalance it without going straight at it.' He might have been describing I.S.I.'s twenty-year strategy against Kabul.

'This will become a revolving door in the south – you'll go in and out, the Taliban will go in and out.'" The Americans, however, "were in no mood to take military advice from Kayani. Petraeus became aggravated. The last person he wanted to take advice from about the war in eastern Afghanistan was a general whose refusal to tear down the Taliban leadership in Quetta or to clean their militias out of North Waziristan was itself undermining N.A.T.O. strategy enormously. Pakistan's sanctuaries were probably the biggest vulnerability in their military plan. [...] Petraeus made his irritation plain and Kayani went outside to cool off with a smoke." (p. 369)

A long history of schizophrenia

Overall, Coll describes the relationship between Washington and the Pakistani army as being one of "a long history of schizophrenia."(p. 314) Apart from the dependence on Pakistan for transit traffic supplying the troops in Afghanistan, a major reason for the US's continued wooing of Pakistani generals with aid and consultations was Pakistan's nuclear arsenal: "The [Bush] administration had 'regular' reports of Al Qaeda and other groups plotting to steal nuclear weapons. They did not want to do anything that would destabilize Pakistani command and control." (p. 312). The Obama administration, in spite of mounting pressure to deal more harshly with Pakistani counterparts, by and large follows the same pattern. In his conclusion, Coll states: "America failed to achieve its aims in Afghanistan for many reasons: under investment in development and security immediately after the Taliban's fall; the drains on resources and the provocations caused by the U.S.-led invasion of Iraq; corruption fed by N.A.T.O. contracting and C.I.A. deal making with strongmen; and military hubris at the highest levels of the Pentagon. Yet the failure to solve the riddle of the I.S.I. and to stop its covert interference in Afghanistan became, ultimately, the greatest strategic failure of the American war." (p. 667)

Conclusions

The conclusions drawn in "Directorate S" are relevant. As the Afghan war lingers on with yet new decision-makers in Washington, a number of old truths illustrated in the book remain clear. While not always immediately apparent, they are also significant factors in the 25 July national election in Pakistan:

- Geography will not change. Since the 1947 partition, Pakistan has defined its strategic interest as having access westwards, in Afghanistan, in the face of a threat from the East, ie, India. This position has survived periods of great turmoil without any substantial change. The likelihood that this will now change, with China emerging as Pakistan's default supporter, seems remote;

- Relations between Pakistan and India remain at the centre of the regional conflict, which cannot be solved unless the international community works on these relations too – from both sides;

- On the Pakistani side, the strategy should not be continued one-dimensional support to its army, which has a vested interest in maintaining its central role. The democratic process has to be supported, strengthened and used for unlocking the stalemate. "Directorate S" needs a counterweight.

"The US's Greatest Strategic Failure": Steve Coll on the CIA and the ISI. Ann Wilkens. Date: 23 July 2018.

Chapter 7

Directorate S: The C.I.A. and America's Secret Wars in Afghanistan and Pakistan

Barbara Elias

In mesmerizing detail, Steve Coll's Directorate-S documents the tragic policies of the US war in Afghanistan. It is a slow, heart-wrenching history of strategically compromised half-measures and uncoordinated bureaucratic practices, in which US, Pakistani, and Afghan allies have cooperated with and conspired against one another, over time enabling the Taliban to reclaim political and geographic space in Afghanistan. A sequel to Coll's 2005 Pulitzer-winning volume Ghost Wars: The Secret History of the CIA, Afghanistan, and Bin Laden, from the Soviet Invasion to September 10, 2001 (2004) documenting the Soviet intervention in Afghanistan and the rise of the Taliban until 2001, Directorate S ambitiously and impressively provides a post-September 11 "history of how the C.I.A., ISI [Pakistan's Inter-Services Intelligence], and Afghan intelligence agencies influenced the rise of a new war in Afghanistan after the fall of the Taliban, and how that war fostered a revival of Al Qaeda, allied terrorist networks, and, eventually, branches of the Islamic State" (p. 7). The book is named after Directorate S, the vexingly effective wing of the ISI that secretively and steadfastly assists the Taliban insurgency against US forces.

Dean of Columbia University's School of Journalism, Coll draws on over five hundred interviews and hundreds of primary source documents to provide an outstanding narrative of a staggeringly complex conflict. The book combines such details as verbatim transcripts of tapped phone conversations between ISI officials with sweeping synopses on the cumulative effects of Pakistani, Afghan, and American policies. For example, in a section discussing US resistance to an Afghan request for expanded support for its intelligence agencies to help Kabul monitor Pakistani support of insurgents, Coll comments that this is a prime example of the American approach to Afghanistan, "deliberate minimalism, followed by tentative engagement, followed by massive investments only when it was very late to make a difference" (p. 192). Unlike the war itself, the book is superbly organized and beautifully composed. In a chapter examining the early years of American intervention, titled "Catastrophic Success," Coll writes, "Thirty years of war—and now, after Operation Enduring Freedom, thousands of additional bombs dropped on the country—had left Afghanistan prostrate.... The country's only real equities were international goodwill and some collective memory of a multiethnic country that had once been peaceful" (p. 111).

As a veteran specialist on Af-Pak issues, Coll readily complicates overly simplistic narratives. For instance, while providing ample evidence documenting the disastrous consequences for Islamabad's duplicity supporting and undermining US counterinsurgency efforts, Directorate S also contextualizes ISI motivations to support Afghan insurgents. Aside from explaining that the Afghan Taliban was a way for Pakistan to hedge its bets against Indian influence in Afghanistan, Coll also documents how the more the ISI helped Washington by isolating the Taliban and other non-state entities, the more Islamabad risked being targeted by those groups. According to Coll, Pakistani intelligence was likely compelled to continue to support extremists, "to prove to its own restive clients that it was not going soft, and that it should not be considered the enemy. After I.S.I. lost control of important sections of its militant clients in 2007, not only were its offices targeted in suicide bombings, [but] its legitimacy was increasingly ridiculed within radical Islamist circles" as well (p. 346).

Coll also takes a nuanced approach to Afghan, American, and Pakistani bureaucracies. He documents how they were at times highly effective institutions (the ISI, for instance, was able to squeeze astronomical sums from Washington while never fully cooperating with American agendas) while proving to be demonstrably ineffectual in other circumstances. "In Washington, it was increasingly common for policy makers and members of Congress to talk of I.S.I. as an omnipotent, malign, highly effective force, when in fact the rise of domestic terrorism in Pakistan could be just as well understood as profound evidence of I.S.I.'s incompetence.... The intelligence showed that at the lower levels of I.S.I., in the field, officers pursued their own plans without necessarily informing the army brass in advance of every operation" (p. 290). Coll provides similar room for the CIA, the Pentagon, and both the George W. Bush and Barack Obama administrations as potent, indecisive, or inept, depending on the given situation and the pressures they were responding to.

Perhaps the most significant contribution of Directorate S is its painful illustration of the ways Islamabad, Kabul, and Washington each supported and undercut one another. Many other works have dissected components of these problematic alliances, mostly focusing on the dysfunctional US-Pakistan partnership, an alliance comedian Jon Stewart characterized as "enemies with benefits."[1] Directorate S instead artfully unravels the dysfunction between Washington, Islamabad, and Kabul as three distinct but codependent players, detailing how Islamabad and Kabul worked for and against one another, as did Kabul and Washington, despite presumptions that Kabul is merely a hapless American client. Being both aided and undermined by allies and responding in kind produces unrelenting strategic dysfunction. Like a Greek tragedy, the process of simultaneously cooperating with and undercutting strategic partners ensured that the war was ill-fated from the start.

This slow march toward defeat is a manifest chorus in Directorate S. Citing Eliot Cohen, for example, Coll comments that over time a pattern emerged in military briefings, as US commanders at the start of a rotation would say, "'this is going to be difficult.' Six months later, they'd say, 'We might be turning a corner.' At the end of their rotation, they would say, 'We have achieved irreversible momentum.' Then the next command group coming in would pronounce, 'This is going to be difficult'" (p. 298). Adding to the circular tragedy is a host of familiar characters who have reemerged in the Donald Trump era, including Michael Flynn, H. R. McMaster, and Zalmay Khalilzad. Khalilzad is a particularly fascinating and pivotal figure in the early history of US intervention, who according to Coll, personally "invented American policy from day to day during the long hours he spent huddling with [Afghan President Hamid] Karzai ... [and] attended [Afghan] cabinet meetings as if he were a member of the government, which, in effect, he was" (p. 189).

A captivating display of Coll's craftsmanship, Directorate S is a 757-page catalogue of cautionary tales. The US should not presume a critical ally will change because it would be terribly inconvenient if they did not. Pakistan should consider the risks of using extremists as extensions of foreign policy, as it pressed Islamabad toward extremism as well. The Afghan state should not be built on institutions it cannot sustain. While some areas of the book rehash well-trodden topics (from 2003 to 2007 Iraq distracted US policymakers at a critical moment in the war in Afghanistan), other sections detail often-overlooked dynamics, including, for example, Afghan intelligence (National Directorate of Security, NDS) attempts to play Pakistan's "hide-my-neighbor's-insurgent-as-a-way-to-gain-leverage-game" by protecting "armed Baluch separatists from the Bugti tribe who were fighting the Pakistan Army in Pakistan's Baluchistan Province. One Bugti leader lived in a safe house on Street 13 in Kabul under N.D.S. protection. Baluch fighters trained in Kandahar" (p. 428).

Not only were Afghan, Pakistani, and US allies often working at cross-purposes, but US policy itself was also often contradictory and counterproductive. Tactics were misaligned with US strategic and political goals. The US was paying off warlords while lamenting endemic corruption, implementing "hearts and minds" campaigns while mistreating prisoners, jailing corrupt figures who were on the payrolls of its intelligence agencies, and simultaneously announcing both surging and withdrawing from a war that the US did not want to lose but was not sure was worth what it would take to win. As Vice President Joe Biden once rashly snapped at Afghan President Karzai when Karzai pressed Biden to do more for Afghanistan against Pakistan's meddling, "Mr. President, Pakistan is fifty times more important than Afghanistan for the United States" (p. 352). The US was not willing to fully address the failing effort, and the war would continue to slowly sink toward some ignoble conclusion.

How US bureaucracies persistently pulled policy in opposite directions is another key expression of American contractions detailed in Directorate **S**. As Coll summarizes, both Bush's and Obama's approaches to Afghanistan "tolerated and even promoted stovepiped, semi-independent campaigns waged simultaneously by different agencies of American government.... It is hardly surprising that policies riddled with such internal contradictions and unresolved analytical questions failed to achieve the extraordinarily ambitious aim of stabilizing war-shattered Afghanistan. The war became a humbling case study in the limits of American power. It became a story of mismatched, means and ends" (p. 666).

Directorate S lays bare the costs and consequences of losing this war. US interventions in Iraq and Afghanistan revived and sustained al-Qaeda, as Iraq, Pakistan, and Afghanistan remain "embroiled in civil violence directly set off by the American-led invasions that followed September 11" (p. 661). US and Pakistani experiences in the war have likely irreparably damaged the relationship between Washington and Islamabad. The US will not soon forget how Pakistan's covert (and not so covert) support for insurgents led to the killing of Americans in Afghanistan and how their duplicity doomed the American effort. Similarly, the US operated unilaterally to kill Osama bin Laden in Abbottabad, which cornered the ISI into a lose-lose situation as they could either admit they knew bin Laden's whereabouts and provided sanctuary or deny they were aware of bin Laden's compound in Pakistan, effectively admitting incompetence. The fact the ISI had failed to prevent or respond to a foreign military applying lethal force within its territory was deeply problematic for the military. As the director-general of the ISI Ashfaq Kayani told the US chairman of the Joint Chiefs of Staff Mike Mullen, "it will forever remain a very deep scar in our national memory and our military's memory, which we failed to detect the raid.... By the same token, it will never fade from our national memory that you guys did it" (p. 546).

To add nuclear weapons to the litany of bad news compiled in Directorate S, there is also the question of Pakistan's weapons of mass destruction. Directorate S recalls in gripping detail the efforts of Pakistani navy lieutenant Zeeshan Rafiq who coordinated with al-Qaeda to attempt to hijack a nuclear-capable seven-story Pakistani frigate in September 2014. While the plot was unsuccessful as Rafiq and the collaborators were killed in a firefight boarding the ship, the perpetrators had gotten too close for comfort, using inside connections to duplicate keys to the missile room and successfully stashing weapons on board. Also important on a grand strategic level is China's involvement. The "fallout from the Afghan war also persuaded Pakistan's leaders, after 2011, to give up on any strategic partnership with Washington and to deepen ties to Beijing. This effectively opened Pakistani territory to Chinese companies and military planners, to construct transit corridors and bases that might improve China's regional influence and links to the Middle East. Overall, the war left China with considerable latitude in Central Asia, without having made any expenditures of blood, treasure, or reputation" (p. 663). As Iran gained regional influence as a result of US failures in the war in Iraq, China is gaining from US failures in Afghanistan.

Considering that one of the most impressive accomplishments of Directorate S is how it gracefully dissects and reconnects the confluence of disasters that has led to this moment in the US war in Afghanistan, it is curious why Coll named the book Directorate S, signaling a focus on Pakistani intelligence, as opposed to a more comprehensive title that would have encompassed the expansive scope of the volume, akin to Ghost Wars. Relatedly, Coll concludes Directorate S by stating, "the failure to solve the riddle of I.S.I. and to stop its covert interference in Afghanistan became, ultimately, the greatest strategic failure of the American war" (p. 667). While the prevailing US effort was doomed as long as Pakistan supported the Afghan Taliban insurgency, it would also likely have been impossible for the US to win without the right governance processes in place in Kabul and/or a coherent US strategy within and toward Afghanistan. After reading 700+ pages of fatal errors and impending tragedy, some involving the ISI, some not, there is plenty of blame and misfortune to go around. Directorate S is an astoundingly readable and comprehensive narrative of the complex processes that have doomed the "good war" in Afghanistan—just don't read it on a day you need an uplifting story.

Chapter 8

The Political and Military Involvement of Inter Services Intelligence in Afghanistan

During the Afghan Jihad in 1980s, jihadists poured into Pakistan from across the Muslim world, including Palestinian teacher and preacher Abdullah Azzam, who had taught in Jordan and Saudi Arabia, preaching Muslims' duty to wage jihad against non-Muslims.[1] In 1990, The ISI diverted its attention towards Kashmir, and established training camps for Kashmiri mujahideen to engage India in an unending proxy war.[2] General Pervez Musharraf played an instrumental role in drafting Pakistan's role in the Afghan civil war. From 1996 to 2001 Osama Bin Laden and Ayman al-Zawahiri remained in Afghanistan. However, the US invaded Afghanistan in October 2001.[3] The Inter Services Intelligence (ISI) of Pakistan had been heavily involved in covertly running military intelligence programs in Afghanistan before and after the US invasion. The United States, along with the ISI and Pakistan's government of Prime Minister Benazir Bhutto became the primary source of support for Hekmatyar in his 1992–1994 bombardment campaign against the Islamic State of Afghanistan. Hollingsworth, Christopher L and Sider, Joshua has noted changing political and military involvement of Pakistan in Afghanistan:

"Pakistan's support of the Afghan Taliban has numerous layers that have morphed into the current relationship that exists today. This relationship originates from Pakistan's ties to the mujahideen who fought the Soviet occupation of Afghanistan between 1979 and 1989. Following the Soviet withdrawal in 1989, Afghanistan was thrust into a civil war between the Soviet-backed Najibullah regime and Afghan warlords who fought to govern the country. This conflict left Pakistan caught between its rival, India, and an increasingly unstable Afghanistan. When the Taliban formed from these mujahideen fighters in 1994, Pakistan viewed the organization as a possible method of stabilizing Afghanistan. Their support contributed to the Taliban rapidly seizure (90%) of Afghanistan between 1994 and 1996. The events between the Taliban's rise to power and today are well documented. The Taliban remained in control of most of the country until after the attacks on September 11, 2001. Since the U.S. and Northern Alliance removed them from power, the Taliban now control more territory than at any point since 2001. Many observers of the Afghan conflict have blamed poor security and governance in Afghanistan for the resurgent Taliban.4 The Taliban benefits from the government of Afghanistan's lack of control, but the support of Pakistan remains a significant source of their resurgence. Pakistan, through the Inter-Services Intelligence (ISI), has continued to support the Taliban post 9/11 for many reasons. The ISI was instrumental in the creation of a coalition of seven Afghan mujahideen parties known as the Tanzeemat and influenced the formation of the Afghan Interim Government to oppose the Soviet-backed Najibullah government in Afghanistan, but complete acquiescence to Pakistani national interests was unattainable".[4]

The ISI established relationship with numerous political organizations in Afghanistan, but its persisting policy inside the country causes distrust. The ISI wants Indian intelligence-RAW to curtail its presence in Afghanistan, and close terror training camps inside the country.[5] Indian intelligence RAW's proxy war against Pakistan prompted deep political and security crisis in Afghanistan. The ISI never tolerated the Indian RAW presence in Afghanistan, the reason that its role in managing several anti-India proxy networks was also unmistakable.[6] Pakistan's military establishment supported militant groups to destabilize the region and maintain Pakistan's sovereignty and national identity. However, civilian institutions also facilitated militants by routinely legitimizing expansive executive powers, limiting judicial oversight, and violating civil liberties in the name of the national interest.[7] Militants who sat across the table with American officials in Doha and Islamabad were trained in Pakistan. Agreement for Bringing Peace to Afghanistan between the Islamic Emirate of Afghanistan which was not recognized by the United States as a state and known as the Taliban and the United States of America signed on 29, February, 2020. Afghans have only seen wars and there is little hope that their miseries will end soon. India has enjoyed a long period of primacy in Afghanistan but a growing Chinese interest in the war-ridden country is poised to upset that delicate arrangement. The China-India competition has many of the smaller neighboring countries in the region concerned about getting caught between the two Asian giants. China wants to build a small military base in Badakhshan to counter any insurgency spillover. In addition to its training efforts, India has also donated Mi-25 and Mi-35 helicopters to Afghanistan, which have proved invaluable for counter-militant operations. On 07 May 2018; Javid Ahmad in his article revealed so many new things about the ISI role in Afghanistan:

"In Afghanistan, ISI's Afghan operations are undertaken by at least three units. The first is Directorate S, the principal covert action arm that directs and oversees the Afghan policy, including militant and terrorist outfits and their operations. The second unit is, the Special Service Group (SSG), also known as the Pakistani SS, and is the army's Special Forces element that was established in the 1950s as a hedge against the communists. Today, some SSG units effectively operate as ISI's paramilitary wing and have fought alongside the Taliban until 2001. In other instances, SSG advisors have allegedly been embedded with Taliban fighters to provide tactical military advice, including on special operations, surveillance, and reconnaissance. In fact, encountering ISI operatives fighting alongside the Taliban in Afghanistan has become a common occurrence that no longer surprise Afghan and American forces. The third ISI unit is the Afghan Logistics Cell, a transport network inside Pakistan facilitated by members of Pakistan's Frontier Corps that provide logistical support to the Taliban and their families. This includes space, weapons, vehicles, protection, money, identity cards and safe passage. Such ISI support networks have been designed to break Afghanistan into pieces and then remold it into a pliant state. The objective is to complicate Afghanistan's security landscape and drive its political climate into an uncharted constitutional territory to create a vacuum, which inevitably places the Taliban in the driving seat. These support actions have visibly made the group more effective. However, the Pakistani mantra is that they maintain contacts with the Taliban but exercise no control over them".[8]

However, after the Soviet intervention in Afghanistan, CIA and ISI established close relationship to fit their forces to the fight against Russian forces. General Abdul Rehman Khan further adorned the agency with modern intelligence technology, and benefited from the covert war operation of ISI. General Zia-ul-Haq was also trying to make the agency professionalize to counter the Indian influence in Afghanistan. He was committed to make the ISI one of the strongest intelligence agencies in South Asia, but unfortunately, he used the agency against political forces.[9] When Benazir took over as Prime Minister; she removed General Hamid Gul due to his jihadist concepts, and appointed General Shamsul Rehman Kallue as the Chief of ISI, but General Aslam Beg never allowed Benazir to manage the Kashmir and Afghan policy. Pakistan like other countries has professional management of its intelligence agencies. This is evident from the fact that in over five decades of nationhood, there have been six committees to review their function.[10]In his research paper, Dr. Bidanda M. Chengappa explains the strategies of ISI against democratic governments to protect the interests of miltablishment:

"During this period there was an uneasy relationship between the military and the political leadership when the country last experienced a decade of democracy. While the military did not directly intervene in the political process the generals used the ISI as a lever to manipulate the course of politics to suit their interests. Essentially the generals wanted a civilian government that would not curtail their power and to that extent such democracy came to be termed 'limited', 'guided' or Islamic democracy. The ISI was variously used to prop up friendly political persona who enjoyed good relations with the military leadership and conversely to minimise the chances of success for a hostile leader through the creation of unfavourable conditions. It was also involved with the creation of new parties or split existing ones in order to act as a counter-weight against other parties. Apparently the ISI proved to be more useful to the military leadership—in the post-Zia decade—which could not exercise its power over state and society overtly but had to do so covertly…….However Benazir said that the ISI was involved against her government which could be analysed in terms of the power of information".[11]

There are different perceptions about the ISI and its support to Taliban in Afghanistan. Some politicians view the function of ISI in the country as interference in the internal affairs of Afghanistan, and some view it as a terrorist campaign against the country. on 19 September 2019, Afghan human rights activist Bilal Sarwary accused Inter-Services Intelligence (ISI) of providing institutional support to terrorist groups operating in Afghanistan. The activist — Bilal Sarway was addressing the tail-end session of the United Nations Human Rights Council (UNHRC) when he made this claim. According to a report by news agency ANI, Sarwary said that the Haqqani Network, the Afghan insurgent group is a 'veritable arm' of ISI's and held it responsible for some of the worst attacks in Kabul. "Pakistan-sponsored terrorism has resulted in the deaths of the Afghan military personnel, international aid workers, civilians, children, and very often entire families have vanished due to these attacks. "Our cities, schools, clinics, funerals, and weddings have been targeted in these brutal terrorist attacks". Sarwary said.[12] Javid Ahmad (07 May 2018-The National Interests) in his article highlighted the ISI operations in Afghanistan through different units. He also spotlighted three important units of the ISI operating in Afghanistan in different directions:

In Afghanistan, ISI's Afghan operations are undertaken by at least three units. The first is Directorate S, the principal covert action arm that directs and oversees the Afghan policy, including militant and terrorist outfits and their operations. The second unit is the Special Service Group (SSG), also known as the Pakistani SS, and is the army's Special Forces element that was established in the 1950s as a hedge against the communists. Today, some

SSG units effectively operate as ISI's paramilitary wing and have fought alongside the Taliban until 2001. In other instances, SSG advisors have allegedly been embedded with Taliban fighters to provide tactical military advice, including on special operations, surveillance, and reconnaissance. In fact, encountering ISI operatives fighting alongside the Taliban in Afghanistan has become a common occurrence that no longer surprise Afghan and American forces. The third ISI unit is the Afghan Logistics Cell, a transport network inside Pakistan facilitated by members of Pakistan's Frontier Corps that provide logistical support to the Taliban and their families. This includes space, weapons, vehicles, protection, money, identity cards and safe passage. Such ISI support networks have been designed to break Afghanistan into pieces and then remold it into a pliant state. The objective is to complicate Afghanistan's security landscape and drive its political climate into an uncharted constitutional territory to create a vacuum, which inevitably places the Taliban in the driving seat. These support actions have visibly made the group more effective. However, the Pakistani mantra is that they maintain contacts with the Taliban but exercise no control over them".[1]

Since 2001, posing as an indispensable ally in the war against terrorism, Pakistan has been benefitting from a lavish US military and development aid, while continuing to provide a safe haven for the Taliban and the Haqqani network. Mullah Abdul Salam Zaeef was arrested by Pakistan's security forces, with the help of their American counterparts, ignoring his diplomatic status and his application for political asylum in Pakistan to escape the wrath of Americans in Afghanistan. Another mistake of Pakistan army was to trade in the lives of the Afghans-arresting and killing them, raiding their homes and illegally detaining their relatives and family members.

The arrest of Mullah Abdul Salam Zaeef by Pakistan's law enforcement agencies caused misunderstanding between the people of Afghanistan and Pakistan that a close and friendly neighbour intentionally violated international diplomatic law. No doubt, ISI had a prolexit list of good friends in Afghanistan, but military dictator General Musharraf acted differently. Former

Afghan Ambassador was arrested and handed to the US agencies. He was humiliated by the CIA in the presence of officials in Islamabad. John F. Burns 04 January 2002) published a detailed story of his humiliation and torture in New York Times. Pakistani analyst Ayaz Amir (daily Dawn. 22 September 2006) also noted some aspects of his painful instant:

"We know, to our lasting shame, how our overlords, dazzled by American power, and afraid of God knows what, handed over the ex-Taliban ambassador, Mullah Abdul Salam Zaeef, to the Americans in January 2002—in violation of every last comma of international law. But until now we have not been privy to the details: how exactly did the handing-over take place? Now to satisfy our curiosity, and perhaps outrage our feelings, comes Mullah Zaeef's own account, published in Pashto and parts of which have been translated into Urdu by the Express newspaper. To say that the account is eye-opening would be an understatement. It is harrowing and mind-blowing. Can anyone bend so low as our government did? And can behaviour be as wretched as that displayed by American military personnel into whose custody Zaeef was given? On the morning of January 2, 2002, three officials of a secret agency arrived at Zaeef's house in Islamabad with this message: "Your Excellency, you are no more excellency." One of them said, no one can resist American power, or words to that effect. "America wants to question you. We are going to hand you over to the Americans so that their purpose is served and Pakistan is saved from a big danger." Zaeef could have been forgiven for feeling stunned. From the "guardians of Islam" this was the last thing that he expected, that for the sake of a few "coins" (his words) he would be delivered as a "gift" to the Americans. Under heavy escort he was taken to Peshawar, kept there for a few days and then pushed into his nightmare. Blindfolded and handcuffed, he was driven to a place where a helicopter was waiting, its engines running. Someone said, "Khuda hafiz" (God preserve you).[14]

Not only Mullah Zaeef was tortured by Pakistani agencies, many Pakistani citizens were detained incommunicado in undisclosed places of detention. Their families distressed about the lack of information on the whereabouts and fate of their loved ones. Ayaz

Amir noted his painful journey, and mental and physical torture by the ISI and CIA, and noted Pakistan's constraints as well. This was Pakistan's biggest mistake that changed mind of every Afghan about the country's hostile attitude towards Afghanistan. Mullah Abdul Salam Zaeef, the Taliban government's ambassador to Pakistan in his book "My Life with the Taliban" has described his heartbreaking story:

"When we arrived in Peshawar I was taken to a lavishly-fitted office. A Pakistani flag stood on the desk, and a picture of Mohammad Ali Jinnah hung at the back of the room. A Pashtun man was sitting behind the desk. He got up, introduced himself and welcomed me. His head was shaved — seemingly his only feature of note — and he was of an average size and weight. He walked over to me and said that he was the head of the bureau. I was in the devil's workshop, the regional head office of the ISI. He told me I was a close friend —a guest —and one that they cared about a great deal. I wasn't really sure what he meant, since it was pretty clear that I was dear to them only because they could get a good sum of money for me when they sold me. Their trade was people; just as with goats, the higher the price for the goat, the happier the owner. In the twenty-first century there aren't many places left where you can still buy and sell people, but Pakistan remains a hub for this trade. I prayed after dinner with the ISI officer, and then was brought to a holding-cell for detainees.........Finally, after days in my cell, a man came, tears flowing down his cheeks. He fainted as his grief and shame overcame him. He was the last person I saw in that room. I never learnt his name, but soon after—perhaps four hours after he left — I was handed over to the Americans. Even before I reached the helicopter, I was suddenly attacked from all sides. People kicked me, shouted at me, and my clothes were cut with knives. They ripped the black cloth from my face and for the first time I could see where I was. Pakistani and American soldiers stood around me. The Pakistani soldiers were all staring as the Americans hit me and tore the remaining clothes off from my body. Eventually I was completely naked, and the Pakistani soldiers — the defenders of the Holy Qur'an — shamelessly watched me with smiles on their faces, saluting this disgraceful action of the Americans"[15]

Abdul Salam Zaeef was mentally tortured by the US agencies. He was sold by General Musharraf and his sarcastic friends to the US just for handful money, and never thought that his vivacity will alienate Afghans forever from Pakistan. Before this occurrence, they killed former President of Afghanistam, Dr. Muhammad Najibullah in Kabul. Analyst Ayaz Amir narrates Mullah Zaeef's wearisomeness when he was undressed:

"There were some people speaking in English. "Suddenly I was pounced upon and flung on the ground, kicked and pummelled from all sides. So sudden was the attack that I was dumbfounded... My blindfold slipping, I saw a line of Pakistani soldiers to one side and some vehicles including one with a flag...My clothes were stripped from my body and I was naked but 'my former friends' kept watching the spectacle. The locks on their lips I can never forget... The (Pakistani) officers present there could at least have said he is our guest, in our presence don't treat him like this. Even in my grave I will not be able to forget that scene." Zaeef suffered unspeakable tortures at the hands of his American captors. He was kept in Bagram, and then taken to Kandahar and from there flown eventually to Guantanamo. He was released from Guantanomo and flown to Kabul in September 2005, charged with nothing, nothing having been proven against him. He remained in American captivity for close to four years".[16]

Mullah Abdul Salam Zaeef suffered inexpressible pain at the hands of CIA within Afghanistan and the United States. Moreover, Pakistan perpetrated one more crime by killing former President Dr. Najeebullah inside the Presidential palace in Kabul in the presence of merchant of fear General Hamid Gul. This way of treating a neighbouring state prompted bigger political and diplomatic challenges for Pakistan. On 26 September 2016, Tolonews TV reported an Afghan research centre divulgence on the 20th anniversary of the death of former Afghan President Dr. Najibullah Ahmadzai. The TV report indicated that former leader was killed based on an intelligence plan, drafted by regional countries and adopted by Pakistan's Inter-Services Intelligence (ISI). Deputy Chief of Afghanistan's Strategic and Scientific Research Center, Aimal Liyan, said that evidence existed to this effect: "There is evidence which shows that famous Pakistani generals from Pakistan's intelligence agency such as Aslam Beg, Gen. Hamid Gul the former head of Pakistan's Inter-Services Intelligence (ISI), Nasirullah Babur and others and besides that, there were other intelligence officials from other countries. The plan to kill Najibullah was implemented by ISI," he said.

"Dr. Najibullah was in favor of unity among Afghans. He wanted peace in the country but he was killed." He added. Meanwhile, Suleiman Layiq, one of Najibullah's supporters, said: "He [Najibullah] had good relations with people. He was an honest man." However, Aryan Khabir said that: "Twenty years after Najibullah's death we see that his demands which were unity among the people have not been fulfilled yet," Dr. Najibullah was President of Afghanistan from 1987 to 1992. He then lived in the United Nations headquarters in Kabul until 1996, when the Taliban took control of Kabul. Tolonews reported. Moreover, analyst Dr. Muhammad Taqi (September 2014, Daily Times) also quoted paragraphs from the book of US former special envoy to Afghanistan, Peter Tomsen who narrated story of Dr. Najeebullah murder in his book, 'The Wars of Afghanistan': "Four Taliban, including, by one account, a Pakistani ISI officer disguised as Taliban, drove directly to the UN compound in a Japanese Datsun pickup. Their mission was to lure the former Afghan President out of the diplomatically protected UN premises." Mullah Abdul Razzaq was the Taliban ringleader who carried out the torture, killing, mutilation and desecration of the corpses—a war crime by any definition—at the behest of his Pakistani minders".[17]

Pakistan's intelligence agencies and the Army support the ISIS terrorist networks inside Afghanistan, Central Asia, and Russia

Pakistan's intelligence agencies are supporting the ISIS terrorist networks in various districts of the country. The country has a long history of promoting terrorism in the name of Pakistan's geostrategic interests. Author Gordon Thomas stated that, "Pakistan still sponsored terrorist groups in the Indian state of Jammu and Kashmir, funding, training and arming them in their war of attrition against India". However, Mr. Stephen Schwartz noted several terrorist groups were receiving support from Pakistani army, and the ISI. Afghanistan is not the only state where Pakistani supports terrorist groups. The country is also supporting terrorists in Kashmir. Moreover, Military dictator, General Musharraf admitted that his army trained militant groups to fight India in Kashmir, and his government had turned a blind eye. Musharraf said: "Inter-Services Intelligence directorate (ISI) cultivated the Taliban after 2001 because Karzai's government was dominated by non-Pashtuns, who are the country's largest ethnic group, and by officials who were thought to favour India".

The Daesh prodigy in 2015 provoked and agitated Pakistan's landscape, while a video message from the Hafsa Madrassa in Islamabad surfaced, in which students of the madrassa invited the Daesh Chief Abu Bakar al-Baghdadi to Pakistan to teach a lesson to Pakistan army. After this video appeared in print media, Daesh declared its presence in the country. There are speculations that The Fauji Foundation of Pakistan army has contributed more than 5,000 retired army soldiers and officers in the army of the ISIS terrorist groups. Major (retd) Agha Amin, a Lahore-based Defense analyst, revealed that Pakistani fighters went to Syria and Iraq with the support of the army and government. The army, Agha Amin said, allowed General Hamid Gul to take former Pakistani soldiers to Iraq and Syria. In 2014, a three member Daesh delegation reached Pakistan from Syria. The delegation was headed by Zubair Al Kuwaiti and included Uzbek Commander Fahim Ansari and Sheikh Yusuf from Saudi Arabia (Akbar 2015). They met Pakistan's based terrorist groups.

Daily Khabrain, Pakistan's Urdu newspaper (29th December, 2015) reported the statement of former Foreign Minister of Pakistan Sardar Asif Ahmed Ali's, and on December 29, 2015, the newspaper reported that some Pakistani travel agents were recruiting youth to fight in the Middle East. However, Senator General (Retd.) Abdul Qayyum demanded action against the travel agents. General Abdul Qayyum also said that women were being exported for sex trade. Another Senator Javed Abbasi told the Senate that there were 17 illegal networks involved in exporting youth to the

Middle East and these networks are making profits to the tune of 927 million dollars.[18] Dr. Yunis Khushi (ISIS in Pakistan: A Critical Analysis of Factors and Implications of ISIS Recruitments and Concept of Jihad-Bil-Nikah-26 June 2017) exposed relationship of government authorities and the Islamic terrorist State in Pakistan:

"A sort of high level game is going on, on the political, foreign policy and law-enforcement levels regarding the presence of ISIS in Pakistan1. The politicians, Foreign Ministry, Interior Ministry, and Law Enforcement Agencies are singing different tunes regarding the presence, recruitments and migration of jihadis or mujahids and jihadi wives from Pakistan to Syria to join the ISIS2. It seems that publicly, the Pakistani Government has refused Saudi Government to send Pakistani armies to Saudi Arabia to fight against Houthi rebels, but silently some private groups have been allowed to recruit youth to join Saudi Armies to fight against Houthis and also against ISIS, which are a major threat against not only Saudi Empire, but also against Arab Emirates and other Middle Eastern Kingdoms. The recruitments for ISIS have been going on in Pakistan for the past more than 3 years, but the Foreign and the Interior Ministries of Pakistan have been constantly denying the presence and activities of ISIS in Pakistan. Law Enforcement agencies have very recently arrested many people from Lahore, Islamabad, Karachi and Sialkot who were associated with ISIS networks. Men have been recruited as jihadis or mujahids and women as jihadi wives to provide sexual needs of fighters who are fighting in Syria, Iraq and Afghanistan. Many women, impressed and convinced through brainwashing with the concept of Jihad-Bil-Nikah, got divorce from their Pakistani husbands and went to marry a Mujahid of ISIS for a certain period, came back gave birth to the child of Mujahid, and remarried their former husband. Some decide to continue that marriage for rest of their lives".[19]

However, Sex business in Pakistan's Sialkot district, and parts of Bahawalpur, Rahim Yar Khan and Central Punjab, and the involvement of different groups and individuals in its raised important questions that why Pakistan and its army support the ISIS group in Syria and Iraq, and why the women brigade of the ISIS army was allowed to recruit women in Sialkot district? Dr.

Yunis Khushi has highlighted this illegal business in his paper and noted that the ISIS terrorist group is paying something around RS. 50,000 to 60,000 per month to every warrior, which is a hefty amount for an unemployed youth suffering in unemployment, poverty and inflation here in Pakistan:

"All of this is being done to obtain worldly wealth and later eternal life in Heaven because ISIS is paying something around RS. 50,000 to 60,000 per month to every warrior, which is a hefty amount for an unemployed youth suffering in unemployment, poverty and inflation here in Pakistan, which is ruled by corrupt ruling elite for the past 68 years and masses only got poverty for being true Muslims and patriot Pakistanis. Most secret and law-enforcement agencies have behaved like a silent bystander to the activities of ISIS in the country. Is this an unofficial channel of providing soldiers to provide the Saudi demands for fighters to fight on behalf of Saudi armies in Yemen and Syria? Whose interests are being protected by the Minister for Interior by his constant denial of the presence of ISIS in the country? Is he afraid of opening his mouth against ISIS? Is he instructed by his bosses to keep his mouth shut? Has he been paid huge sums of Riyals for keeping his mouth shut? Why is Sharif Government closing its eyes to the reality of ISIS in Pakistan? Is Sharif family obliging Saudis as close allies and relatives? Is Sharif family repaying the debt for the 1.5 billion US dollars that were given by the Saudi Government? Is some sort of underground large scale recruitment going on for Saudi Empire? This paper will also try to find answers to different responses of the different State institutions and find an answer to the question of "why has the government adopted an attitude of indifference and taken different position on this serious issue? Also why do youth opt for becoming paid warriors away from their homeland on the foreign lands fighting the war that is not theirs, and why do women and girl are driven crazy to accept the concept of Jihad-Bil-Nikah, leave their husband along with their young children and go to the Syrian war front to become the wives of blood thirsty mujahideen who do not believe in the words like mercy or forgiveness and have no respect for human life, human dignity, modesty and honour of women and do not believe in human rights of anyone except for themselves"?[20]

On 19 June 2019, ToloNews reported former Indian ambassador to Afghanistan, Amar Sinha, asseverations against Pakistan that Daesh permanently remained a tool of the Pakistani army. The army fabricated it to put pressure on the Afghan government. Talking to Tolonews, the former Indian envoy said: "that assessments which are carried out by the Afghan institutions have found that over 70 percent of Daesh fighters are coming from Pakistan's tribal regions. "Now the thing is, is it the new version of Taliban when the Taliban gets reintegrated, mainstreamed? Is this new terror grouping another instrument of Pak[istan] military policy? My hunch is yes. But I guess more research will have to be done both intelligence agencies and we have to look carefully at the origin, at the source of funding and the source of support," he explained. Sinha confirmed that some Indian citizens had also joined Daesh, adding that the Afghan government extradited some of these militants back to their home country. Pakistan has always denied claims of supporting or sponsoring Daesh in Afghanistan"[21]

However, in February 2018, Voice of America reported warning of Russian government that the US army turning Northern Afghanistan into a "resting base" of international terrorism and a "bridgehead" for establishing its "destructive" caliphate in the region. "The "international wing of Daesh" is spearheading the effort of terrorists spilling over the borders of Syria and Iraq and moving worldwide, asserted Russian Ambassador to Pakistan, Alexey Dedov". However, he said: "With clear connivance, and sometimes even with direct support of certain local and outside sponsors, thousands of militants of various nationalities are consolidating under the banners of Daesh there (in northern Afghanistan), including jihadis from Syria and Iraq," Dedov told a seminar in Islamabad. Moreover, Iranian military General also alleged that the U.S. was transferring ISIS militants to Afghanistan to fuel regional instability and justify its presence in the region[22]

In 2019, there were speculations that the Islamic State gained foothold in Baluchistan to train its fighters. On 18 September

2019, in his Samaa News analysis, Roohan Ahmad noted developments of Daesh recruitment in Pakistan: "The Islamic State militant group has named a former Karachi police constable Daud Mehsud the leader of its newly created Wilayah Pakistan, after separating Pakistan from its Khorasan province. Mehsud was a munshi or constable at Karachi's Quaidabad police station, one of them said, requesting anonymity because he is not authorized to speak to reporters. "Previously, he was based in Afghanistan," he added. It is believed that he has moved to Balochistan after Daesh formed its Wilayah Pakistan in May 2019. The official said that there is no direct link between Daesh's Pakistan group and the group's central leadership in Iraq and Syria. According to him, the decisions are made in Syria or Iraq and conveyed to Pakistan through Khorasan (Afghanistan). Mehsud has a history. He started out with the proscribed Tehreek-e-Taliban Pakistan group led by the group's slain leader Hakimullah Mehsud and rose in the ranks to its Karachi chief under Mullah Fazlullah. He had to leave Pakistan after law-enforcement agencies geared up an operation against militant groups. In 2017, Mehsud left the TTP and pledged allegiance to the then Daesh's Khorasan group. According to DIG Goraya, Mastung, Quetta, Kalat, Khuzdar and Lasbela were the most affected parts. These areas are used as a "transit, lodging and boarding point," he added. "Some presence [was] also reported in Bolan and Dera Murad Jamali," the CTD official said".[23]

The so-called Islamic state with the support of Pakistan army and the ISI has established strong terror network - recruiting new jihadists to fight holy war in Russia and Central Asia. The group has also established strong relationship with the terrorist and extremist groups of Pakistan, and recruiting young poor girls from villages for its women brigade in Sialkot and Southern districts of Punjab. Prominent analyst and journalist Kunwar Khuldune Shahid (Asia Times, 27 November 2019) has noted some important aspects of the establishment of the ISIS group, and its recruitment process in Pakistan:

"Multiple interviews with security and government officials from the region reveal that yet to be located ISIS sleeper cells exist in the former Federally Administered Tribal Areas (FATA) and

Balochistan. The development comes in the aftermath of security forces recently busting ISIS-affiliated cells in the two most populous provinces of Punjab and Sindh. In May this year, the Islamic State unveiled its new wilayah (provinces) in India and Pakistan within the then-Islamic State of Khorasan Province (ISKP), which had been based along the Af-Pak border. The announcement came immediately after the group led gun raids in Shopian district of Indian-administered Kashmir. In the month leading up to the announcement, the Islamic State claimed two terror attacks in Balochistan's cities of Mastung and Quetta. "The idea behind creating the new wilayah was to separate it from Daesh's base in the region, which is Afghanistan. Daesh wants a group that is solely focused on South Asia and is eying jihadist allies in the volatile areas like Balochistan, [former] FATA and Indian-occupied Kashmir," a senior security official from Balochistan explains. Experts underline that this year's Easter bombings in Sri Lanka deployed the Islamic State's modus operandi for South Asia a month before the group announced its new wilayah. While the attacks were carried out by National Thowheeth Jama'ath and Jammiyathul Millathu Ibrahim, both of these jihadist groups are affiliates of ISIS in Sri Lanka, which simultaneously claimed the attack. "ISIS deploys local foot-soldiers from their affiliated groups to launch attacks on targeted locations, and then they claim these attacks. That means that the core group doesn't exist in the areas they are targeting, but the local militants work under the ISIS umbrella. This helps the recruitment for these affiliates," says Major General (retd) Saad Khattak, a former army officer based in Balochistan who has been appointed as Pakistan's High Commissioner to Sri Lanka"[24.]

On 17 May 2019, the Nation reported the establishment of the ISIS branch in Pakistan. The newspaper noted the ISIS announcement that it has established its branch in Baluchistan. Since its establishment on May 2015, the group claimed its activities in Balochistan. "The state of Pakistan has been claiming that there's no organised presence of Daesh in the country and that some local militant groups have allied them with IS after their parent organisations were dismantled in the military and intelligence-based operations. However, Daesh has succeeded in proving its footprint by not only carrying out several attacks in the volatile north-western Balochistan but also making some hits in relatively much secure areas of the country. A senior government official insisted that Daesh doesn't have its own infrastructure and recruits in Pakistan; rather, it hires and uses local militants who were associated with different militant outfits in the past. "This means IS has no direct presence in the country [as it is trying to portray by announcing its chapter in Pakistan]," the newspaper reported.[25]

On 23 December 2017, a Pakistani political figure said that following the collapse of the Daesh (ISIS or ISIL) terrorist group in Syria and Iraq, the US government was equipping Daesh militants in border areas of Pakistan with weapons. Speaking to the Tasnim News Agency, Shabir Hussein Sajedi, a member of the Majlis Wahdat-e-Muslimeen (MWM), a Shiite political organization, said the activities of Daesh have increased in northwestern Pakistan. He added that the terror group is recruiting members on Pakistani soil and is beginning some movements in the country. He further warned that the US is providing Daesh terrorists with weapons and other military equipment in border areas.[26] However, on 01 January 2020, Tribal News Network reported the surrender of women and children of Daesh fighters from merged tribal district to Jalalabad authorities.

"In a video released by the official media centre of the Nangarhar government, it can be seen that Pakistani relatives have come to receive the women and children of Daesh militant group fighters. The video states that a centre for families of surrendered Daesh fighters was formed in Jalalabad city where they were provided all facilities. It says that the legitimate 50 women and 76 children of Daesh fighters were to be handed over to their Pakistani relatives on Thursday after verification. Afghan officials say the women and children coming from Afghanistan hail from Tirah Valley, Orakzai, Bajaur and Peshawar. An elderly person in the video says he has come to receive three women and four children of his family. He says these women had gone to Afghanistan five years ago. Afghan officials claim that thousands of Daesh fighters had come to Afghanistan from tribal districts of Pakistan and they also brought their wives and children later. They were living in areas under the control of the militant group in Nangarhar. Malik Usman, a tribal elder from Jalalabad, told media after a Jirga that women and children will only be handed over to their family members from Pakistan. In November 2019, Afghan President Ashraf Ghani had announced in Jalalabad that the family members of the fighters will be handed over to their Pakistani relatives through a tribal Jirga"[27]

Chapter 9

Pakistan Army and the Pashtun Tahafooz Movement

........Journalist, M. Ilyas Khan (Uncovering Pakistan's secret human rights abuses, BBC journalist M Ilyas Khan confirmed atrocities of Pakistan army in his BBC News report: "In May 2016, for example, an attack on a military post in the Teti Madakhel area of North Waziristan triggered a manhunt by troops who rounded up the entire population of a village. An eyewitness who watched the operation from wheat field nearby and whose brother was among those detained told the BBC that the soldiers beat everyone with batons and threw mud in children's mouths when they cried. A pregnant woman was one of two people who died during torture, her son said in video testimony. At least one man remains missing". (BBC News, Dera Ismail Khan, 02 June 2019).

The Pashtun Tahafooz Movement is the only well banded together movement that created awareness within the Pashtun communities about the atrocities and war crimes of Pakistan army in FATA and Waziristan. However, it started long marches, and rallies to divert the attention of international community towards the forced disappearances of its workers and leaders by the agencies. Frequently, they used social media as a bridge of communication. Originally, its demands included the release of missing persons and an end to extra-judicial killings of Pashtuns, stopping humiliation of passengers at security checkpoints, and removal of landmines in

FATA.[1] On 13 January 2018, Naqeebullah Mehsud was kidnapped and killed in a fake police encounter in Karachi.[2]

The PTM is the latest manifestation of decades of Pashtun protest against state brutalities. Its origin can be traced back to 2014 when student leaders of Gomal University in the Khyber Pakhtunkhwa (KP) province were propelled into activism to protect the rights of Pashtuns.[3] The PTM is a nonviolent movement led by Manzoor Pashteen against the alleged enforced disappearances, extra-judicial killings, as well as the mistreatment of the Pakhtun community by security forces. Madiha Afzal (07 February 2020) interviewed leaders of PTM for her book in Lahore, highlighted the PTM demand in her book:

"The movement alleges grave human rights violations by Pakistan's military against Pashtuns in the country's northwest. It says that Pashtuns have been the target of violence at the hands of both the Taliban and the Pakistani military for two decades. The movement claims that the military has killed innocent civilians in its operations against the Pakistani Taliban, and that it needs to answer for "missing persons." It also contends that Pashtuns are regularly harassed at checkpoints and treated with suspicion, and that landmines continue to make their lives insecure. These complaints festered for years before the movement was officially created in 2018. In 2015, while conducting interviews for my book, I met Pashtun students in Lahore who told me that the army's ongoing, multi-year military operation—Zarb-e-Azb—was not what it seemed from outside the tribal areas. The PTM demands a truth and reconciliation commission to address claims of extrajudicial killings and missing persons. The movement also claims that the military supported Pakistani Taliban (also known as Tehreek-e-Taliban Pakistan, or TTP) militants, and its leaders have said—most explosively — that after the military claims to have decimated the Pakistani Taliban in Zarb-e-Azb, "the Taliban are being allowed to return" to the tribal areas in a "secret deal with the military."[4]

Torture and humiliation in Waziristan couldn't undermine Talibanization, extremism, and terrorism, it alienates citizens from the state. Manzoor never targeted Pakistan army, and never killed a single soldier of security forces; he is fighting for the fundamental rights of the residents of Waziristan and FATA regions. On 11 February 2019, in his New York Times article, PTM leader Manzoor Pashteen gave an account of his struggle for the recovery of kidnapped Pashtun activists by Pakistan's military establishment:

"The government ignored us when these militants terrorized and murdered the residents. Pakistan's military operations against the militants brought further misery: civilian killings, displacements, enforced disappearances, humiliation and the destruction of our livelihoods and way of life. No journalists were allowed into the tribal areas while the military operations were going on. Pashtuns who fled the region in hopes of rebuilding their lives in Pakistani cities were greeted with suspicion and hostility. We were stereotyped as terrorist sympathizers. I was studying to become a veterinarian, but the plight of my people forced me and several friends to become activists. In January 2018 Naqeebullah Mehsud, an aspiring model and businessman from Waziristan who was working in Karachi was killed by a police team led by a notorious officer named Rao Anwar. Mr. Anwar, who is accused of more than 400 extrajudicial murders, was granted bail and roams free. Along with 20 friends, I set out on a protest march from Dera Ismail Khan to Islamabad, the capital. Word spread, and by the time we reached Islamabad, several thousand people had joined the protest. We called our movement the Pashtun Tahafuz Movement or the Pashtun Protection Movement".[5]

Mr. Manzoor Pashteen holds responsible Pakistan army for the disinformation campaign against his movement, and complained that agencies also concocted stories of the involvement of RAW and NDS in his campaign for the recovery of kidnapped men, women and children from the custody of the police and agencies. He, however, accused the army and police for the killing of his workers. PTM leader also lamented military establishment and the police for the harassment of social media activist, and the arrest of Alamzaib Khan Mehsud, (an activist who was gathering data and advocating on behalf of victims of land mines and enforced disappearances), activist Hayat Preghal, and Gulalai Ismail:

"The military unleashed thousands of trolls to run a disinformation campaign against the P.T.M., accusing us of starting a "hybrid war." Almost every day they accuse us of conspiring with Indian, Afghan or American intelligence services. Most of our activists, especially women, face relentless online harassment. A social media post expressing support for our campaign leads to a knock from the intelligence services. Scores of our supporters have been fired from their jobs. Many activists are held under terrorism laws. Alamzaib Khan Mehsud, an activist who was gathering data and advocating on behalf of victims of land mines and enforced disappearances, was arrested in January. Hayat Preghal, another activist, was imprisoned for months for expressing support from our movement on social media. He was released in October but barred from leaving the country and lost his pharmacist job in Dubai, his sole source of income. Gulalai Ismail, a celebrated activist, has been barred from leaving Pakistan. On Feb. 5, while protesting against the death of Mr. Luni, the college teacher and P.T.M. leader, she was detained and held incommunicado in an unknown place for 30 hours before being released. Seventeen other activists are still being detained in Islamabad".[6]

On 17 February 2020, the Print published yell of Gul Bukhari against the ISI wing of Pakistan Embassy in the UK. Gul Bukhari complained that the ISI wing was sniffing for her home address in London. "I am at a loss, I can't understand what is it about me that fascinates the Pakistani government or makes it obsess over me so much. I left Pakistan in December 2018 and am leading a quiet life in the UK. Yet, the establishment hasn't stopped hounding me. Just a few days ago, a friend sent me some screenshots of Pakistani media channel ARY and asked what the case against me was, and what 'dehshatgardi' I had done. I was stunned. I asked around if these were fake screenshots. "No, Gul, this is breaking news on ARY right now," I was told. According to the news, Pakistan's Federal Investigation Agency (FIA) had sent a notice, asking me to appear before it and explain myself. And if I fail to do so, I would be slapped with charges under cyber crime and anti-terror laws, my properties in Pakistan would be seized, and I would be extradited via the Interpol". Gul said.[7]

Gul Bukhari also kicked up the fuss that the PTI government requested the UK government to expel her from London as soon as possible. The PTI government wrote directly to the government in the UK, hoping that action will be taken against her here, but the UK government does not prosecute asylum seekers, and the PTI government cannot force the UK government in any case because Gul Bukhari is a human rights activist:

"The Pakistan Tehreek-e-Insaf (PTI) government wants the UK to take action against me under the country's hate speech and anti-terrorism laws. And the Pakistani establishment, according to journalist Ali Shah, has sent this letter to 10 Downing Street, the Foreign Office, the Home Office, and to the local police. It was another shock to me. As reported by the journalist, the language used in the letter (which I haven't seen yet) contained typical fauji terms like "inimical activities", and seeks an investigation into my "lifestyle". Having realised it may not be successful in bringing me back to Pakistan via the FIA, the Imran Khan regime wrote directly to the government in the UK, hoping that action will be taken against me here. I am wondering if those in power in Pakistan think the UK government is as big a duffer as they are. Yes, we have Boris Johnson at the helm here but he is not the one and all. Murtaza spat out his Coke laughing while reading the letter, but the serious concerns are these: they are hounding me; slapping me with made-up charges or trying to get that done by the UK government; the Inter-Services Intelligence (ISI) wing of the Pakistan embassy in the UK is trying to sniff out my residential address. They are trying anything and everything.........I was in their safe house and under their control in 2018 when they asked me if I would toe their line if they put me on prime time TV. I said no. Then they asked me again in the car (when they were taking me back home after my abduction) and also threatened me with my son's life, "Aitchison jatahaina (he goes to Aitchison, doesn't he?)", they said, referring to his school. "Uss ko kuchh ho gayatoh hum se nagilakarna (if something happens to him, then don't complain to us)." I replied,

"No, you must be out of your minds." They literally threatened to kill my son" Gul Bukhari grumbled.[8]

Having commented on her tearful complaints against Pakistan Embassy in London, prominent journalist Aurang Zeb Khan Zalmay (17-02-2020) in his facebook account criticised agencies for their campaign against Pakistani human rights activists in Britain and Europe: "The Pakistani monster is constantly following and intimidating journalists and human-rights activists across Europe and Middle East. This project to hound rights-activists was launched by Gen. Bajwa on his official visit to Pakistan High Commission in London in Jun 2019. Since that day the Pakistan's embassies in Europe and their spies and stooges are active to stop voices of the voiceless. Last month, they attacked one of our friends in Rottardam in front of his home. They can't intimidate us with their cowardice and cheap tactics, they are in self-deception, and we will never give up our peaceful rights activism".[9]

The PTM activist, Gulalai Ismail was also accused of treason, but human rights defenders said allegations were bogus and she was being targeted for highlighting abuses committed by Pakistan's military. Notwithstanding her arrival in New York, she still lives in consternation. She was arrested and harassed by intelligence agencies to change her opinion on the war crimes of the army in FATA and Waziristan, but she strongly refused to become reticent. In his New York Times article, Jeffrey Gettleman (19 September, 2019) reported that Gulalai Ismail had been advocating the rights of raped women, kidnapped and tortured Pashtuns, Punjabis and Balochs since years:

"Her account of being chased out of the country does not help the government's efforts to win diplomatic support at a time when the economy is tanking and Pakistan is begging the world to censure India for its recent moves on Kashmir, a disputed territory claimed by both Pakistan and India. It has taken Ms. Ismail some time to feel safe even in New York, she said, but she has begun to meet with prominent human rights defenders and the staffs of congressional leaders. "I will do everything I can to support Gulalai's asylum request," said Senator Charles Schumer, Democrat of New York.

"It is clear that her life would be in danger if she were to return to Pakistan." Pakistani security officials said they had suspected for some time that Ms. Ismail had slipped through their fingers. "Our guys have been after her, by all means, but she is not traceable," said a Pakistani intelligence agent who spoke on the condition of anonymity, citing intelligence protocols. "She has gone to a place beyond our reach."........Ever since she was, Ms. Ismail has been speaking out about human rights abuses, focusing on the plight of Pakistani women and girls who suffer all kinds of horrors including forced marriages and honor killings. In January, she aired accusations, on Facebook and Twitter, that government soldiers had raped or sexually abused many Pakistani women. She has also joined protests led by an ethnic Pashtun movement that Pakistan's military has tried to crush. Pakistani officials have accused Ms. Ismail of sedition, inciting treason and defaming state institutions".[10]

While Gulalai reached New York, her father also suffered torment due to his daughter's campaign for the rights of oppressed Pakistani citizens. According to the CIVICUS, systematic attacks against the PTM with scores of peaceful protesters arbitrarily arrested, detained and prosecuted on spurious charges, while protests by the PTM have been obstructed by security forces. In his interview with CIVICUS, Professor Mohammed Ismail said: "I have been targeted because of my daughter's activism. In May 2018, my daughter Gulalai Ismail, a women's rights activist, visited South Waziristan, an area on the border with Afghanistan, which was once a hub for international terrorism. Residents of the area have been complaining that the Pakistani army was protecting the militants, killing peaceful citizens and destroying their property".

Gulalai Ismail was arrested three times, harassed and mentally tortured by FIA in Islamabad. Her name was put on ECL but her arrest in Islamabad Press Club enraged journalist and intellectual community across Pakistan. The CIVICUS analysis of her struggle to save lives of innocent women and children noted her pain and industrious struggle. Some newspapers also published stories about her zeal and pluckiness. Gulalai led a protest in Islamabad against police brutality and misconduct and spoke up about sexual harassment of women and girls of tribal areas. Due to her activism, the government brought two criminal cases against Gulalai for attending gatherings of the PTM, but these were quashed by the courts:

"Gulalai visited an area named Khaisoor along with a group of women human rights activists. Women and girls shared their stories about sexual harassment by army personnel. Gulalai assured them that she would highlight their situation and work on the issue of sexual harassment of women and girls in conflict areas. In May 2019, a nine-year-old girl whose parents had been internally displaced from tribal areas experiencing conflict was raped and killed in Islamabad, the capital of Pakistan. The police refused to file a first information report (FIR) of the incident, and instead abused and harassed the father and brother of the child in the police station. Gulalai led a protest in Islamabad against police brutality and misconduct and spoke up about sexual harassment of women and girls in tribal areas and of the internally displaced population from tribal areas. Due to her activism, the government brought two criminal cases against Gulalai for attending gatherings of the PTM, but these were quashed by the courts. On 12 October 2018, Gulalai was arrested at Islamabad Airport by the Federal Investigation Agency (FIA) on her arrival from London and her name was put on the Exit Control List (ECL), which bans her from travelling outside the country. In February 2019, Gulalai was picked by security agencies at the Islamabad Press Club while she was attending a protest for the release of PTM activists, but her name was not on the list of people arrested and she went missing for 36 hours. She was produced and released by the Pakistani army after the Prime Minister of Pakistan interceded".[11]

PTM was helped by social media in circulating its message across the globe. Without the help of the social media and international press, information about the military operation in Waziristan was inaccessible. Known scholar and journalist Daud Khattak (Foreign Policy, 30 April 2019) in his well-written analysis of Pashtun Tahafuz Movement (PTM) has noted some aspects of PTM's challenges in demanding justice for families whose relatives were kidnapped by the army:

"Pashtun Protection Movement came to prominence in early 2018 in Waziristan, a remote outpost along Pakistan's rugged border with Afghanistan. Although the grievances PTM tapped into—discrimination against tribal people, violence by the Taliban, and military presence in the area—were long-standing, the trigger for the group's recent explosion was the extrajudicial killing of an aspiring model and artist from Waziristan in the city of Karachi in January 2018. Despite a media blackout—the major news channels have refrained from covering PTM gatherings or running interviews with its leadership, allegedly because of bullying and arrests by the intelligence agencies—Pashteen's protest is gaining ground. In February 2018, the PTM staged a sit-in in Islamabad, which was followed by more protests against the military in all major Pakistani cities. In February this year, for example, hundreds of young men and women marched in Lahore, the country's second-largest city, to demand freedom of expression, respect for the country's constitution, and civil rights. The name of their rally—Shehri Tahafuz March, or Citizen Protection March—was homage to PTM. And in April, tens of thousands of people demonstrated under the PTM banner in the North Waziristan city of Miran Shah".[13]

The agencies intercepted all newspapers and electronic media from reporting PTM's protests across Pakistan. Tehrik Insaf's government has a turbulent relationship with media under Imran Khan, elected as Prime Minister with strong backing from the military. Journalists are living in a climate of consternation and suppression. Scholar and journalist Daud Khattak also noted some incidents of kidnapping of PTM leaders and workers by Pakistani intelligence agencies. He also noted statement of General Ghafoor, in which he accused PTM leadership of getting money from Indian and Afghan intelligence agencies:

"In early February, for example, Ammar Ali Jan, a college teacher and PTM supporter, was picked up by law enforcement agencies from his house in Lahore in the middle of night on charges of supporting the PTM. In response, dozens of Punjab-based activists launched a social media campaign for his release. A few days after his release, Jan explained his ordeal in an op-ed. He clarified that he is not an ethnic Pashtun but has supported the PTM in its broader struggle against human rights violations. Facing widespread protest, the Pakistani military has resorted to its old playbook and condemned the PTM and other emerging movements as "fifth-generation warfare"—that is, hybrid warfare against the state. Meanwhile, the military has also linked Pashteen and others to foreign governments and intelligence agencies. Addressing a news conference on April 29, Pakistani military spokesman Maj. Gen. Asif Ghafoor accused the PTM leadership of getting money from Indian and Afghan intelligence. "But tell us how much money did you get from the NDS [Afghan National Directorate of Security] to run your campaign?" he asked. "How much money did RAW [India's Research and Analysis Wing] give you for the first dharna [sit-in] in Islamabad?"[14]

War criminal General Raheel Sharif protected terrorists, and accommodated them in guest houses, and ordered the killing and kidnapping of young men, women and children, and used sophisticated weapons in the region. He never allowed maimed, disabled and mutilated children to treat their wounds, or leave the region safely. Extrajudicial killings in FATA and Waziristan by his forces and illegal torture of children and women by his cronies caused permanent consternation and schizophrenic diseases in North Waziristan. More than 1,000 women and girls were kidnapped, and 2,000 tribal leaders have been disappeared by the army in FATA and Waziristan since 2004. Reftworld in its recent report highlighted cases of torture, humiliation, ill-treatment and unlawful arrest and detention in Pakistan:

"Irrespective of the "war on terror", the people of Pakistan suffer widespread violations of their civil and political rights. In Pakistan, torture and ill-treatment are endemic; arbitrary and unlawful arrest and detention are a growing problem; extrajudicial executions of criminal suspects are frequent; well over 7,000 people are on death row and there has recently been a wave of executions. Discriminatory laws deny the basic human rights of women and of minority groups. To this dismal human rights record, Pakistan's actions in the "war on terror" have added a further layer of violations. Hundreds of people suspected of links to al-Qaeda or the Taleban have been arbitrarily arrested and detained. Scores have become victims of enforced disappearance (for a definition see section 6); some of these have been unlawfully transferred (sometimes in return for money) to the custody of other countries, notably the USA. Many people have been detained incommunicado in undisclosed places of detention and tortured. Their families, distressed about the lack of information on the whereabouts and fate of their loved ones, have been harassed and threatened when seeking information. The right to habeas corpus has been systematically undermined as state agents have refused to comply with court directions or have lied in court. The fate of some of the victims of arbitrary arrest, detention and enforced disappearance has been disclosed – some have been charged with criminal offences unrelated to terrorism, others have been released without charge, reportedly after being warned to keep quiet about their experience, while some have been found dead".[15]

Journalist, M. Ilyas Khan (Uncovering Pakistan's secret human rights abuses, M Ilyas Khan, BBC News, Dera Ismail Khan, 02 June 2019) has confirmed atrocities of Pakistan army in his BBC News report: "In May 2016, for example, an attack on a military post in the Teti Madakhel area of North Waziristan triggered a manhunt by troops who rounded up the entire population of a village. An eyewitness who watched the operation from wheat field nearby and whose brother was among those detained told the BBC that the soldiers beat everyone with batons and threw mud in children's mouths when they cried. A pregnant woman was one of two people who died during torture, her son said in video testimony. At least one man remains missing".[16]

Human Rights Commission of Pakistan in its report "State of Human Rights in 2018" noted the scourge of enforced disappearances in Pakistan and reported the statement of Sardar Akhtar Mengal of the BNP-M, who warned that the situation in Naya Pakistan didn't changed as 235 people, including nine women gone missing from Balochistan:

"Families had received 45 dead bodies during the period from 25 July to 30 October 2018 and as many as 5,000 people are still reportedly missing from Balochistan. According to him, people were afraid to register FIRs if any of their family went missing because, if they did, they received threats from law enforcement agencies. Sardar Akhtar claimed that human rights activists, nationalists, and anyone who raised the issue of enforced disappearances on social media were also picked up by intelligence agencies. In their Bi-annual Report 2018 The State of Balochistan's Human Rights, the Baloch Human Rights Organisation and Human Rights Council of Balochistan said they had received 'partial reports' of 541 cases of enforced disappearances in the first half of the year. In the majority of cases 'the persons were picked up by security forces from their homes, in front of the entire families and villagers'. According to Amnesty International in March, the UN Working Group on Enforced or Involuntary Disappearances had more than 700 pending cases from Pakistan. Addressing a press conference at the Quetta Press Club in April, Hamida Baloch, sister of missing Saghir Baloch, appealed to the government of Pakistan, the Supreme Court, the Human Rights Commission of Pakistan, and civil society to raise their voice for the safe recovery of her brother. Saghir, a student of BS Political Science at the University of Karachi, went missing on 20 November 2017.[17]

In April 2019, Al Jazeera reported Pakistan army allegations against PTM leaders that it received funds from foreign intelligence services, warning its leaders that "their time is up". Major General Asif Ghafoor, speaking at a press conference at the military's headquarters in Rawalpindi levelled allegations that the Pashtun Tahafuz Movement (PTM) had been funded by RAW and NDS: "The way they are playing into the hands of others, their time is up," he said. "No one will be hurt and nothing illegal will be done. Everything will be done according to the law. Whatever liberties you could take, you have taken." General Ghafoor said. PTM leaders denied the charges, saying they were ready to present the group's accounts before parliament or other accountability bodies to be examined. "These accusations are being levelled against us only because we are demanding accountability," said Mohsin Dawar, a PTM leader and Member of Parliament, on the floor of Pakistan's National Assembly hours after Ghafoor's press conference. "We want accountability for targeted killings, for extrajudicial killings, for missing persons, people who have been held without charge or crime by the government. Whenever anyone speaks of these issues, they are accused of being foreign-funded," he said.[18]

However, Pakistani army attacked PTM workers near the border of Afghanistan, leaving at least three people dead and scores wounded. Leaders of the Pashtun movement said they exercised their right to protest peacefully, but the military saw the movement as being propped up by foes of the state and accuses neighboring Afghanistan and India of trying to stir up unrest with support of the movement in areas straddling the Afghan border. "You have enjoyed all the liberty that you wanted to," Maj. Gen. Asif Ghafoor, the military spokesman, warned P.T.M. leaders in a news conference. However, on 01 May 2019, Zahid Hussain noted General Ghafoor warning and the army bitterness against Pashtuns:

"Notwithstanding the conscious efforts of some elements to turn to chauvinism, the movement has so far remained peaceful, and there have not been incidents of any violence in its protest rallies, which is quite a rare phenomenon in Pakistani politics. The move to turn it into an anti-state movement can only be criticised, and the use of force would fuel negative propaganda. There is no denying the sacrifices rendered by Pakistan's security forces in eliminating militancy and bringing the former tribal areas into the national mainstream. It is wrong to blame the security establishment for everything that has gone wrong in the strife-torn region. But any attempt to suppress the protests will only widen alienation. It may be true that in this age of hybrid war, hostile foreign intelligence agencies are exploiting discontent for their own vested interests. But the inept handling of the situation will only help their agenda. Any rash action could be disastrous for the country. Warnings of the sort given at the briefing can only make people angrier. It is an issue that must be dealt with politically. The prime minister has taken the right approach in handling the problem. The allegation of foreign funding is very serious and no state can tolerate foreign meddling in its internal matters. There is an urgent need to investigate the matter and action must be taken if the charges are substantiated. More important, however, is that the blackout of the PTM should be lifted. The Senate committee has done a right thing by hearing the PTM leaders. This kind of dialogue must continue. A rational dialogue is the only way out of the problem".[19]

Pakistan army needs to adopt new strategy of counterinsurgency, instead of killing and kidnapping innocent people in Pakistan. This policy of oppression and humiliation will turn the region into an endless war, and foreign involvement will also challenge the authority of the state. On 30 May 2019, Human Rights Watch demanded the investigation of the North Waziristan atrocities:

"Pakistan authorities should impartially investigate the deaths of at least three people during violence between Pashtun activists and the army in North Waziristan on May 26, 2019, Human Rights Watch said. Both the army and supporters of the Pashtun Tahaffuz Movement (PTM), which campaigns for the rights of ethnic Pashtuns in the former tribal areas bordering Afghanistan, accuse the other of initiating a clash at a military checkpoint at KharKamar. In addition to the deaths, several people, including soldiers, were injured. "The uncertainty surrounding the deaths at KharKamar requires a prompt, transparent, and impartial investigation by Pakistani authorities," said Brad Adams, Asia director. "Upholding the rule of law is critical for maintaining security and protecting human rights in North Waziristan." The incident arose during a protest at the checkpoint by local residents following the arrest of two men after a military search operation. The search operation was in response to two attacks on army personnel, on May 6 and May 24, that killed one soldier and injured three others. A key PTM leader, Mohsin Dawar, told the media that as the group's elected representative, he and his supporters had gone to meet the demonstrators at the checkpoint. Dawar said that while he was meeting with the protesters, soldiers opened fire without provocation. After the incident, the army issued a statement that a group led by Dawar and Ali Wazir, another leader of the Pashtun group attacked the military checkpoint to force the release of a suspected terrorist facilitator. "In exchange of fire," the statement said, "three individuals who attacked the post lost their lives and 10 got injured." The prime minister's office endorsed the military's statement. The authorities registered a criminal case against Wazir and eight other PTM members who have been arrested. On May 27, the army issued a statement that five more bodies were found close to the area where the clash occurred".[20]

Pakistan's Armed Forces have been implicated in torture and other ill-treatment cases of individuals detained over the last decade of so called counter-insurgency operations in Waziristan and FATA. As the state practices have moved away from traditional counterinsurgency operations to sporadic clashes with local population since 2014, security and law and order situation is consecutively deteriorating in the region. With this shift in focus, Amnesty International became increasingly concerned about the treatment of detainees. Charles Pierson in his Wall Street Journal article noted the killing of 20 truck drivers by Pakistan army:

"Only three months ago, the Journal reported on an army massacre of unarmed civilians. This earlier story quoted local residents, three of them named, who told how an army unit ordered more than 20 men out of a restaurant in North Waziristan and then killed them execution style. No trial, no jury. The restaurant owner said that the men killed were truck drivers".[21] Raheel Sharif inflicted huge fatalities on civilian population in North Waziristan. His army kidnapped women and children, and humiliated tribal leaders. On 02 May 2019, Kunwar Khuldune Shahid in his analysis noted the resentment of Gen Ghafoor and the army against Pashtuns:

"Pakistan Army's spokesperson, Major General Asif Ghafoor, has warned the leadership of the Pashtun Tahafuz Movement (PTM) that their "time is up." Ghafoor dedicated most of his press conference on April 29 to the PTM–a nationalist movement dedicated to safeguarding the rights of the Pashtun community–accusing the group of receiving funds from Indian and Afghan intelligence agencies. While Ghafoor failed to substantiate his allegations, he laid the onus of disproving the Army's claims against the PTM on the movement's leadership. He put forth a questionnaire for the PTM, demanding answers regarding the group's responsibilities in the tribal areas, their overseas activities, collaborators in Kabul and New Delhi, narrative against the military, and income sources. At the same time, Ghafoor categorically told the media not to invite the movement's leadership on their channels to answer his own questions, amid the continued blanket ban on covering the PTM. In the same press conference, the spokesperson had earlier said with a straight face that the Army does not tell the media what to air and what not to air. When Member of the National Assembly (MNA) Mohsin Dawar, a PTM leader, tried to respond to the Army spokesperson's questions, his speech was cut short by the NA speaker. But there was enough time for Dawar to express his readiness for accountability, asking the military establishment if it could similarly come clean. On April 26, the PTM's elected MNAs from Waziristan, Dawar and Ali Wazir, weren't allowed to hold a press conference at the Islamabad Press Club, where they were going to address similar accusations that Prime Minister Imran Khan had levelled against them during a rally in the Orakzai tribal district on April 19. The Pakistan state habitually touts any emerging ethno-nationalist movements as a threat to national unity, remaining completely oblivious to the reality that it is actually through addressing valid grievances, like the ones that the PTM has taken up, that the state can overcome centrifugal forces and maintain its integrity".[22]

The army strived to undermine the leadership of Pashtuns in Waziristan but failed, and clefts appeared within the army ranks. Jaibans Singh in his analysis of the Pashtun Tahafooz Movement noted responses of Pashtun leaders and activists to the former ISPR Chief tweets:

"DG-ISPR's comments, especially on the missing persons, created a twitter storm. "The whole presser was horrendous. But this was the OMG moment. This confession will sink the military image. He is admitting to crime against humanity on television, OMG," wrote well known journalist, Gul Bukhari, in a tweet after the press conference. Screenshot of Pakistani Journalist Gul Bukhari's tweet in response to DG-ISPR Maj. Gen. Asif Ghafoor's admission that Pakistan Army has been responsible for missing Pakistani citizens. Gulali Ismail, a well known Human Rights Activist from Khyber Pakhtunkhwa tweeted, "I consider this Press Conference not an attack on PTM, but an attack on the Parliament of Pakistan, an attack on the Democracy of Pakistan and an attack on the Constitution of Pakistan PTM Zindabad." In fact, there are thousands of tweets on the same line with PTM Zindabad which, by now, must be giving nightmares to the Pakistan Army. They are also generating debates on the role of social media across the country. It will not come as a surprise if the DG-ISPR is soon transferred from the post. It is now apparent that the PTM and its leadership are not going to be cowed down by the usual pressure tactics of the Pakistan Army based on rising of anti-National, anti-Islam bogeys. These calls for accountability of the actions taken by the Army are going to increase and also envelope other trouble-torn areas of the country like Balochistan and Pakistan Occupied Kashmir (POK)".[23]

On 14 January 2020, the News International reported leaders of Pakistan's political parties to work with Pashtun Tahafuz Movement (PTM) for the protection of the rights of Pakhtuns. PTM chief Manzoor Pashteen at a public rally in Bannu announced the formation of a jirga to convince Pakhtun leaders to collectively work for Pakhtuns rights. Jamaat-e-Islami (JI) leader Senator Mushtaq Ahmad Khan told The News that he had raised the problems being faced by Pakhtuns at the highest forum in the country. "Pakhtuns rights are being violated at every level in Pakistan, adding that their undisputed rights provided in the Constitution were made disputed," he added. He said that he all parties' conference would be convened on January 29, 2020.[24]

Senator Mushtaq Ahmad Khan also said that he had raised the issues of net hydel profit, gas and others. He said Khyber Pakhtunkhwa was denied the rights to use its gas resource, which had been ensured in article 158. "They are making their own interpretation of this article to deny our rights," Mushtaq said. Jamiat Ulema-e-Islam-Fazl (JUI-F) leader Maulana Attaur Rehman said that they could respond on the possibility of cooperation after the PTM leaders present their demands. "The party leaders could take a decision on whether or not to work with PTM when we meet them and know their position," he added.[25] PTM held the public gathering in Bannu after a break of seven months and reiterated its demand of de-mining of the erstwhile FATA, end to enforced disappearances and constitution of truth and reconciliation commission.[26]

However, Mohsin Dawar, a leading member of Pashtun Tahafuz Movement (PTM) and Pakistani parliamentarian, termed the PTM rally in Bannu as a bigger success, adding that participation of thousands of Pashtuns in the rally showed that Pashtuns want their rights and could not remain silent. Mohsin Dawar said that since the starts of the PTM, a number of issues faced by Pakhtun in Pakistan have been resolved: "Cases of forced disappearances as well as violence in tribal districts reduced and PTM is getting more attention. However, he added, When the pressure is reduced, they (Security forces) will yet again resort to their old ways". Talking to Radio Ashna, Dawar added that the Bannu meeting was according to their expectations. Other political parties have not organised such a huge gathering in the region. "Our issues would automatically be resolved if they properly implement the constitution of the Pakistan," Dawar argued, and said: "We would continue our non-violent protests and would keep pressurising the government to accept the PTMs' demands," He said. Before the Banu PTM conference, on 22 February 2019, Senator Farhatullah Babar in his Friday Times analysis argued that the military culture of torture must undermine. He also noted that new legislation will limit the right of free trial, and the army will be operating with impunity:

"Due to conflict zones in Balochistan and erstwhile tribal areas, new legislation limiting the right to free trial, opaque detention centres under control of the military and increasing reliance on so called 'doctrine of exceptionalism' has blurred focus on the culture of impunity of torture in Pakistan. However, two recent developments should help return our focus on this issue and can serve as a catalyst for criminalising torture and ending the widespread impunity of the crime in the country. First, a recent Peshawar High Court verdict overturning scores of convictions awarded by military courts on grounds that suggested questionable ways of confessions extracted possibly under torture. Second, a report jointly prepared by the National Commission of Human Rights (NCHR) and Justice Project of Pakistan (JPP) on systematic torture by police in Faisalabad over a seven-year period covering three different administrations. Although Pakistan signed the

Convention against Torture (CAT) in 2008 and also ratified it in 2010, it has still not made domestic legislation that defines and criminalises torture. Pakistan's official report to the third Universal Periodic Review (UPR) in 2017 of its human rights record, referring to articles of the Constitution and penal laws, claimed that torture had already been eliminated and no one was tortured in the country. Referring to the Extradition Act, the official report claimed fool proof guarantees against handing over suspects to other parties who could subject them to torture. 1,424 cases of torture and other forms of cruel, inhuman and degrading treatment by the police were documented. No official inquiry was launched by any government body into any of these cases."[29]

However, Maj General Asif Ghafoor's irresponsible tweets, comments and conferences against the Pashtun nation left a black contemptuousness blot on the face of Pakistan army that the army only represents a club of Punjabi Generals. Gen Asif Ghafoor acted like a vandal and warlord that put the army in ordeal by challenging the Pushtun nation of Pakistan. The fact is, his resentment against Pashtuns, and his immature statement issued from the flatform of ISPR couldn't attract civil society in Pakistan. His past history and lose character show that he has often been swimming in a contaminated water where he adopted an abusive language. A man of shameless character created numerous controversies while his childlike statements and tweets caused misunderstading between Pakistan army and the Pashtun population across the border. On 15 January 2020, he shamelessly warned Pashtun nation that Pakistan army will butcher their children again. These and other artless statements and tweets forced GHQ to replace him by Maj General Babar Iftikhar.[30]

Chapter 10

Double Game: Why Pakistan Supports Militants and Resists U.S. Pressure to Stop

Sahar Khan

Executive Summary

The United States and the international community have accused Pakistan of sponsoring militant groups in Afghanistan and Indian-administered Jammu and Kashmir for decades—a charge Pakistan vehemently denies. Pakistan does, in fact, support three prominent jihadi militant groups in Jammu and Kashmir: the Hizb-ul-Mujahideen, Lashkar-e-Taiba, and Jaish-e-Mohammad, even though these groups are officially banned by the Pakistani government. The United States has also routinely criticized Pakistan for supporting the Afghan Taliban and Haqqani Network (a U.S.-designated terrorist group), both of which frequently attack U.S. troops and coalition forces in Afghanistan.

Why does Pakistan continue to sponsor militant groups in the face of considerable U.S. pressure to stop? This question has plagued U.S.-Pakistan relations for decades. President Trump has rebuked Pakistan, inflaming an already tense relationship when he tweeted about decades of U.S. aid to Pakistan with "nothing but lies & deceit" in return. The Trump administration subsequently reduced security and military aid to Pakistan, campaigned to add Pakistan to an intergovernmental watchlist for terrorism financing, and imposed sanctions on seven Pakistani firms involved in prohibited nuclear activities.

Unfortunately, these policies are unlikely to be effective in changing Pakistan's behavior. Pakistan's military establishment and intelligence agencies consider militant sponsorship an important mechanism for maintaining Pakistan's sovereignty and national identity. Pakistan's civilian institutions, too, have evolved to facilitate militant sponsorship by routinely legitimizing expansive executive powers, limiting judicial oversight, and violating civil liberties in the name of the national interest. Pakistan's civilian and military institutions, therefore, are much more closely aligned on matters of state sponsorship of militant groups than most U.S. policymakers and academics think, and therefore less susceptible to outside pressure.

However, the pervasiveness of militant sponsorship should not deter the United States from pursuing a productive relationship with Pakistan. The United States and Pakistan have a shared interest in ending the war in Afghanistan. This objective will continue to elude Washington unless policymakers better understand the motivations behind Islamabad's support for militant groups in Afghanistan and Kashmir. Therefore, policymakers should focus less on trying to change Pakistan's security policies and instead find ways to leverage its existing strategic perspective in pursuit of U.S. interests.

Introduction

On January 1, 2018, President Trump tweeted: "The United States has foolishly given Pakistan more than 33 billion dollars in aid over the last 15 years, and they have given us nothing but lies & deceit, thinking of our leaders as fools. They give safe haven to the terrorists we hunt in Afghanistan, with little help. No more!"[1] The president's message was clear: the United States will no longer tolerate Pakistan's policy of aiding and abetting militant groups, specifically the Afghan Taliban and the Haqqani Network.

Pakistan reacted swiftly—and angrily. Foreign Minister Khawaja Muhammad Asif blamed the United States for undermining the

U.S.-Pakistan alliance,[2] while the Ministry of Defense retorted that the United States ignores "cross-border safe havens of terrorists who murder Pakistanis."[3] On January 2, 2018, Prime Minister Shahid Khaqan Abbasi called an emergency session of the National Security Commission, the principal federal forum for Pakistan's civilian and military leadership for foreign policy.[4] After detailed discussions, the Commission stated that it would continue cooperation with the United States because stability in Afghanistan is one of Pakistan's core objectives, along with curbing terrorism.[5] Yet, as it became clear that the United States would be suspending military aid,[6] Pakistan retaliated by suspending intelligence-sharing, specifically of human intelligence gathered from ground sources that provides crucial support to ongoing U.S.-led operations in Afghanistan.[7]

Trump had criticized Pakistan on these grounds before. In August 2017, while announcing his strategy in Afghanistan and South Asia, he asserted that his administration intended to change the U.S. approach to Pakistan.[8] The president reproached Pakistan for continuing to provide refuge to terrorist groups at the risk of regional stability, citing 20 U.S.-designated foreign terrorist organizations operating in Pakistan and Afghanistan, the most in any region of the world, he claimed.[9] The National Security Strategy, which the administration released on December 18, 2017, reinforced the president's remarks, stating that the United States "will press Pakistan to intensify its counterterrorism efforts" while also "demonstrating that it is a responsible steward of its nuclear assets."[10]

Trump is hardly the first president to call Pakistan out for sponsoring militant groups. While unveiling his strategy for Afghanistan and Pakistan in 2009, President Barack Obama charged that al Qaeda was planning attacks on the U.S. homeland from its safe haven in Pakistan.[11] Similarly, President George W. Bush wrote in his memoir that he remained skeptical of Pakistan's insistence that it was acting against militant groups operating within its borders.[12] Neither is Trump the first president to cut security aid to Pakistan. In 2011, the Obama administration suspended $800 million in security aid that included the provision of U.S. equipment to the

Frontier Corps, a paramilitary organization based in the tribal region, and a $300 million reimbursement to Islamabad for its counterinsurgency expenditures.[13]

However, the U.S.-Pakistan relationship is currently at an all-time low. The Trump administration has already begun to implement a tougher approach toward Pakistan, which may include cutting military and security funding, stripping Pakistan of its designation as a non-NATO ally, and officially labeling Pakistan as a state sponsor of terror.[14] A U.S.-led campaign aims to add Pakistan back on to the terrorism financing watchlist of the Financial Action Task Force (FATF), an intergovernmental body intended to combat international money laundering and terrorism financing.[15] In March 2018, the Department of Commerce imposed sanctions on seven Pakistani firms for engaging in illicit nuclear trade.[16] Yet these policies are unlikely to change Pakistan's behavior or deter it from sponsoring militant groups, mainly because they are based on a faulty understanding of how militant sponsorship has evolved in Pakistan.

In Washington, the conventional wisdom on Pakistan correctly links militant sponsorship with the state's military establishment and intelligence agencies, principally the Inter-Services Intelligence (ISI). U.S. policies to combat militant sponsorship therefore largely focus on cutting aid to the military. However, when it comes to the issue of counterterrorism and national security, Pakistan's civilian institutions are more closely aligned with the military than Washington acknowledges.[17] This civil-military alignment is a result of the Pakistan Army's dominance as one of the strongest institutions in the country.[18] Civil institutions not only are subordinate, but also develop policies and bureaucratic routines of their own that reinforce the military's policy of sponsoring violent nonstate actors.

This paper is divided into three sections. The first section discusses the history of U.S.-Pakistan relations, highlighting how changes in the international order have created unrealistic expectations and divergent security calculations on both sides. The second section briefly describes Pakistan's counterterrorism bureaucracy, providing an institutional roadmap for how civilian counterterrorism structures have facilitated the state's policy of sponsoring militant groups. The final section explains the limitations of the Trump administration's hardline approach toward Pakistan and presents policy recommendations aimed at finding areas for cooperation.

US Pakistan Relations

The tension in the U.S.-Pakistan relationship stems from two key events: the end of the Cold War and the onset of the Global War on Terror (GWOT). The Cold War altered the structure of the international system and profoundly affected Pakistan. As Afghanistan's neighbor, Pakistan found itself at the center of the U.S.-Soviet rivalry when the Soviet Union invaded Afghanistan in 1979. In 1980, the United States and Pakistan supported the mujahideen,[19] a group of anti-Soviet tribal warlords funded by the United States and Saudi Arabia and directed by Pakistan's leading intelligence service, the ISI, to fight Soviet forces in Afghanistan.[20] These tribal groups claimed they were conducting jihad against the godless, communist Soviets. After almost a decade of seemingly unlimited funding and arms, the mujahideen drove Soviet forces out of Afghanistan. As the Soviet Union collapsed and the Cold War ended, so did support for the mujahideen. Pakistan now had at its disposal well-armed, religiously motivated, Sunni-dominated militants that were essentially unemployed after the Cold War.

Scholars disagree about how Pakistan used the mujahideen in the post–Cold War world. Some argue that Pakistan used them to bolster the anti-Indian insurgency in Kashmir and then to gain favor with the United States.[21] Pakistan's recognition and support of the Taliban (the primary remnant of the mujahideen) as it rose to power in Afghanistan in 1996 was a way to dispel the tensions with Afghanistan over the Durand Line—the disputed border between the two countries.[22] Others argue that Pakistan's use of the mujahideen is not a byproduct of the Cold War or a half-baked strategy to support insurgencies in Kashmir or Afghanistan. Rather, it is the focal point of the Pakistani state's strategy of using jihad to meet the state's geostrategic goals and bolster its security.[23]

The terrorist attacks of September 11, 2001, created a state of panic within the United States.[24] Two days after the attacks, then secretary of state Colin Powell famously called Pakistan's president at the time, General Pervez Musharraf, and stated: "You are either with us or against us."[25] While Musharraf chose to side with the United States, he authorized the rescue of key Taliban members from Afghanistan, allowing them to resettle in Pakistan.[26] As the U.S. war in Afghanistan has continued, U.S.-Pakistan relations have steadily deteriorated because of Pakistan's consistent support of the Taliban and the Haqqani Network.

Pakistan is facing intense backlash against its policy of militant sponsorship, both domestically and internationally. In June 2018, the FATF, the international watchdog on terrorism financing, put Pakistan on its "gray list," concluding that Pakistan's anti-money laundering structure had serious deficiencies.[27]Meanwhile, militant sponsorship also generates domestic political instability.[28] For example, the Pakistan Army's harsh counterinsurgency campaigns in the northwest tribal region have sparked a Pashtun civil rights movement, leading to concern in Islamabad but also abroad about the fragility of the state's political system.[29]

At the same time, the U.S. war in neighboring Afghanistan continues unabated. As a candidate, Trump pledged, "I will never send our finest into battle unless necessary, and I mean absolutely necessary, and will only do so if we have a plan for victory with a capital V."[30] Yet, as president, he increased the number of troops in Afghanistan,[31] and NATO soon followed.[32] As of June 2018, there are 14,000 U.S. troops in Afghanistan.[33] In April, the Special Investigator General for Afghanistan Reconstruction concluded that overall U.S. reconstruction efforts are going poorly: corruption remains rampant while the economy is heavily dependent on foreign aid, and the Afghan National Security Forces continue to lack capacity to provide security.[34]

The legacies of the Cold War and the GWOT continue to influence the relationship between Islamabad and Washington, and Afghanistan has been at the center of the relationship from the beginning. From the U.S. perspective, the main question that should be dominating the relationship with Pakistan is this: How can the U.S. successfully conclude its war in Afghanistan? Both states want the war to end, but each has a very different idea of what the end state should look like.

Washington's Perspective on US-Pakistan Relations

Washington essentially left Afghanistan in the hands of Pakistan and Saudi Arabia after the Soviets withdrew. With respect to Pakistan, U.S. policymakers favored military dictator General Zia ul-Haq, who had proved to be a key U.S. ally during the Cold War. But as the Soviets were preparing to withdraw from Afghanistan, Haq died in a plane crash in 1988. On the way to attending Haq's funeral, Secretary of State George Shultz, Under Secretary of State for Political Affairs Michael Armacost, Assistant Secretary of Defense for International Security Richard Armitage, and Rep. Charlie Wilson (D-TX) devised a U.S. strategy for Pakistan that consisted of deepening ties with Pakistan's military establishment and intelligence agencies while also supporting democratic developments such as general elections.[35]

Soon after the Soviet withdrawal, Afghanistan devolved into a civil war that ended when the Taliban took over and established what they called the Islamic Emirate of Afghanistan.[36] U.S. Assistant Secretary of State for South Asia Robin Raphel visited Afghanistan in April 1996 to urge the Taliban to allow Unocal, an American oil company, to build an oil and gas pipeline from Turkmenistan to Pakistan through Afghanistan. Raphel emphasized that the United States wanted to ensure that Afghanistan (and potentially the United States) would not lose any financial and economic opportunities.[37] In turn, Unocal began to provide economic and humanitarian aid to the Taliban.[38]

Sensing U.S. sympathy for the Taliban, Pakistan's then Prime Minister Benazir Bhutto tried to convince Washington to publicly side with the Taliban—and Pakistan. This idea was not radical given the context of U.S. regional policy: Congress had authorized a covert $20 million budget for the CIA to counter Iran's influence in the region.[39] Even though Pakistan and Iran were not enemies—

both had worked to quash the Baloch insurgency in Pakistan since the 1970s—Pakistan considered the United States a more important strategic ally.40 More significantly, Iran opposed the Taliban.[41] The Clinton administration, however, refused to openly support the Taliban. In the meantime, the Taliban leadership hosted al Qaeda's leader, Osama bin Laden, a known threat to U.S security. Taking advantage of its base in Afghanistan, al Qaeda launched simultaneous attacks on U.S. embassies in Tanzania and Kenya in August 1998, killing more than 200 people.[42] President Clinton ordered airstrikes against al Qaeda targets in Afghanistan and Sudan.[43] A few months after the strikes, Unocal withdrew from the oil pipeline project, effectively halting it.[44] By 1999, the alliance between the Taliban and al Qaeda was clear,[45] as was Pakistan's unwavering support for the Taliban.[46]

In 2000, Clinton visited India, Pakistan, and Bangladesh—the first U.S. president to visit South Asia since the end of the Cold War.[47] Clinton's historic visit set the tone for an improved U.S.-India relationship.[48] However, the administration was inflexible toward Pakistan. Clinton publicly lauded the country for striving to be a "beacon of democracy in the Muslim world."[49] But in private he told General Pervez Musharraf, who came to power via a military coup just six months before Clinton's visit, to restore democracy, halt militant sponsorship in Kashmir, and assist the U.S in capturing Osama bin Laden.[50] The George W. Bush administration more or less maintained the Clinton administration's policy toward South Asia until the 9/11 attacks.

In its initial months, the Bush administration hailed the war in Afghanistan as a success: the Taliban were ousted from Kabul, and their airfields and headquarters were destroyed, effectively eliminating their ability to provide physical sanctuary to al Qaeda.[51] World leaders met in Bonn, Germany, to set the course for Afghan reconstruction in an attempt to avoid the neglect that had followed the Soviet withdrawal in 1989. The Bonn Agreement was signed in December 2001, and the Afghan Interim Authority, led by Hamid Karzai (who later was elected and served as Afghanistan's president until 2014), was given a six-month mandate to begin forming a constitution that would lay down the foundation for an Afghan government.[52] The agreement also created the International Security Assistance Force (ISAF), a NATO-led force tasked with training the Afghan National Security Forces.[53]

Pakistan was generally in favor of the Bonn Agreement.[54] Pakistani officials tried to convince the Bush administration to talk with the Taliban, but President Bush was adamantly against any such negotiations.[55] Within a year of the Bonn Agreement, the Bush administration began to turn away from Afghanistan to focus on regime change in Iraq.[56] The Iraq War not only took resources away from Afghanistan at a crucial moment, but also fueled instability across the Middle East.[57] The discovery of the Khan Network further aggravated U.S.-Pakistan relations under the Bush administration.[58] The Khan Network was essentially a black market for nuclear materials, created and led by Pakistan's leading nuclear scientist, Abdul Qadir Khan.

The network helped further nuclear programs in Iran, North Korea, and Libya until its discovery in 2004. While Khan maintained that the Pakistani state knew of these activities, the state denied all knowledge. Even though the Khan Network was dismantled, its lingering impact on nuclear proliferation remains a cause for concern within the U.S. intelligence community[59] Furthermore, U.S. (and Afghan) officials worry about the safety of Pakistan's nuclear arsenal.[60] Pakistan's former minister of foreign affairs Khurshid Mahmud Kasuri (2002–2007), however, maintains that the army has strengthened its oversight over Pakistan's nuclear weapons.[61]

The Obama administration's Afghanistan policy consisted of two overarching goals: defeating al Qaeda in Afghanistan and Pakistan and preventing al Qaeda from establishing a "safe haven" from which to launch another attack on U.S. territory.[62] Like the Bush administration, the Obama administration pursued a military-centric approach. From 2008 to 2011, Obama increased the number of U.S. ground troops from 30,000 to more than 100,000 to fight the insurgency and help train and increase the capacity of the Afghan security forces.[63] However, he also set a withdrawal date of December 2014 in order to dispel expectations that U.S.

involvement in Afghanistan was open-ended. Obama emphasized the need for a peaceful Afghan-led government and the importance of Pakistan in achieving that goal.[64]Yet the U.S.-Pakistan relationship remained tense, especially regarding Pakistan's tacit support of the Afghan Taliban, Haqqani Network, and the Quetta Shura (a Taliban government based in Peshawar, a major city and capital of Pakistan's Khyber Pakhtunkhwa province).

Tensions between the United States and Pakistan reached a high point when, after nine years of searching, bin Laden was found living in a compound with his family in Abbottabad, Pakistan. U.S. Navy SEALs killed bin Laden in a clandestine raid on May 2, 2011. Officials in both Washington and Islamabad say the Obama administration did not inform Pakistan of the raid before it happened.[65] In June 2011, the administration of Asif Ali Zardari (elected in 2008 after Musharraf's downfall) called on the Supreme Court of Pakistan to investigate the events that led up to the raid. After two years, the Abbottabad Commission submitted its report, which was later leaked and published by Al Jazeera in July 2013. The report was 700 pages long, included 200 recommendations and testimonies from more than 300 witnesses, and held both the Pakistani government and the military responsible for incompetence and complicity in hiding bin Laden.[66]

As the trust deficit between the United States and Pakistan deepened, the Obama administration pursued negotiations with the Taliban.[67] Working with Germany, the United States convinced Qatar to allow the Taliban to open a political office in Doha to facilitate peace talks.[68] Direct negotiations between the United States and the Taliban, meanwhile, made Pakistan's military establishment nervous, as officials in Islamabad have much preferred to mediate between the two.[69] Ultimately, the Obama administration pursued a multifaceted policy toward Pakistan that involved temporary cuts to military and security aid, a massive development aid package, and public criticism of Pakistan as a "difficult" partner.[70] For example, when members of the Senate Armed Services Committee asked Admiral James Winnefeld about the nature of U.S.-Pakistan relations during his confirmation hearing to serve as the vice chairman of the Joint Chiefs of Staff, he replied, "Even though this is a difficult partnership, it is an important one."[71] Yet the administration was unable to deter Pakistan from its policy of militant sponsorship.

For those closely following the U.S.-Pakistan relationship in the context of the U.S. war in Afghanistan, Trump's hardline approach toward Pakistan is not new. Whereas frustration with Pakistan is warranted, the Trump administration's policy is misguided, especially if the ultimate goal is to reach a viable political solution with key stakeholders, withdraw U.S. troops from Afghanistan, and protect against potential future threats emerging from Afghanistan in particular and South Asia in general.[72] Like past administrations, the Trump administration views Pakistan largely through the lens of the war in Afghanistan, which has proved to be counterproductive for fostering a cooperative bilateral relationship. Washington tends to devalue the impact that the Cold War and the mujahideen had on Pakistan's strategic calculus.

More significantly, the United States tends to blame Pakistan for the failure of the war in Afghanistan. Pakistan's continued support for the Afghan Taliban and Haqqani Network has certainly played a significant role in sustaining the insurgency and undermining the Afghan government's stability. Yet even if Pakistan abruptly halted all support for these militant proxies, the war would still be going badly because of various factors, including U.S. mismanagement of Afghan reconstruction, lack of coordination between U.S. troops and ISAF, and corrupt Afghani politics.[73] Although it remains unclear whether efficient reconstruction efforts or improved coordination between various ground troops would positively influence the trajectory of the war, one thing is obvious: the Trump administration needs to reorient its expectations of Pakistan.

Islamabad's Perspective on US-Pakistan Relations

From Pakistan's perspective, its relationship with the United States is still dominated by the Cold War, U.S. support for the mujahideen, and a feeling of abandonment once Washington shifted its focus elsewhere after the Berlin Wall fell. In many respects, Islamabad sees the United States as an unreliable ally that continues to ignore the myriad sacrifices Pakistan has made as a key partner in the GWOT. Pakistan's support for the Taliban continues to this day. Yet, when questioned about the policy of militant sponsorship, Pakistani officials deny it and demand evidence. There is, of course, plenty of evidence. Throughout the 1990s, Pakistan provided diplomatic and material assistance to the Taliban as part of its "strategic depth" policy. Strategic depth is loosely defined as the army's strategy for maintaining influence over the Afghan government in Kabul to prevent it from backing Pakistan's domestic insurgencies, such as the Balochi and Sindhi movements and the ongoing Pashtun movement, and to counter India's plans for regional domination.[74]

Over the years, a handful of high-level army officers and ISI agents joined the Taliban.75 An ex-ISI agent, Colonel "Imam" Sultan Amir, advised local Taliban leaders in the 1990s.[76] In 2001, just before U.S. troops were deployed to Afghanistan, the Bush administration approved an ISI plan to airlift Pakistanis in Afghanistan back to Pakistan. In the process of the airlift, the ISI also rescued key members of the Taliban, and relocated them to Baluchistan and Pakistan's tribal areas.[77] Pakistan has also continued to provide safe haven to militant groups waging jihad in Kashmir. Lashkar-e-Taiba (LeT), one of the most prominent anti-India militant groups, remains active in Pakistan despite official state bans.[78] Similarly, Jaish-e-Mohammed (JeM), the group that claimed responsibility for the attacks on Indian army bases in Pathankot and Uri in 2016, is headquartered in southern Punjab.[79] While he was president, Hamid Karzai (2004–2014) continuously accused Pakistan of undermining the Afghan government by sponsoring the Taliban, who routinely attack U.S., ISAF, and Afghan National Security Forces (ANSF) troops in Afghanistan.[80]

Pakistan thinks that it has borne significant costs by being an active participant in the GWOT and believes further that Washington habitually ignores these sacrifices. Pakistan currently hosts more than 1.4 million Afghan refugees, most of whom fled because of the U.S. invasion of Afghanistan following 9/11.[81] Many Taliban escaped to Pakistan and regrouped in the Federally Administered Tribal Areas (FATA) in the northwest, where the mountainous terrain provided the perfect cover. FATA is a majority Pashtun area that consists of seven tribal agencies and six frontier regions that are governed by Pakistan's federal government through colonial-era laws called the Frontier Crimes Regulation, which have granted a measure of autonomy to the region.[82] Consequently, the Pakistani military rarely intruded into FATA.[83] But in 2002, under U.S. pressure, the Pakistan Army began conducting counterinsurgency operations in three of the tribal agencies—Khyber, North Waziristan, and South Waziristan—to weed out the Taliban seeking refuge there.[84]

The ruthless operations left thousands of Pashtuns dead, detained by military authorities, or internally displaced, while 200 tribal elders were killed. In response to the army's operations, some Afghan Taliban members and others formed an umbrella organization called the Tehrik-i-Taliban Pakistan, or Pakistani Taliban, that actively targets both Pakistani security forces and civilians.[85] In one particularly egregious example, the Pakistani Taliban attacked the Army Public School in Peshawar in 2014, killed more than 130 children, and issued warnings of future attacks.[86] Some Pakistani officials, therefore, go so far as to blame the United States for the rise of the Pakistani Taliban.

Since 2002, terrorist groups have killed more than 22,000 Pakistani civilians.[87] In response to repeated threats and attacks by the Pakistani Taliban, the Pakistan Army has continued to launch counterinsurgency campaigns in the tribal areas and the province of Khyber Pakhtunkhwa,[88] also dominated by Pashtuns.[89] Military authorities claimed that more than 3,500 militants were killed in the Zarb-e-Azb (Strike of the Sword) campaign that lasted from June 2014 to April 2016.[90] Radd-ul-Fasaad (Elimination of Strife) is an ongoing operation that began in February 2017 and aimed at eliminating terrorist sleeper cells across the country.[91] These campaigns have continued to displace thousands of Pashtuns and have resulted in numerous cases of "missing persons" and "enforced disappearances."[92] From Pakistan's perspective, it is currently involved in two wars: the GWOT and a domestic counterterrorism war.[93]

Pakistan's feelings of regional insecurity help drive its policy of militant sponsorship. Because of concerns about competing militant groups, tribal cleavages, and domestic unrest, Pakistan seeks to establish a pro-Pakistan government in Kabul via the Taliban.[94] As such, Pakistan is wary of increased Indian engagement in Afghanistan. India has a long history of supporting development projects in Afghanistan.[95] Most recently, India has invested heavily in Iran's Chabahar Port, reducing Afghanistan's reliance on Pakistani ports as a trade route to the Indian Ocean.[96] From Pakistan's perspective, Chabahar is proof of India's scheme to encircle Pakistan.[97] But India's investment in Chabahar is also a way for India to counter China's growing influence within South Asia.[98] As longtime allies, Pakistan and China have a relatively stable relationship, and the ongoing China-Pakistan Economic Corridor (CPEC)—a multi-billion-dollar development project funded and led by China in Pakistan—will most likely increase China's interest in Pakistan's political and economic stability.[99]

Therefore, Pakistan's view of its bilateral relationship with the United States is informed by both domestic security priorities and dynamic regional interests. Pakistan's response to the Trump administration's hardline policy consists of a combination of playing the victim and exercising restraint. Pakistan seeks to persuade the United States by arguing that its counterinsurgency operations in the tribal areas have eliminated all Afghan Taliban and Haqqani Network safe havens. Pakistani officials also emphasize the number of Pakistani civilians that have been killed by the Pakistani Taliban and U.S. drone strikes in the tribal region, highlighting the human costs Pakistanis have borne as a result of the U.S.-led GWOT. Pakistan has also shown restraint by keeping NATO supply routes open after Trump's January tweet (in the past, Pakistan has closed supply routes multiple times).[100] Ultimately, Pakistan does not want to be isolated from the United States and is working to prevent further deterioration in relations.

It is important that the Trump administration maintains a constructive working relationship with Pakistan in order to conclude the war in Afghanistan. But to accomplish this goal, the administration needs to adjust its expectations of Pakistan. Like all past U.S. administrations, the Trump administration's approach is based on the notion that Pakistan's civilian institutions will respond to pressure tactics and push back against the policy of militant sponsorship that is driven by the military establishment and intelligence agencies. But a close examination of Pakistan's civilian counterterrorism bureaucracy demonstrates that the civilian institutions have become complicit in militant sponsorship by expanding executive powers, legitimizing the military's overreach, and refusing to reform.

Pakistan's civilian Counterterrorism Establishment

Washington's attempts to pressure Pakistan to stop supporting militants rest on a faulty assumption that Pakistan's civilian institutions can push back on the military's prerogatives on militant sponsorship. In fact, Pakistan's civilian institutions simply empower the military and intelligence communities and reinforce their perspective on nonstate militants. In particular, three civilian institutions play a key role in supporting militant sponsorship: the legislature, the judiciary, and the police.

Pakistan's anti-terrorism legal regime consists of 16 colonial-era criminal laws and more recent counterterrorism statutes.[101] Both civilian leaders and military dictators have used the anti-terrorism legal regime established by the legislature to increase their power and promote their legitimacy after political crises. For example, soon after gaining power via a military coup in 1999, President Musharraf used the Anti-Terrorism Act of 1997 to discredit then Prime Minister Nawaz Sharif and justify his coup. The Anti-Terrorism Act provides the foundation for Pakistan's counterterrorism bureaucracy.[102] According to the act, those charged with terrorism will be tried in special courts called Anti-Terrorism Courts (ATCs), which operate nationwide.[103]

Sharif, however, had not committed any act of terrorism. Instead, Musharraf amended the law by expanding its jurisdiction to include crimes such as conspiracy, arms trafficking, hijacking, and kidnapping. Musharraf then used these amendments to build a case against Sharif, forcing the former prime minister to be tried in an ATC rather than regular criminal court.[104] Political leaders have also used anti-terrorism statutes to expand executive and military power, providing the military establishment legal cover for questionable practices. For instance, the identical "aid to civil power" regulations for the federally and provincially administered tribal areas legalized the military's previously unauthorized detention of civilians caught during the counterinsurgency campaigns in 2009 and 2010, many of whom are still detained without any charges against them.[105]

The second civilian institution that plays an important role in counterterrorism is the judiciary. In the context of counterterrorism, the judiciary's main responsibility has been to ensure that anti-terrorism statutes do not violate Pakistan's constitution. However, Pakistan's Supreme Court has routinely upheld expansive anti-terrorism laws, citing the doctrine of state necessity.[106] The doctrine of necessity is a commonly used legal principle in commonwealth countries that is used to justify otherwise illegal government action.[107] For example, in 2015 the court used the doctrine to allow civilians charged with terrorism to be tried in military courts.[108] The military courts were established via a constitutional amendment in 2015 after the Pakistani Taliban attacked a school in Peshawar, killing more than 130 children.[109] The civilian government had responded quickly, passing a National Action Plan that included reinstating the death penalty and establishing special trial courts run by the military tribunals for "swift" justice.[110] Human-rights activists argued that trying civilians charged with terrorist acts in military courts was unconstitutional. Pakistan's Supreme Court disagreed.[111]

The judiciary has also accepted the formation of specialized courts like the ATCs, fundamentally agreeing with the legislative branch that a separate court system for those charged with terrorism would be more efficient than the regular criminal justice system.[112] The third civilian institution at the forefront of counterterrorism is the police. According to the Anti-Terrorism Act, the police can use deadly force, detain suspects for up to 90 days, target militant "networks," and confiscate the passports of suspects charged under the statute. The police also have provincial Counterterrorism

Departments, Rapid Response Forces, and high-security prisons to counter terrorist groups.[113] Yet daily police activities are still governed by antiquated colonial laws that affect how the police can gather evidence.[114] For example, under regular criminal laws, a confession to a police officer is not permitted in a court of law, but according to the Anti-Terrorism Act, it is. The police often arrest a suspect under the act regardless of the crime, which in turn has overburdened Anti-Terrorism Courts. Civilian leaders have also been reluctant to reform the police.

Instead, politicians routinely interfere in police investigations, officer recruitment, officer transfers, and basic material purchases— and often uses the police as personal bodyguards, especially in rural areas.[115] As a result, the Pakistani police remain one of the weakest civilian counterterrorism institutions. Pakistan's military establishment and intelligence agencies are primarily responsible for sponsoring groups such as the Afghan Taliban, Haqqani Network, LeT, and JeM. But the tendency of the legislature and the courts to expand the power of the executive and the military, and the police's continued operational weakness and corruption have created a civilian counterterrorism bureaucracy that is beholden to the military and its sponsorship of militant groups. Therefore, each civilian institution involved in counterterrorism— the legislature, judiciary, and police—helps facilitate, rather than counteract, militant sponsorship.

A Pragmatic US Approach Towards Pakistan

Continuous U.S. support of Pakistan's military has only exacerbated the country's civil-military imbalance.[116] The United States needs to adopt a more informed and constructive approach toward Pakistan. The Trump administration has taken a hardline approach toward Pakistan aimed at curbing the state's sponsorship of militant groups. This approach includes military and security aid cuts; a U.S.-led campaign to put Pakistan on FATF's gray list; and targeting LeT, a U.S.-designated terrorist group that operates openly in Pakistan. Cutting U.S. military and security aid to Pakistan in order to pressure the country to stop supporting militant groups has been tried repeatedly throughout the years and has largely failed to change Pakistan's policies.

At the Obama administration's behest, Congress established the Pakistan Counterinsurgency Fund in 2009 to provide U.S. military equipment and combat training to Pakistan's military and paramilitary forces for counterinsurgency operations in the tribal areas.[117] As Pakistan's support for the Taliban and Haqqani Network continued, Congress discontinued the fund soon after it started—a move supported by the Obama White House.[118] The Trump administration is currently withholding Foreign Military Financing, a grant and loan program used by several countries to acquire U.S. arms. Trump has also partially cut the Coalition Support Fund (CSF),[119] established to reimburse Pakistan for America's use of Pakistani military bases to launch ground offensives—and later drone strikes—in the tribal areas.[120] Ending financial support to Pakistan's military establishment is a good thing because taxpayer dollars should not go toward corrupt foreign militaries, particularly those that aid terrorist groups. However, cutting off aid will not alter Pakistan's use of militant proxies.

The United States and India spearheaded a campaign to add Pakistan to the FATF's gray list—a list of countries that can be sanctioned because of their involvement in illicit terrorist financing. To garner some goodwill, Pakistan amended its anti-terrorism law in February 2018 to ban the Jamaat ud Dawa and the Falah-i-Insaniat, charity wings of LeT, the notorious militant group that wages jihad in Kashmir with the Pakistan Army's support.[121] The FATF, however, issued a warning anyway, and eventually added Pakistan to its list in June 2018, opening the possibility of more sanctions.[122] Yet sanctions rarely alter state behavior.[123] In any case, adding Pakistan to the FATF gray list in the hope that authorities would stop sponsoring the Taliban, Haqqani Network, and Kashmiri insurgents has already been tried—and it failed. The Obama administration also advocated adding Pakistan to the FATF's gray list, where it remained from 2012 to 2015. During this period, Pakistan not only continued to sponsor militant groups but managed to stabilize exports and imports. Pakistan also completed its International Monetary Fund program and raised $5 billion in the international bond market.[124]

Being on the FATF list, therefore, hardly hindered Pakistan's economic growth. At best, the pressure could force the government to reform its Anti-Money Laundering Act, a currently dormant law designed to combat the financing of militant organizations and groups operating within Pakistan, with an emphasis on implementation.[125] However, such cosmetic changes will not substantively alter Pakistan's policies. Like past administrations, the Trump administration is also trying to curb Pakistan's sponsorship of the LeT by designating the Milli Muslim League, the political party of LeT, as a global terrorist group.[126] Yet "terrorist" label are more political than practical, and as such, will have minimal impact on Pakistan's sponsorship of the LeT. For its part, Pakistan's election commission has refused to register the party, preventing it from participating in the general elections (though its members are running in the elections as independent candidates).[127] Despite Washington's designation of the group as a terrorist organization, the Pakistani military continues to support the League.[128]

Underlying these U.S. policies is the assumption that Pakistan can be convinced to sever all ties with the Taliban and Haqqani Network. Ambassador Richard G. Olson, who served as U.S. ambassador to Pakistan from 2012 to 2015 and special representative for Afghanistan and Pakistan from 2015 to 2016, argues that the Trump administration should tell Pakistan it must cut all ties with the Taliban and the Haqqani Network in order to repair its damaged relationship with the United States.[129] Yet the United States has never been able to convince Pakistan to stop supporting the Taliban, the Haqqanis, or the Quetta Shura. Many analysts worry that Pakistan will increasingly look toward China as its relationship with the United States worsens, but Pakistan's "drift" toward China is not new. Pakistan's foreign policy has always been influenced by South Asian regional politics, in which China is a significant actor.

China and Pakistan have been allies for decades, with China often providing material and diplomatic support to Pakistan to counter

India. China even played a key role in developing Pakistan's nuclear program. However, the Sino-Pakistan relationship, especially in its current form, should not be a cause of alarm in Washington. In recent years, Beijing has heavily invested in Pakistan through the CPEC, a multi-billion-dollar development project. China, therefore, has an interest in a stable Pakistan. In fact, China has been in talks with Baloch militants to prevent any attacks on Chinese workers and CPEC projects.[130] Rumors that China is planning to build a naval base near Pakistan's Gwadar port, where it signed a 40-year lease in 2017, have been a source of anxiety in Washington, but both China and Pakistan deny any plans to build a base.[131] In any case, such a military base would not necessarily pose a threat to U.S. interests.[132]

The United States and Pakistan may never have an ideal relationship, but they do agree on one fundamental thing: U.S. involvement in Afghanistan needs to end. To achieve this shared objective, the United States must adopt a more pragmatic approach toward Pakistan. The Trump administration should adjust its expectations with respect to Pakistan and its support for militant groups, especially the Taliban. Although the United States has been fighting the Taliban for almost two decades, no enduring resolution to the war in Afghanistan is possible without their cooperation. The Trump administration should pursue an Afghan-led peace process that directly involves the Taliban.[133] While the Taliban have so far refused to participate in Afghanistan's parliamentary elections, scheduled for this fall, they have expressed an interest in negotiating with the United States. Instead of rejecting that offer, the Trump administration should try to leverage talks with the Taliban to mediate the U.S. relationship with the Afghan government, while also planning for a military withdrawal. Pakistan can be a useful partner in such an effort.

The Trump administration should seek common ground with Pakistan while acknowledging areas of disagreement. For example, protecting Pakistan's nuclear arsenal from militant groups is a priority for both countries. According to Gina Haspel's testimony during her confirmation hearing to become CIA director, the CIA remains focused on monitoring any activities between extremist groups and Pakistan's nuclear arsenal, which may provide a good opportunity for American and Pakistani intelligence communities to cooperate.[134] Finding a feasible and lasting end to the war in Afghanistan is also mutually beneficial for the United States and Pakistan. The United States wants to ensure that Afghanistan has a stable government and that the country does not become a launching pad for another terrorist attack on the United States.

However, Washington has ruled out any role for the Taliban in the Afghan government. Pakistan's objective is to ensure a pro-Pakistan government in Kabul, one that will assist it in deterring India, and maintains that the Taliban would be the most reliable actor. Yet the Taliban's pro-Pakistan tendencies are questionable at best. Furthermore, it remains unclear whether Afghanistan can even have a stable government in the next few years. Ongoing U.S. and Pakistani support for an Afghan-led peace process is a step in the right direction. The United States must come to grips with its inability to get Pakistan to stop sponsoring militants and pursue direct talks with the Taliban while the opportunity still exists.

For years, the United States has supported Pakistan's military establishment over its civilian institutions. While Pakistan's civil-military imbalance is a result of numerous domestic factors, U.S. support for the Pakistan Army has aggravated it. The United States has also overlooked the ways in which Pakistan's civilian institutions have evolved to facilitate militant sponsorship, directly or indirectly. The only way the Trump administration can have a positive relationship with Pakistan is recognize the futility of pressuring Pakistan to stop funding militants and partner with Islamabad on terms it can accommodate. A strategic reevaluation of the U.S.-Pakistan relationship is in order.

Conclusion

Pakistan has a long history of militant sponsorship. The military establishment has played a central role in Pakistan's use of militant groups as proxies, but contrary to longstanding presumptions in Washington, Pakistan's civilian establishment by no means serves as a check against these policies. Militant sponsorship has become a kind of whole-of-government principle of Pakistan's security policy and national identity. Punitive U.S. actions to discourage it, therefore, have little chance of success. Washington should incorporate this reality into its policy and look for alternative solutions to securing a durable peace in Afghanistan that can set the stage for a U.S. withdrawal and establish a new and constructive relationship with Pakistan.

Double Game: Why Pakistan Supports Militants and Resists U.S. Pressure to Stop. By Sahar Khan. September 20, 2018, Number 849. Sahar Khan is a visiting research fellow in defense and foreign policy studies at the Cato Institute. She has a PhD in political science from the University of California, Irvine. The views expressed in this paper are those of the author(s) and should not be attributed to the Cato Institute, its trustees, its Sponsors, or any other person or organization. Nothing in this paper should be construed as an attempt to aid or hinder the passage of any bill before Congress. Copyright © 2018 Cato Institute. This work by Cato Institute is licensed under a Creative Commons Attribution-Non Commercial-Share Alike 4.0 International License. The Cato Institute is a public policy research organization — a think tank —dedicated to the principles of individual liberty, limited government, free markets, and peace. Its scholars and analysts conduct independent, nonpartisan research on a wide range of policy issues. Founded in 1977, Cato owes its name to Cato's Letters, a series of essays published in 18th- century England that presented a vision of society free from excessive government power. Those essays inspired the architects of the American Revolution. And the simple, timeless principles of that revolution —individual liberty, limited government, and free markets—turn out to be even more powerful in today's world of global markets and unprecedented access to information than Jefferson or Madison could have imagined. Social and economic freedom is not just the best policy for a free people; it is the indispensable framework for the future.

Notes to Chapters

Introduction Intelligence Agencies, Political and Bureaucratic Stakeholders, JIT, NADRA, NACTA, IB and the ISI

Chapter 1: Pakistan's Intelligence Agencies: Stakeholders, Crisis of Confidence and lack of Modern Intelligence Mechanism

1. The Intelligence War in Afghanistan, Musa Khan Jalalzai, Vij Publishing 2019

2. Ibid

3. Pakistan: Living with a Nuclear Monkey. Musa Khan Jalalzai, Vij Publishing 2018

4. Ibid

5. Florina Cristiana Matei and Carolyn Halladay-2019

6. Pakistan army brass meets amid political turmoil, 01 September, 2014, https://www.rediff.com/news/report/pakistan-army-brass-meets-amidpolitical-turmoil/20140901.htm

7. Musa Khan Jalalzai, Pakistan: Living with a Nuclear Monkey, Vij Books, Delhi, 2018, pp. 1, 2 and.

8. Dr. Julian Richards chapter. The Image of the Enemy: Intelligence Analysis of Adversaries Since 1945, Published 2015 by Georgetown University USA.

9 Ibid.

10. Daniel F. Runde and Richard Olson, "An Economic Crisis in Pakistan again: What is different this Time?" Centre for Strategic and International Studies, October 31, 2018, https://www.csis.org/analysis/economic-crisispakistan-again-whats-different-time.

11. Ibid.

12. Prem Mahadevan research paper, 2011

13. The crisis of Indian intelligence. Musa Khan Jalalzai, Daily Times, 08 September 2016

14. Ibid

15. Musa KhanJalalzai, 2018, op. cit., p. 5

16. Janani Krishnaswamy Thesis-2013

17. Imad Zafar, "The corrosive influence of Pakistan's 'deep state'", Asia Times, March 28, 2018, https://www.asiatimes.com/2018/03/opinion/redline-needs-redefined-power-corridors/.

18. Muhammad Taqi, 13 March 2019

19. Mapping Pakistan's internal dynamics Implications for State Stability and Regional Security. Mumtaz Ahmad, Dipankar Banerjee, Aryaman Bhatnagar, C. Christine Fair, Vanda Felbab-Brown, Husain Haqqani, Mahin Karim, Tariq A. Karim, Vivek Katju, C. Raja Mohan, Matthew J. Nelson, and Jayadeva Ranade, Te National Bureau of Asian Research, February 2016.

20. Military-Intelligence Militant Nexus in Pakistan: Fighting a War of Asymmetry against India Focus, Sanjeeb Kumar Mohanty and Jinendra Nath Mahanty. Journal of Defence Studies, Vol. 5 No. 4 October 2011

21. Ibid

22. Hassan Abbas, "Reform of Pakistan's Intelligence Services", Belfer Center for Science and International Affairs, March 15, 2008, https:// www. belfercenter.org/publication/reform-pakistans-intelligence-services.

23. A Pakistani Fifth Column? The Pakistani Inter-Service Intelligence Directorate's Sponsorship of Terrorism, Grant Holt David H. Gray, Global Security Studies, Winter 2011, Volume 2, Issue 1.

24. How much strong really is Pakistani ISI? Rajesh Bhushan, January 12, 2019

25. Pakistan's Secret Power: The Inter Services Intelligence. Dr Bidanda M Chengappa, South Asian Terrorism Portal, 2001.www.satp.org › idr › vol.15(1) › dr_bidanda_m_chengappa

26. Musa Khan Jalalzia, "Pakistan: Reorganization of Intelligence infrastructure", Daily Times, March 24, 2014, https://dailytimes.com.pk/105378/pakistan-reorganisation-of-intelligence infrastructure/.

27. Ibid

28. Musa Khan Jalalzai, "Pakistan: fixing the intelligence machine", Daily Times, April 14, 2014, https://dailytimes.com.pk/105114/pakistan-fixingthe-intelligence-machine/.

29. Musharraf-era spy bosses in hot seat: Taliban-Afghan-US negotiations are biggest challenge for Pakistan's new Interior Minister. Taha Siddiqui, 06 May 2019, Firstpost.

30. Musa Khan Jalalzia, "Pakistan: Reorganization of Intelligence infrastructure", op. cit.

31. B.Raman research paper No-287

32. Musa Khan Jalalzai, 2018, op. cit., pp. 172-173.

33. Inter Services Intelligence: Pakistan's Secret Power: The Inter Services Intelligence. Dr Bidanda M Chengappa, South Asia Terrorism Portal, 2001

34. Abbas Nasir, "Pakistan's Intelligence Agencies: The inside Story", Herald, September 14, 2017, https://herald.dawn.com/news/1153827.

35. Musa Khan Jalalzai, 2018, op. cit. p. 162.

36. Musa Khan Jalalzia, "Pakistan: Reorganization of Intelligence infrastructure", op. cit.

37. Pakistan's Intelligence Agencies: The inside Story. Abbas Nasir, Herald-Dawn 14 September, 2017

38. Ibid

39. Musa Khan Jalalzia, The Prospect of Nuclear Jihad in Pakistan, Algora Publishing, New York, 2015, p.184.

40. Inter Services Intelligence: Pakistan's Secret Power: The Inter Services Intelligence. Dr Bidanda M Chengappa, South Asia Terrorism Portal, 2001

41. Musa Khan Jalalzai, "Pakistan: Reorganization of Intelligence infrastructure", op. cit.

42. B.Raman research paper No-287

43. The ISI Role in Pakistan's Politics, Dr. Bidanda M. Chengappa, Senior Fellow, IDSA

44. Ibid

Chapter 2: Militarization of Intelligence, Dematerialization of Civilian Intelligence and a War of Strength between the Military and Cvilian Spy Agencies

1   Musa Khan Jalalzai, 2018, op. cit. p. 174.

2   F. M. Shakil, "The growing 'tug of war' between Pakistan's Spy Agencies", Asia Times, October 4, 2017, http://www.atimes.com/article/growing-tugwar-pakistans-spy-agencies/.

3   Abbas Nasir, "Pakistan's Intelligence Agencies: The Inside Story", op. cit.

4   Hassan Abbas, op. cit.

5   Musa Khan Jalalzai, 2018, op. cit. pp. 165-167.

6.   Dr Niaz Murtaza. Dawn. 22 October, 2019

7.   Joint Intelligence Directorate", National Counter Terrorism Authority NACTA Pakistan, Government of Pakistan, https://nacta.gov.pk/jointintelligence-directorate-jid/.

8.   Musa Khan, The Afghan Intel Crisis: Satellite State- War of Interests and the Blame Game, Algora Publishing, New York, 2017, p.133.

9.   New Delhi Times, 25 September 2017

10. On 22 July, 2018, Mr. Justice Shaukat Aziz Siddiqui levelled serious allegations against ISI that the agency's interference in judicial affairs badly affected independence of judiciary, Dawn newspaper, Pakistan.

11. Ibid

12. Supreme Judicial Council No. 347 of 2018. Inquiry against Mr. Justice Shaukat Aziz Siddiqui. LEAP-Pakistan in Case Reports, October 16, 2018

13. Ibid

14. Ibid

15. IHC judge sacked for accusing ISI of interference, Malik Asad, Dawn 12 October 2018

16. Ibid

17. Dr. Faqir Hussain, 30 April 2019, Pakistan Today

18. Global Village, 21 October, 2018

19. Musa Khan Jalalzai, 2018, op. cit., p. 133.

20. Ibid.

21. The Challenges of Civilian Control over Intelligence Agencies in Pakistan, Frederic Grare, 18 December 2015. Book Chapter: Bangladesh Institute of Law and International Affairs.

22. ISI cultivated Taliban to counter Indian action against Pakistan: Musharraf. Dawn.com February 13, 2015. The Guardian, February 13, 2015

23. Imad Zafar, "Dawn Leaks: A Tweet that Underscored the State within State", The Nation, May 1, 2017, https://nation.com.pk/01-May-2017/ dawn-leaks-a-tweet-that-underscored-the-state-within-a-state.

24. Why Pakistan supports terrorists Groups" Vanda Felbab-Brown, Brookings, January 5, 2018, https://www.brookings.edu/blog/order-fromchaos/2018/01/05/why-pakistan-supports-terrorist-groups-and-why-theus-finds-it-so-hard-to-induce-change/.

25. Issue Brief, N0-3, 2008, Dr. Suba Chandran is Deputy Director of the Institute of Peace and Conflict Studies (IPCS). The Centre for Land Warfare Studies (CLAWS), New Delhi

26. Civilian-military Relations during the Zardari Regime (2008-2012) in Pakistan, internal and external factors. A Dissertation Submitted to The School of Politics and International Relations Quiad-i- Azam University Islamabad In Partial Fulfillment of the Requirement for the Degree of Doctor of Philosophy Nasreen Akhtar, 2017

27. Musa Khan Jalalzai, 2018, op. cit., p. 4.

28. Civilian-military Relations during the Zardari Regime (2008-2012) in Pakistan, internal and external factors. A Dissertation Submitted to The School of Politics and International Relations Quiad-i- Azam University Islamabad In Partial Fulfillment of the Requirement for the Degree of Doctor of Philosophy Nasreen Akhtar, 2017

29. Causes of Military Intervention in Pakistan: A Revisionist Discourse Muhammad Hassan. http://pu.edu.pk/images/journal/studies/PDF-FILES/Article-3_V_12_No_2_Dec11.pdf

30. National Security Committee agrees to recalibrate foreign policy, initiate economic partnerships", February 28, 2019, Dawn, https://www.dawn. Com/news/1392089.

31. Musa Khan Jalalzai, 2018, op. cit., p. 4.

32. New Internationalist, 01 July 2007

33. Is the mullah-military nexus crumbling? Mubashir Zaidi, Dawn. 11 November, 2013

34. Pervez Hoodbhoy, "Mainstreaming Jihad: Why Now?", Dawn, December 16, 2017, https://www.dawn.com/news/1376805.

35. Reuters, 22 November 2008

36. Civilian-military Relations during the Zardari Regime (2008-2012) in Pakistan, internal and external factors. A Dissertation Submitted to The School of Politics and International Relations Quiad-i- Azam University Islamabad In Partial Fulfillment of the Requirement for the Degree of Doctor of Philosophy Nasreen Akhtar, 2017

37. The Armed Forces in the Muslim World, Italian Institute for International Political Studies.2014

38. Contemporary Pakistan: Political System, Military and Changing Scenario. Dr. Nitin Prasad. Vij Books India Pvt Ltd, 20 February, 2016

39. Dawn, Pakistan's Supreme Court in 2012 remarked that the entire state machinery.

40. Ibid

41. Samson Simon Sharaf, the Nation 03 August, 2012

42. ISI Wrongfully Accused of Killing Journalist? Washington's vengeful accusations lead us one step closer to war with Islamabad. John R. Schmidt, The National Interest, July 11, 2011.

43. Dhruva Jaishankar, Foreign Policy, 15 February 2019

44. ISI Wrongfully Accused of Killing Journalist? Washington's vengeful accusations lead us one step closer to war with Islamabad. John R. Schmidt, the National Interest, July 11, 2011.

45. Amir Hamza Marwan October 2015, PP-25

46. The CIA, the ISI and the Next Bin Laden. The man next in line to lead al-Qaeda has close ties to the ISI. Almost as close as the ties between the ISI and the CIA, John R. Schindler, May 12, 2011

Chapter 3: The Challenges of Civilian Control over Intelligence Agencies, Democratic Governments, Military Establishment and a War of Strength

1. Financial Times-12 January 2012

2. Musa Khan Jalalzai, 2015, op. cit., p. 111.

3. The intelligence and agencies of Pakistan (Part I), By Ali K Chishti, 11 February 2011

4. Musa Khan Jalalzai, 2015, op. cit., p. 111.

5. The Challenges of Civilian Control over Intelligence Agencies in Pakistan, Frederic Grare, 18 December 2015. Book Chapter: Bangladesh Institute of Law and International Affairs.

6. Pakistan's Supreme Court tells military and intelligence agencies to stay out of politics, Agence France-Presse, 07 Feb, 2019Agence France-Presse,07 February 2019

7. Ibid

8. Ibid

9. 26 January 2020, daily Dawn

10. Ibid

11. Ibid

12. Privacy International, July 2015

13. The Intelligence War in Afghanistan, Musa Khan Jalalzai, 2019, Vij Publishing India

14. Privacy International, July 2015

15. Economic Times, 25 July 2019

16. Dhruv C. Katoch, "Pakistan's Armed Forces: Impact on the Stability of the State", Journal of Defence Studies, Volume 5, Number 4, 2011, p. 72.

17. Pakistan's Inter-Services Intelligence Contributes to Regional Instability. Alexandra Gilliard December 18, 2018

18. Dawn newspaper, 06 October 2016,

19. Ibid

20. Ibid

21. Musa Khan Jalalzai, 2015, op. cit., p. 111.

22. Ibid.

23. Alok Bansal, "Radicalisation of Pakistani Armed Forces", CLAWS, June 28, 2011, https://www.claws.in/624/radicalisation-of-pakistani-armed-forcesalok-bansal.htm.

24. Yunis Khushi, "Pakistan's Internal and External Enemies", Annals of Social Sciences & Management studies, Volume 1, Issue 4, 2018, p. 1.

25. Ibid

26. The Intelligence War in Afghanistan, Musa Khan Jalalzai, 2019, Vij Publishing India

27. Ibid

28. Pakistan's Inter-Services Intelligence Contributes to Regional Instability. Alexandra Gilliard On December 18, 2018

29. The Intelligence War in Afghanistan, Musa Khan Jalalzai, 2019, Vij Publishing India

30. Ibid

31. Dawn, 29 September 2017

32. Ibid

33. Frontier Post, May 18, 1994

34. Dawn, 25 April, 1994

35. Azaz Syed, 28 September 2018

36. The Intelligence War in Afghanistan, Musa Khan Jalalzai, 2019, Vij Publishing India

37. Ibid

38. Ibid

39. Ibid

40. 26 September 2017, Dawn newspaper

41. Ibid

42. Economic Times, 26 September 2017

43. Ibid

44. Ibid

45. Ibid

46. Ibid

47. Dawn Newspaper, 26 September 2017

48. 30 September 2017, Abhinandan Mishra article

49. Sunday Guardian, 30 September 2017

50. Ibid

51. Cyril Almeida's principled patriotism - Times of India, 17 February 2017

52. On April 29, 2019, Major General Asif Ghafoor, the spokesman of Pakistan army's Inter-Services Public Relations (ISPR) department, expressed his institution's dissatisfaction over the government's probe into the leak that put military and the civilian government on a collision course. Daily Dawn.

53. General Ghafoor Twitter, Dawn, 29 April 2017

54. Scholar Frederic Grare Paper, 18 December 2015

55. The News International, November 27, 2013

56. Pakistan: Living with a Nuclear Monkey, Musa Khan Jalalzai, 2018, Vij Publishing, India

57. BBC, 02 June 2019

58. New book offers important insights on Pakistani military: The launch of acclaimed author Shuja Nawaz' latest work 'The Battle for Pakistan' was blocked by the authorities. Imad Zafar, Asia Times, 31 December 2019.

59. Ibid

60. Ibid

61. Pakistan: Living with a Nuclear Monkey, Musa Khan Jalalzai, 2018, Vij Publishing, India

62. Ibid

63. Mapping Pakistan's internal dynamics Implications for State Stability and Regional Security. Mumtaz Ahmad, Dipankar Banerjee, Aryaman Bhatnagar, C. Christine Fair, Vanda Felbab-Brown, Husain Haqqani, Mahin Karim, Tariq A. Karim, Vivek Katju, C. Raja Mohan, Matthew J. Nelson, and Jayadeva Ranade, Te National Bureau of Asian Research, February 2016.

64. Dawn Leaks: A tweet that shows a "State within a State". Who is at the helm of affairs in Pakistan? Every single sane person knows it. It is a fact that the civilian governments in Pakistan are always dependent on the defence establishment's mandate rather than depending on the mandate of the masses. Imad Zafar, May 1, 2017

65. Scholar Frederic Grare, 18 December 2015

Chapter 4: Military Courts, Fair Trials Violations, Confessions without Adequate Safeguards against Torture, Rough-Handling of Prisoners, and Denial of Public Hearing.

1. Twenty-points National Action Plan (NAP) approved by Parliament, The News International, 24 December 2014

2. A perspective on Military Courts. Mohsin Raza Malik. 22 January, 2019

3. Dr. Muhammad Zubair, 28 January 2019

4. Military Courts in Pakistan: Will they return? What are the implications? D. Suba Chandran, National Institute of Advanced Studies (NIAS) Strategic Forecast, 11, December 2017.

5. Watchdog: Pakistan's Military Courts 'Disaster' for Human Rights. Ayaz Gul. January 16, 2019

6. On 16 January 2019, International commission of jurists deeply criticised the illegal function of military courts in Pakistan.

7. On 12 January 2019, Dr. Mehdi Hasan, Chairperson of the Human Rights Commission of Pakistan (HRCP) expressed grave concern at the government's decision to table a bill in favour of extending the tenure of military courts, which were otherwise due to end their term, Press release of the Human Rights Commission of Pakistan (HRCP). 12 January 2019.

8. Dawn, 06 Mar, 2017

9. Amnesty international in its report, 27 March 2019

10. Pak Army's confession of enforced disappearances.19 May 2019, Rahim Baloch

11. General Ghafoor admitted in a Press conference on 29 April, 2019

12. Ibid

13. Imad Zafar. Asia Times, 17 September 2019

14. January 2018, Human Right Watch Report

Chapter 5: The Pakistani Godfather: The Inter Services Intelligence and the Afghan Taliban 1994-2010, Adrian Hanni and Lukas Hegi

1. Ahmed Rashid, Taliban: AfghanistansGotteskrieger und der Dschihad, Munich: Droemer, 2002, p. 56.

2. For a detailed portrayal of the ISI see Ishtiaq Ahmed, "The Pakistan Inter-Services Intelligence: A Profile", ISAS Insights, No. 35, 15.08.2008; Hein G. Kiessling, ISI und R&AW: Die GeheimdienstePakistans und Indiens: KonkurrierendeAtommächte, ihrePolitik und der InternationaleTerrorismus, Berlin: Koster, 2011.

3. Rashid, Taliban, p. 58.

4. Ibid. p. 62.

5. Ibid. p. 69.

6. Ibid, p. 71 and Anthony Davis, "How the Taliban became a Military Force", in: William Maley (ed.), Fundamentalism reborn? Afghanistan and the Taliban, London: NYU Press, 1998, pp. 43ff.

7. Davis, "How the Taliban became a Military Force", p. 46.

8. "Developments in Afghanistan", Memo to Ron McMullen, U.S. Department of State, 05.12.1994.Copies of all primary sources cited in this article may be requestedfrom the authors' private archive.

9. Rashid, Taliban, p. 73. All English translations by the authors

10. Memo to Ron McMullen.

11. Cf. Jason Burke, Al-Qaeda: The True Story of Radical Islam, London: I.B. Tauris, 2004, pp. 125f.

12. Human Rights Watch, Afghanistan: Crisis of Impunity, July 2001, p. 24.

13. Rashid, Taliban, p. 79.

14. Davis, "How the Taliban became a Military Force", pp. 52f.

15. Ibid. p. 54. Tanai had been a general in the Afghan army and Defence Minister during the Soviet occupation. In 1990 he organized a coup with the help of Hekmatyar but failed. Tanai then fled to Hekmatyar in Pakistan. Pakistan was allegedly also implicated in this coup. Benazir Bhutto, for instance, had called upon the country to assist Tanai.

16. Ibid. p. 61.

17. Rashid, Taliban, p. 79; cf. also "Letter of GOP PERMREP to SYG on Afghanistan", Cable from U.S. Mission USUN New York to RUEHC/ Secretary of State, 01.11.1995.

18. "Pakistan Afghan Policy: Anyone but Rabbani/Masood – Even the Taliban", Cable from U.S. Embassy Islamabad to Secretary of State, U.S. Department of State, October 1995, p. 2.

19. Rashid, Taliban, p. 91.On the role of Colonel Imam in the establishment of the Taliban see also Carlotta Gall, "Former Pakistani Officer Embodies a Policy Puzzle", New York Times, 03.03.2010.

20. Rashid, Taliban, p. 94.

21. Ibid. p. 96.

22. Ibid. p. 97.

23. Ibid. p. 108f.

24. Human Rights Watch, Afghanistan, p. 23.

25. Ibid.

26. Abdul Salam Zaif, My Life with the Taliban, New York: Columbia University Press, 2010.See alsoJonathan Steele, "Gesucht: Taliban für den Frieden", Le Monde Diplomatique [German edition], Nr. 9312, 08.10.2010, pp. 12f.

27. Ahmed Rashid, Descent into Chaos: The U.S. and the Disaster in Pakistan, Afghanistan, and Central Asia, New York: Penguin Books, 2008, p. 26; "Pakistan Involvement in Afghanistan", Information Report to DIA Washington, Defense Intelligence Agency, U.S. Department of Defense, November 1996 (re money); "Scenesetter for Your Visit to Islamabad: Afghan Angle", Cable from U.S. Embassy Islamabad to Secretary of State, U.S. Department of State, January 1997, p. 9 (re military advisors); "Afghanistan: X Describes Pakistan's Current Thinking, Cable from U.S. Embassy Islamabad to Secretary of State, U.S. Department of State, March 1998, pp. 2f,7 and 9 (re weapons).

28. Human Rights Watch, Afghanistan, p. 23; "Pakistan Interservice Intelligence", Information Report to DIA Washington, Defense Intelligence Agency, U.S. Department of Defense, 22.10.1996 (re ammunition, fuel); "Afghanistan: X Describes Pakistan's Current Thinking", pp. 2f,7 and 9 (re ammunition and fuel); "Afghanistan: Pakistanis to Regulate Wheat and Fuel Trade to Gain Leverage over Taliban", Cable from U.S. Embassy Islamabad to Secretary of State, U.S. Department of State, 13 August 1997, p. 7 (re fuel); "Afghanistan: Taliban seem to have less Funds and Supplies this Year, but the Problem does not appear to be that acute", Cable from U.S. Embassy Islamabad to Secretary of State, U.S. Department of State, February 1999 (re fuel); "Scenesetter for Your Visit to Islamabad", pp. 2 and 9 (re diplomatic support); "Official Informal – For SA Assistant Secretary Robin Raphel and SA/PAB", Cable from U.S. Embassy Islamabad to Secretary

of State, U.S. Department of State, March 1997, p. 4 (re diplomatic support).

29. See for example Rashid, Taliban, pp. 183-195 and Davis, "How the Taliban Became a Military Force", pp. 43ff.

30. Rashid, Descent into Chaos, pp. 29 and 52.

31 . Afghan-PAK Border Relations at Torkham Tense, Cable from U.S. Consulate Peshawar to Secretary of State, U.S. Department of State, 02.10.1996.

32. Afghanistan: X Briefs the Ambassador on his activities. Pleads for Greater Activism by U.N. , Cable from U.S. Embassy Islamabad to Secretary of State, U.S. Department of State, 27.08.1997. In 1996, 20 million Pakistani rupees were the equivalent of nearly half a million US dollars.

33. "Afghanistan: Taliban seem to have less Funds and Supplies this Year, but the Problem does not appear to be that acute", Cable from U.S. Embassy Islamabad to Secretary of State, U.S. Department of State, February 1999, p. 1.

34. Human Rights Watch, Afghanistan, p. 27.

35. Ibid. p. 28; based in part on an interview conducted in June 1999with MollinNayim, the Afghan intelligence chief during the Taliban regime.

36. "Pakistan Involvement in Afghanistan", Information Report to DIA Washington, Defense Intelligence Agency, U.S. Department of Defense, November 1996.

37. Ibid.

38. Human Rights Watch, Afghanistan, pp. 30f; Mohammed Yousaf and Mark Adkin, The Bear Trap: Afghanistan's Untold Story, London: L. Cooper, 1992, pp. 40-42.

39. Rashid, Descent into Chaos, p. 46. Apparently, the support of Pakistan for the Taliban had been declining since 1998, because the Pakistani government, buffeted by economic problems and economic sanctions that were imposed as a result of nuclear tests in 1998, had less money to allocate. See also "Afghanistan: Taliban Seem to Have Less Funds and Supplies This Year",p. 1.

40. Rashid, Descent into Chaos, p. 50.

41 . For more information on Ahmad, Aziz and Usmani see Rashid, Descent into Chaos, pp. 24 and 28f.

42. "Pakistan Support for Taliban", Cable from Secretary of State to U.S. Embassy Islamabad, U.S. Department of State, 26.09.2000, p. 1.

43. Ibid. p. 2.

44. Human Rights Watch, Afghanistan, p. 26; based on interviews with Taliban officials and diplomatic sources in Kabul and Islamabad. See also Rashid, Descent into Chaos, p. 60.

45. "The Situation in Afghanistan and Its implications for International Peace and Security", Report of the Secretary General A/55/633-S/2000/1106, U.N. Secretary General, United Nations, 20.11.2000.

46. Rashid, Descent into Chaos, p. 25.

47. Ibid. p. 60.

48. Human Rights Watch, Afghanistan, p. 23; based on interviews and e-mail communication with sources in Afghanistan and Pakistan. The number of 30 ISI trucks per day is also given by Rashid, Descent into Chaos, p. 60.

49. "Mahmud Plans 2nd Mission to Afghanistan", Cable form U.S. Embassy Islamabad to Secretary of State, U.S. Department of State, 24.09.2001; Saif, My Life with the Taliban,quoted in: Steele, "Gesucht", p. 13.

50. Ibid.; "Deputy Secretary Armitage – Mamoud Phone Call – September 18, 2001", Cable from Secretary of State to U.S. Embassy Islamabad, U.S. Department of State, 18.09.2001; Rashid, Descent into Chaos, p. 77.

51. "Deputy Secretary Armitage's Meeting with General Mahmud: Actions and Support Expected of Pakistan in Fight Against Terrorism", Cable from Secretary of State to U.S. Embassy Islamabad, U.S. Department of State, 14.09.2001; "Musharraf Accepts the Seven Points", Cable from U.S. Embassy Islamabad to Secretary of State, U.S. Department of State, 14 September 2001.

52. See for example Thomas Ruttig, the Other Side: Dimensions of the Afghan Insurgency: Causes, Actors and Approaches to Talks, Afghanistan Analysts Network, July 2009; Antonio Giustozzi (ed.), Decoding the New Taliban Insights from the Afghan Field, New York: Columbia University Press, 2009.

53. Rashid, Descent into Chaos, pp. 221, 223 and 244.

54. Matt Waldman, "The Sun in the Sky: The Relationship between Pakistan's ISI and Afghan insurgents", Crisis State Research Centre Discussion Papers, No. 18, June 2010, p. 17.

55. Rashid, Descent into Chaos, p. 242.

56. Ibid. pp. 221 and 241.

57. Ibid. p. 219.

58. Carlotta Gall, "Pakistani Military Still Cultivates Militant Groups, a Former Fighter Says", New York Times, 4 July 2011.

59. Sultan Amir Tarar, best known as Colonel Imam,wasalso Consul General in Herat andan officer in the Special Service Group (SSG) of the Pakistani Army. Hehad trained and mentoredthe Taliban as well as other militant groups. Abbasi had planned and executed attacks on positions of the Indian army as commander of the Pakistani army in Kashmir and been convicted of involvement in an attempted coup against the government of Benazir Bhutto in 1995.

60. Waldman, "The Sun in the Sky", p. 13.

61. For the following details on ISI support for the Taliban see Rashid, Descent into Chaos, pp. 222f. Rashid's analysis is based on confirmed U.S. and NATO intelligence reports, which are, amongst other sources, based on observations of American soldiers from bases along the eastern Afghan border, recordings by U.S. drones and SIGINT from the U.S. base at Bagram.

62. See also ibid. pp. 249f. The JUI is the largest Islamic party in the Pashtun areas of Pakistan.

63. Ibid. pp. 221f.

64. "Pakistan: Fixing Coalition Support Funding", Cable from U.S. Embassy Islamabad to RHMFISS/CDR USCENTCOM MACDILL, U.S. Department of State, 15 December 2007.

65. "Counterterrorism Activities (Neo-Taliban)", Issue Paper for Vice President of the United States (VPOTUS), U.S. Department of State, 9 December 2005, p. 1.

66. Rashid, Descent into Chaos, p. 360.

67. "Insurgency and Terrorism in Afghanistan: Who is Fighting and Why?" [June 2006], in: Special Security Initiative of the Policy Action Group, Papers Presented to President Karzai at the Meeting of the Policy Action Group, Kabul, 9 July 2006.

68. Rashid, Descent into Chaos, p. 364.

69. Mark Mazzetti, Jane Perlez, Eric Schmitt, and Andrew W. Lehren, "Pakistan Aids Insurgency in Afghanistan, Reports Assert", New York Times, 25 July 2010.

70. MTG, Field report from the Afghan War Diary, Regional Command East, Tracking Number 2007-045-142245-0241, 12 February 2007.

71. See for example Rashid, Descent into Chaos, p. 406; Mazzetti et al., "Pakistan Aids Insurgency".

72. "Scenesetter for PM Gilani's Visit to Washington", Cable from U.S. Embassy Islamabad to Secretary of State, U.S. Department of State, 25.07.2008.

73. Ibid.

74. "Terrorist Finance: Action Request for Senior Level Engagement on Terrorism Finance", Cable from Secretary of State to RUEHIL/U.S. Embassy Islamabad, U.S. Department of State, 30.12.2009.

75. "Special Advisor to SRAP with Saudi Intel: What To Do about the Taliban? ", Cable from U.S. Embassy Riyadh to RUEHC/Secretary of State, U.S. Department of State, 23.01.2010.

76. Waldman, "The Sun in the Sky".

78. Tobias Matern, "Pakistan erwartetGegenleistungfürFestnahme-hoher Taliban", Tages-Anzeiger, 22.03.2010.

79. Tobias Matern, "Pakistan entdeckt den neuenFeind", Tages-Anzeiger, 20.08.2010. Spanta's statement has of course to be taken with a grain of salt, since at least parts of the Afghan government consider Pakistan an enemy.

80. This conclusion is also reached by Seth Jones, In the Graveyard of Empires: America's War in Afghanistan, New York: W.W. Norton & Co., 2009, p. 266.

81. Waldman, "The Sun in the Sky", p. 12. These statements are of course to be interpreted with extreme care, because the interviewed Taliban commanders perhaps wanted to give the responsibility for particularly unscrupulous attacks, such as extremely unpopular attacks on Afghan civilians, to Pakistan as a foreign scapegoat.

82. Ibid. pp. 15f.

83. Ibid. p. 6 (interview conducted in March 2010).

84. Ibid. (interview conducted in May 2010).

85. Ibid. p. 10 (interview conducted in March 2010).

86. Tribal Analysis Center, the Quetta Shura: A Tribal Analysis, Williamsburg, 2009, p. 6.

87. Pakistanis at Kandahar Border Flag Meeting – The Quetta Shura Is a Fabrication, Cable from U.S. Embassy Kabul to RUEHC/Secretary of State, U.S. Department of State, 7.10.2009. The Pakistani delegation, led by Brigadier General Sejaad, also included three ISI officials.

88. Waldman, "The Sun in the Sky", pp. 16-20.

89. Ibid. pp. 5 and 8f.

90. Jones, Graveyard of Empires, who could, however, not yet base his study on the comprehensive source material analysed in this article.

91. Christine Fair, "The Time for Sober Realism: Renegotiating US Relations with Pakistan", the Washington Quarterly 32/2 (2009), pp. 161-163. Furthermore, the American analysts Thomas Johnson and M. Chris Mason recognize the involvement of Pakistan's civilian government in supporting the Afghan resistance. See Thomas H. Johnson and M. Chris Mason, "No Sign until the Burst of Fire: Understanding the Pakistan-Afghanistan Frontier", International Security 32/4 (2008), pp. 41-77.

92. For example Prime Minister Gilani during a visit to Washington in the summer of 2008. See "Scenesetter for PM Gilani's Visit to Washington".

93. "Scenesetter for General Kayani's Visit to Washington", Cable from U.S. Embassy Islamabad to RUEHC/Secretary of State, U.S. Department of State, 19.02.2009.

94. "Security Environment Profile Questionnaire (SEPQ) – Peshawar", Cable from U.S. Consul Peshawar to Secretary of State, U.S. Department of State, 28.02.2009.

95. "Reviewing Our Afghanistan – Pakistan Strategy", Cable from U.S. Embassy Islamabad to Secretary of State, U.S. Department of State, 23.09.2009.

96. See for example "Datenleck: Obama spieltBedeutung der Afghanistan-Dokumenteherunter", Spiegel Online, 27.07.2010. On the ISI's relationship with the Taliban see in particular Mazzetti et al., "Pakistan Aids Insurgency"; Matthias Gebauer et al., "EnthüllungbrisanterKriegsdokumente: Die Afghanistan-Protokolle" Spiegel Online, 25.07.2010; Nick Davies and David Leigh, "Afghanistan war

logs", The Guardian, 25.07.2010.The 76'911 documents could not be systematically evaluatedwithin the scope of this study. The authors had to limit themselves to selective reading.

97. Mazzetti et al., "Pakistan Aids Insurgency".

98. Onthe role of Gul in the Afghan resistance against the Karzai government see ibid.

99. Ibid.

100. Waldman, "The Sun in the Sky", pp. 10ff.

101. Mark Mazzetti and Dexter Filkins, "Secret Joint Raid Captures Taliban's Top Commander", New York Times, 15.02.2010.

102. "Profile: Mullah Abdul GahniBaradar", BBC News, 17.02.2010.

103. Ron Moreau, "America's New Nightmare", Newsweek, 24.07.2009.

104. Mazzetti and Filkins, "Secret Joint Raid".

105. Moreau, "America's New Nightmare".

106. Bette Dam, "Mullah Baradar: friend or foe? ", Radio Netherlands Worldwide, 16.02.2010.

107. Moreau, "America's New Nightmare".

108. "Taliban Commander Mullah Baradar 'seized in Pakistan'", BBC News, 16.02.2010.

109. Martin Killian, "Pakistan verhaftete Taliban-Chef, um Krieg in Afghanistan zuverlängern", Tages-Anzeiger, 24.08.2010, p. 9; Dexter Filkins, "Pakistanis Tell of Motive in Taliban Leader's Arrest", New York Times, 22.08.2010.

110. Filkins, "Pakistanis Tell of Motive".

111. Mazzetti and Filkins, "Secret Joint Raid".

112. Pir Zubair Shah and Dexter Filkins, "Pakistani Reports Capture of a Taliban Leader", New York Times, 22.02.2010.

113. David Ignatius, "To Pakistan, almost with love", Washington Post, 04.03.2010.

114. Ashley J. Tellis, "Beradar, Pakistan, and the Afghan Taliban: What Gives?", Carnegie Endowment for International Peace, Policy Outlook, 24.03.2010. Tellis lists no fewer than 17 names.

115. Waldman, "The Sun in the Sky", p. 7; Dean Nelson and Ben Farmer, "Hamid Karzai Held Secret Talks with Mulla Beradar in Afghanistan", Telegraph, 16.03.2010.

116. Tellis, "Beradar, Pakistan, and the Afghan Taliban", p. 5.

117. Thomas H. Johnson and M. Chris Mason, "Down the AfPak Rabbit Hole", Foreign Policy, 01.03.2010.

118. Matt Waldman, Dangerous Liaisons with the Afghan Taliban, United States Institute of Peace, Special Report No. 256, 18.10.2010.

119. Filkins, "Pakistanis Tell of Motive".

120. Ibid.

121. John Rollins, Osama bin Laden's Death: Implications and Considerations, Report for Congress, Congressional Research Service, 05.05.2011.

122. "Remarks by the President in Address to the Nation on the Way Forward in Afghanistan and Pakistan", Barack Obama, the White House, 01.12.2009.

123. "Report on Progress toward Security and Stability in Afghanistan and United States Plan for Sustaining the Afghanistan National Security Forces", Report to U.S. Congress, U.S. Department of Defense, April 2010, p. 5.

124. Alan K. Kronstadt, Direct Overt U.S. Aid and Military Reimbursements to Pakistan, FY2002-FY2014, U.S. Congressional Research Service Report, 11.04.2013; Alan K. Kronstadt, Major U.S. Arms Sales and Grants to Pakistan since 2001, U.S. Congressional Research Service Report, 07.03.2013.

125. "Pakistan: Fixing Coalition Support Funding", Cable from U.S. Embassy Islamabad to RHMFISS/CDR USCENTCOM MACDILL, U.S. Department of State, 15 December 2007.

126. Report on Progress toward Security and Stability in Afghanistan, pp. 7 and 32.

127. Rashid, Descent into Chaos, p. 25.

128. Tellis, "Beradar, Pakistan, and the Afghan Taliban", p. 8.

129. Rashid, Descent into Chaos, p. 248; Waldman, "The Sun in the Sky", p. 5.

130. Ibid

131. "Reviewing Our Afghanistan – Pakistan Strategy", Cable from U.S. Embassy Islamabad to Secretary of State, U.S. Department of State, 23.09.2009.

132. Rashid, Descent into Chaos, pp. 248f and 417; Waldman, "The Sun in the Sky", p. 5.

133. "Indian Views on Afghanistan: Eager for Increased USG Coordination, Wary of Pakistani Scheming, Skeptical on R/R", Cable from U.S. Embassy New Delhi to Secretary of State, U.S. Department of State, 23.02.2010.

134. Rashid, Descent into Chaos, pp. 267f. For the Durand Line and its historical impact on Pakistan and Afghanistan, see also Georges Lefeuvre, "AfghanischePatrioten: Die Paschtunen, die Nation und die Taliban", Le Monde Diplomatique [German edition], Nr. 9312, 08.10.2010, pp. 14f.

135. Rashid, Descent into Chaos, p. 8; Steele, "Gesucht", p. 13; Waldman, "The Sun in the Sky", p. 5. About 25 million Pashtuns live in Pakistan, approximately twice as many as in Afghanistan.

136. Waldman, "The Sun in the Sky", pp. 5-7 and 9; Tellis, "Beradar, Pakistan, and the Afghan Taliban", p. 5.Hamid Karzai, for example, is a Durrani Pashtun; Mullah Omar was aGhilzai-Pashtun. Most of the Taliban fighters mobilized originally by the ISI were from the Ghilzai tribes. See Ashley J.Tellis, Pakistan and the War on Terror: Conflicted Goals Compromised Performance, Carnegie Endowment for International Peace, 2008, 6.

Bibliography Chapter 5

Ahmed, Ishtiaq, the Pakistan Inter-Services Intelligence: A Profile, ISAS Insights, No. 35, 15. August 2008.

Burke, Jason, Al-Qaeda: The True Story of Radical Islam, London, 2004.

Davis, Anthony, How the Taliban Became a Military Force, in: Maley, William (Ed.), Fundamentalism Reborn? Afghanistan and the Taliban, London, 1998, 43-71.

Fair, Christine, the Time for Sober Realism: Renegotiating US Relations with Pakistan, the Washington Quarterly 32, 2 (2009), 149-172.

Filkins, Dexter, Pakistanis Tell of Motive in Taliban Leader's Arrest, New York Times, 23 August 2010, 1.

Gall, Carlotta, Pakistani Military Still Cultivates Militant Groups, a Former Fighter Says, New York Times, 4 July 2011, www.nytimes.

com/2011/07/04/world/asia/04pakistan.html?_r=1&ref=asia   (7 August 2011).

Gebauer, Matthias; Goetz, John; Hoyng, Hans; Koelbl, Susanne; Rosenbach, Marcel; Schmitz, Gregor Peter, Die Afghanistan-Protokolle: EnthüllungbrisanterKriegsdokumente, Spiegel Online, 25. July 2010, www.spiegel.de/politik/ausland/0,1518,708311,00.html (31 December 2010).

Giustozzi, Antonio (Ed.), Decoding the New Taliban Insights from the Afghan Field, London, 2009.

Human Rights Watch, Afghanistan: Crisis of Impunity: The Role of Pakistan, Russia, and Iran in Fueling the Civil War, Washington D.C. et al., July 2001.

Johnson, Thomas H.; Mason, M. Chris, No Sign until the Burst of Fire: Understanding the Pakistan-Afghanistan Frontier, International Security 32, 4 (2008), 41-77. Down the AfPak Rabbit Hole, Foreign Policy, 1. March 2010, www.foreignpolicy.com/articles/2010/03/01/down_the_afpak_rabbit_hole (31 December 2010).

Jones, Seth, In the Graveyard of Empires: America's War in Afghanistan, New York, 2009.

Khalilzad, Zalmay, The Great Pakistan Rethink, The National Interest, 5 May 2011, http://nationalinterest.org/commentary/great-pakistan-rethink-node-5263Document1 (12 May 2011).

Lefeuvre, Georges, and AfghanischePatrioten: Die Paschtunen, die Nation und die Taliban, Le Monde Diplomatique [German edition], and Nr. 9312, 8 October 2010, 14-15.

Mazzetti, Mark; Perlez, Jane; Schmitt, Eric; Lehren, Andrew W., Pakistan Aids Insurgency in Afghanistan, Reports Assert, New York Times, 25 July 2010.

Rashid, Ahmed, Taliban: AfghanistansGotteskrieger und der Dschihad, München, 2002. Descent into Chaos: The U.S. and the Disaster in Pakistan, Afghanistan, and Central Asia, New York, 2008.

Rollins, John, Osama bin Laden's Death: Implications and Considerations, Report for Congress, Congressional Research Service, 05 May 2011.

Ruttig, Thomas, The Other Side: Dimensions of the Afghan Insurgency: Causes, Actors and Approaches to Talks, Afghanistan Analysts Network, July 2009.

Saif, Abdul Salam, My Life with the Taliban, London, 2010.

Steele, Jonathan, Gesucht: Taliban für den Frieden, Le Monde Diplomatique [German edition], Nr. 9312, 8 October 2010, 12-13.

Tellis, Ashley J., Pakistan and the War on Terror: Conflicted Goals Compromised Performance, Carnegie Endowment for International Peace, Washington D.C. et al., 2008. Beradar, Pakistan, and the Afghan Taliban: What Gives? Carnegie Endowment for International Peace, Policy Outlook, Washington D.C., March 2010.

Tribal Analysis Center, the Quetta Shura: A Tribal Analysis, Williamsburg, 2009.

Waldman, Matt, The Sun in the Sky: The Relationship Between Pakistan's ISI and Afghan Insurgents, Crisis State Research Centre Discussion Papers, No. 18, June 2010. Dangerous Liaisons with the Taliban: The Feasibility and Risks of Negotiations, United States Institute of Peace, Special Report, No. 256, Washington D.C., October 2010.

Yousaf, Mohammed; Adkin, Mark, The Bear Trap: Afghanistan's Untold Story, London, 1992.

Chapter 6: Directorate S: The C.I.A. and America's Secret Wars in Afghanistan and Pakistan. Barbara Elias

Chapter 7: Directorate S: The C.I.A. and America's Secret Wars in Afghanistan and Pakistan. Barbara Elias

Chapter 8: The Political and Military Involvement of Inter Services Intelligence in Afghanistan

1. Bin Ladin, Palestine and al-Qa'ida's Operational Strategy. Asaf Maliach. Middle Eastern Studies, Vol. 44, No. 3 (May, 2008), pp. 353-375

2. Intelligence war in Afghanistan, Musa Khan Jalalzai, 2018, Vij Books India

3. Ibid

4. Disrupting the ISI-Taliban relationship: A Principal-Agent Approach. Hollingsworth, Christopher L. and Sider, Joshua, 2018-Monterey, CA; Naval Postgraduate School. http://hdl.handle.net/10945/61387

5. Ibid

6. The Afghan Intel Crisis, Musa Khan Jalalzai, 2017, New York USA

7. Ibid

8.   The National Interest, 07 May 2018; Javid Ahmad's article

9.   The Afghan Intel Crisis, Musa Khan Jalalzai, 2017, New York USA

10. Pakistan: Living with a Nuclear Monkey, Musa Khan Jalalzai, Vij Publishing, India, 2018

11. Dr. Bidanda M. Chengappa Research paper, The ISI Role in Pakistan's Politics-2001. Military governments, the ISI and political hybridity in contemporary Pakistan: from independence to Musharraf, Kunal Mukherjee, 07 Apr 2017.

12. 19 September 2019, Afghan human rights activist Bilal Sarwary accused Inter-Services Intelligence (ISI) of providing institutional support to terrorist groups operating in Afghanistan.

13. -Pakistan's Secret War Machine: Pakistani intelligence has mainstreamed terrorism and political violence in the region. Javid Ahmad, May 07, 2018

14. Ayaz Amir (daily Dawn. 22 September 2006

15. My Life with the Taliban, Mullah Abdul Salam Zaeef, and Alex Strick Van Linschoten (Editor), 01 Jul 2011, C Hurst & Co Publishers Ltd.

16. The ordeal of Mullah Zaeef, Ayaz Amir, Dawn, September 22, 2006

17. 26 September 2016, Tolonews reported Deputy Chief of Afghanistan's Strategic and Scientific Research Center, AimalLiyan, allegations against ISI.

18. Daily Khabrain, Pakistan's Urdu newspaper (29th December, 2015)

19. Dr. Yunis Khushi. ISIS in Pakistan: A Critical Analysis of Factors and Implications of ISIS Recruitments and Concept of Jihad-Bil-Nikah-26 June 2017

20. Ibid

21. 19 June 2019, ToloNews

22. February 2018, Voice of America

23. 18 September 2019, Samaa News, Roohan Ahmad

24. Kunwar Khuldune Shahid, Asia Times, 27 November 2019

25. 17 May 2019, the Nation

26. 23 December 2017, a Pakistani political figure said that the US government was equipping Daesh militants in border areas of Pakistan with weapons. Tasnim News Agency

27. 01 January 2020, Tribal News Network

Chapter 9: Pakistan Army and the Pashtun Tahafooz Movement

1. Rights Movement in Pakistan Vows to Continue Its Protests, VOA News, May 13, 2018

2. Naqeebullah was killed in 'fake encounter', had no militant tendencies: police inquiry finds, Imtiaz Ali, Dawn newspaper, January 20, 2018

3. Impact of the Pashtun Tahafuz Movement on Pakistan's. takshashila. org. S Ramachandran, 2018

4. Madiha Afzal (07 February 2020) interviewed leaders of PTM for her book in Lahore.

5. On 11 February 2019, in his New York Times article, PTM leader Manzoor Pashteen gave an account of his struggle for the recovery of kidnapped Pashtun activists by Pakistan's military establishment. The Military Says Pashtuns Are Traitors. We Just Want Our Rights: Pakistan's powerful military is trying to crush a nonviolent movement for civil rights. Manzoor Ahmad Pashteen. 11 February 2019.

6. Ibid

7. The Print, 17 February 2020, the Print published yell of Gul Bukhari, a Pakistani human rights activist. Gul Bukhari complained that the ISI wing of Pakistan embassy in UK was sniffing for her home address in London.

8. Ibid

9. On 17-02-2020, prominent journalist Aurang Zeb Khan Zalmay in his facebook comment criticised Pakistani agencies for their campaign against Pakistani human rights activists in Britain and Europe.

10. In his New York Times article, Jeffrey Gettleman reported that Gulalai Ismail had been advocating the rights of raped women, kidnapped and tortured Pashtuns, Punjabis and Balochs since years. New York Times, 19 September, 2019.

11. On 12 October 2018, Gulalai was arrested at Islamabad Airport by the Federal Investigation Agency (FIA) on her arrival from London and her name was put on the Exit Control List (ECL), which bans her from travelling outside the country. In February 2019, Gulalai was picked by security agencies at the Islamabad Press Club while she was attending a protest for the release of PTM activists, but her

name was not on the list of people arrested and she went missing for 36 hours.

12. The CIVICUS analysis of her struggle to save lives of innocent women and children noted her pain and industrious struggle. Some newspapers also published stories about her zeal and plcukiness.

13. Journalist DaudKhattak, Foreign Policy, 30 April 2019

14. Ibid

15. Pakistan: Human rights ignored in the "war on terror". Pakistan Human rights ignored in the "war on terror", Refworld. www.refworld. org . Journalist, M. Ilyas Khan (Uncovering Pakistan's secret human rights abuses, M Ilyas Khan, BBC News, Dera Ismail Khan, 02 June 2019.

17. Human Rights Commission of Pakistan report: "State of Human Rights"2018

18. Al Jazeera, April 2019

19. Dawn. 01 May 2019, Zahid Hussain article

20. Pakistan: Investigate North Waziristan Deaths: Uphold Rights of Region's Pashtun Population. Human Rights Watch, 30 May 2019.

21. Charles Pierson in his Wall Street Journal, Pakistani Army. 31, 2014

22. Pakistan Declares War on Pashtun Nationalism: The Pakistani military is trying to sound the death knell of the Pashtun Tahaffuz Movement. By Kunwar Khuldune Shahid, the Diplomat--May 02, 2019

23. Pashtun Tahafuz Movement: The game changer for Pakistani politics, Jaibans Singh, June 2019

24. 14 January 2020, the News International

25. Ibid

26. Ibid

27. PTM is on a peaceful quest to free all Pakistanis from oppression: The Pakistani state's repeated attacks on us only strengthen our resolve. Mohsin Dawar. Al Jazeera, 6 Dec 2019.

28. PTM will continue pressurizing government for Pakhtuns' rights: Dawar, Syhoon New, 16 February, 2010

29. Friday Times, 22 February 2019, Senator Farhatullah Babar

30. 15 January 2020, General Ghafoor shamelessly humiliated Pashtun nation that Pakistan army will butcher their children again.

Chapter 10: Double Game: Why Pakistan Supports Militants and Resists U.S. Pressure to Stop. Sahar Khan

1.   Donald Trump, Twitter post, January 1, 2018, 4:12 a.m., https://twitter.com/realDonaldTrump/status/947802588174577664.

2.   Saeed Shah, "Pakistan Foreign Minister Says U.S. Has Undermined Countries' Ties," WALL STREET JOURNAL, January 5, 2018, https://www.wsj.com/articles/pakistan-says-alliance-with-u-s-is-over-1515155860.

3.   Minister of Defense, Pakistan, Twitter post, January 1, 2018, 6:53 a.m., https://twitter.com/PakMnstrDefence/status/947843255286353921.

4.   DAWN, "Pakistan Has Given Us Nothing but Lies and Deceit: US President Donald Trump," January 2, 2018, https://www.dawn.com/news/1380148/pakistan-has-given-us-nothing-but-lies-and-deceit-us-president-donald-trump; and Scott Neuman, "Pakistani Leaders Fire Back at Trump Tweet Accusing Them of 'Lies & Deceit,'" National Public Radio, January 2, 2018, https://www.npr.org/sections/thetwo-way/2018/01/02/575025799/pakistani-leaders-fire-back-at-trump-tweet-accusing-them-of-lies-deceit.

5.   "NSC Decides Not to Take Measures in Haste Post Trump Statement," Geo News, January 2, 2018, https://www.geo.tv/latest/174935-pm-to-chair-nsc-meeting-following-trump-tweet.

6.   KrishnadevCalamur, "Pakistan's Week Keeps Getting Worse," THE ATLANTIC, January 4, 2018, https://www.theatlantic.com/international/archive/2018/01/us-suspends-security-aid-pakistan/549731/; Arhsad Mohammed and Jonathan Landay, "U.S. Suspends At Least $900 Million in Security Aid to Pakistan," Reuters, January 4, 2018, https://www.reuters.com/article/us-usa-pakistan-aid/u-s-suspends-at-least-900-million-in-security-aid-to-pakistan-idUSKBN1ET2DX; and Missy Ryan, Annie Gowen, and Carol Morello, "Piling on Pressure over Safe Havens, U.S. Suspends Military Aid to Pakistan," WASHINGTON POST, January 4, 2018, https://www.washingtonpost.com/world/national-security/feud-between-us-and-pakistan-flares-up-after-trumps-lies-and-deceit-tweet/2018/01/04/7cb457b8-f08a-11e7-97bf-bba379b809ab_story.html?utm_term=.5f05d8671fb2.

7.   Farhan Bokhari, Katrina Manson, and Kiran Stacey, "Pakistan Halts Intelligence-Sharing with US after Aid Suspension," FINANCIAL TIMES, January 11, 2018, https://www.ft.com/content/59969778-f6b1-11e7-88f7-5465a6ce1a00.

8. Remarks by President Trump on the Strategy in Afghanistan and South Asia, Fort Myer, Arlington, Virginia, August 21, 2017, https://www.whitehouse.gov/briefings-statements/remarks-president-trump-strategy-afghanistan-south-asia/.

9. President Trump's statement is incorrect. From the list of Foreign Terrorist Organizations, the following 10 are either headquartered in Pakistan or operate from both Pakistan and Afghanistan: Harakat ul-Mujahidin (HUM), al Qaeda, Jaish-e-Mohammad (JeM), Lashkar-e-Taiba (LeT), Islamic Jihad Union (IJU), Harakat ul-Jihad-i-Islami (HUJI), Tehrik-e-Taliban Pakistan (TTP), Islamic State-Khorasan (ISIL–K), al Qaeda in the Indian Subcontinent, and Hizbul Mujahideen (HM). See U.S. Department of State, "Foreign Terrorist Organizations," https://www.state.gov/j/ct/rls/other/des/123085.htm.

10. National Security Strategy of the United States, December 2017, p. 50, https://www.whitehouse.gov/wp-content/uploads/2017/12/NSS-Final-12-18-2....

11. President Barack Obama, Remarks on a New Strategy for Afghanistan and Pakistan, March 27, 2009, https://obamawhitehouse.archives.gov/the-press-office/remarks-president-a-new-strategy-afghanistan-and-pakistan.

12. George W. Bush, Decision Points (New York: Broadway Books, 2010), pp. 214–20.

13. Karen DeYoung, "U.S. Withholding Military Aid to Pakistan," WASHINGTON POST, July 10, 2011, https://www.washingtonpost.com/world/asia-pacific/us-withholding-military-aid-to-pakistan/2011/07/10/gIQAZdJH7H_story.html?utm_term=.83ec91550339.

14. See Husain Haqqani and Lisa Curtis, "A New Approach to Pakistan: Enforcing Aid Conditions without Cutting Ties," Hudson Institute, February 6, 2017, https://www.hudson.org/research/13305-a-new-u-s-approach-to-pakistan-enforcing-aid-conditions-without-cutting-ties; and Bruce Riedel, "Trump Is Right: Pakistan Is a Terrorist Haven. But What Will He Do about It?" ORDER FROM CHAOS, Brookings Institution, January 4, 2018, https://www.brookings.edu/blog/order-from-chaos/2018/01/04/trump-is-right-pakistan-is-a-terrorist-haven-but-what-will-he-do-about-it/.

15. Kay Johnson and DrazenJorgic, "Global Watchdog to Put Pakistan Back on Terrorist Financing Watchlist: Source," Reuters, February 23, 2018, https://www.reuters.com/article/us-pakistan-militants-

financing/global-watchdog-to-put-pakistan-back-on-terrorist-financing-watchlist-sources-idUSKCN1G70X7.

16. DrazenJorgic, "U.S. Sanctions Pakistani Companies over Nuclear Trade," Reuters, March 26, 2018, https://www.reuters.com/article/us-pakistan-usa-sanctions/u-s-sanctions-pakistani-companies-over-nuclear-trade-idUSKBN1H20IO.

17. This paper stems from my dissertation, for which I conducted field-work in Karachi, Lahore, Islamabad, and Rawalpindi throughout 2015. The primary data consist of in-person interviews, parliamentary debates on anti-terrorism legislation, terrorism-related case law, local think tank reports, unclassified statistical information and presentations, and local language newspaper articles. I conducted 92 interviews, 60 percent of which were anonymous, while the rest were on the record.

18. See Ayesha Siddiqa, Military Inc.: Inside Pakistan's Military Economy (London: Pluto Books, 2007); Aqil Shah, The Army And Democracy: Military Politics In Pakistan (Cambridge, MA: Harvard University Press, 2014); and C. Christine Fair, Fighting To The End: The Pakistan Army's Way Of War (New York: Oxford University Press, 2014).

19. Mujahideen is the plural of mujahid, a person who is conducting jihad, which is loosely defined as struggle in the name of Islam.

20. Steve Coll, Ghost Wars: The Secret History Of The Cia, Afghanistan, And Bin Laden: From The Soviet Invasion To September 10, 2001 (New York: Penguin, 2004); and Shuja Nawaz, Crossed Swords: Pakistan, Its Army, And The Wars Within (Oxford: Oxford University Press, 2008).

21. Robert G. Wirising, India, Pakistan, And The Kashmir Dispute (New York: St. Martin's Press, 1998); International Crisis Group, "Kashmir: The View from Islamabad," Report no. 68, December 4, 2003, https://www.crisisgroup.org/asia/south-asia/kashmir/kashmir-view-islamabad; and Stephen P. Cohen, Idea of Pakistan (Washington: Brookings Institution, 2004).

22. Ahmed Rashid, Taliban: Militant Islam, Oil And Fundamentalism In Central Asia (New Haven: Yale University Press, 2000), p. 187.

23. Jacob N. Shapiro and C. Christine Fair, "Understanding Support for Islamist Militancy in Pakistan," International Security 34, no. 3 (Winter 2010): 79–118; Fair, Fighting To The End; Stephen Tankel, "Beyond the Double Game: Lessons from Pakistan's Approach to

Islamist Militancy," Journal Of Strategic Studies (June 2016): 1–31; and S. Paul Kapur and SumitGanguly, "The Jihad Paradox: Pakistan and Islamist Militancy in South Asia," INTERNATIONAL SECURITY 37, no. 1 (Summer 2012): 111–41.

24. Before 9/11, the only other large-scale attack on U.S. soil was Pearl Harbor in 1941, which killed more than 2000 Americans and resulted in the United States' involvement in World War II.

25. Pervez Musharraf, In The Line Of Fire: A Memoir (London: Free Press, 2006), p. 201. Various high-level U.S. officials were involved in convincing Pakistan to participate in OEF. Deputy Secretary of State Richard Armitage met with Pakistan's ambassador to the U.S. Maleeha Lodhi and the director general of the ISI Lt. Gen. Mahmood Ahmed in Washington, while U.S. Ambassador to Pakistan Wendy Chamberlain met with Musharraf in Islamabad. See Ahmed Rashid, Descent Into Chaos: The U.S. And The Disaster In Pakistan, Afghanistan, And Central Asia (New York: Penguin, 2008), p. 27; Musharraf, IN THE LINE OF FIRE, pp. 204–7.; and CNN, "Bush Administration Puts Pressure on Pakistan," September 13, 2001, http://www.cnn.com/2001/WORLD/asiapcf/central/09/13/pakistan.us.bush/.

26. Seymour M. Hersh, "The Getaway: Questions Surround a Secret Pakistani Airlift," NEW YORKER, January 28, 2002, https://www.newyorker.com/magazine/2002/01/28/the-getaway-2; Ayesha Jalal, The Struggle For Pakistan: A Muslim Homeland And Global Politics (Cambridge, MA: Harvard University Press, 2014), p. 327.

27. The first time was in 2008, while the second time Pakistan was on the list from 2012 to 2015. See Usman Hayat and Shahid Karim, "Pakistan on FATF's Grey List: What, Why, and Why Now?" DAWN, July 6, 2018, https://www.dawn.com/news/1418143.

28. Abbas Nasir, "The Good and Bad Taliban," AL JAZEERA, July 30, 2015, https://www.aljazeera.com/indepth/opinion/2015/07/good-bad-taliban-mullah-omar-malik-ishaq-150730070225207.html; and Thomas E. Ricks, "The Long-Term Dangers for Pakistan of Believing in 'Good' and 'Bad' Taliban," Foreign Policy, September 29, 2015, http://foreignpolicy.com/2015/09/29/the-long-term-dangers-for-pakistan-of-believing-in-good-and-bad-taliban/.

29. Abubakar Siddique, "New Nationalist Movement Emerges from Pakistan's Pashtun Protests," Gandhara, April 11, 2018, https://gandhara.rferl.org/a/new-nationalist-movement-emerges-from-Paki-

stan--pashtun-protests/29159389.html; and Sahar Khan, "Pashtun Protests Reflect Pakistan's Tensions with U.S., Afghanistan," AXIOS, April 16, 2018, https://www.axios.com/pashtun-protests-reflect-pakistans-tensions-with-us-afghanistan-59a00747-5833-4bb9-a15a-5117697be90d.html.

30. Ryan Teague Beckwith, "Read Donald Trump's 'America First' Foreign Policy Speech," TIME, April 27, 2016, http://time.com/4309786/read-donald-trumps-america-first-foreign-policy-speech/.

31. Alex Ward, "Trump Is Sending More Than 3,000 Troops to Afghanistan," VOX, September 17, 2017, https://www.vox.com/world/2017/9/19/16227730/trump-afghanistan-3000-troops-mattis; and David Welna, "Defense Secretary Mattis Sends More Troops to Afghanistan with Hopes to End War," All Things Considered, National Public Radio, March 14, 2018, https://www.npr.org/2018/03/14/593609862/defense-secretary-mattis-sends-more-troops-to-afghanistan-with-hopes-to-end-war.

32. Robin Emmott, "NATO to Send More Troops to Afghanistan after U.S. Shift," Reuters, November 7, 2017, https://www.reuters.com/article/us-nato-afghanistan/nato-to-send-more-troops-to-afghanistan-after-u-s-shift-idUSKBN1D71E0.

33. Council on Foreign Relations, "War in Afghanistan," Global Conflict Tracker, June 11, 2018, https://www.cfr.org/interactives/global-conflict-tracker#!/conflict/war-in-afghanistan.

34. Congress created the Special Investigator General for Afghanistan Reconstruction (SIGAR) in 2008 and tasked the office with conducting independent and objective oversight of U.S. reconstruction efforts in Afghanistan. SIGAR submits a quarterly report to Congress, as mandated by law, which summarizes U.S. reconstruction efforts, including U.S. commitments, expenditures, and revenues. The second quarterly report of 2018 was released on April 30 and summarizes Afghanistan's reconstruction effort from January 1 to March 31, 2018. See Sigar, Quarterly Report To The United States Congress, April 30, 2018, https://www.sigar.mil/pdf/quarterlyreports/2018-04-30qr.pdf. Also see James Clark, "The War in Afghanistan Is (Still) going terribly," TASK AND PURPOSE, May 1, 2018, https://taskandpurpose.com/war-afghanistan-continues-go-terribly/.

35. Coll, GHOST WARS, pp. 169–79.

36. Rashid, Descent Into Chaos, pp. 11–13.

37. Coll, GHOST WARS, p. 305, and Rashid, TALIBAN, p. 45. Also see "Statement by Robin Raphel, Assistant Secretary of State for South Asian Affairs before the Senate Foreign Relations Committee on Near Eastern and South Asian Affairs,"March 7, 1995, https://www.mtholyoke.edu/acad/intrel/raphael.htm.

38. Rashid, Descent Into Chaos, p. 15. According to Steve Coll, Pulitzer prize–winning journalist, it was reasonable for the Taliban to view Unocal as an arm of the U.S. government. See Coll, GHOST WARS, p. 364; and Rashid, TALIBAN, p. 179.

39. Rashid, TALIBAN, p. 46.

40. For more information on the Pakistan-Iran relationship in the context of Baluchistan, see Ahsan Butt, Secession And Security: Explaining State Strategy Against Separatists (Ithaca: Cornell University Press, 2017), p. 73; Chris Zambelis, "A New Phase of Resistance and Insurgency in Iranian Baluchistan," CTC SENTINEL 2, no. 7 (July 2009), https://ctc.usma.edu/a-new-phase-of-resistance-and-insurgency-in-iranian-baluchistan/; Alex Vatanka, Iran And Pakistan: Security, Diplomacy And American Influence (London: I.B. Tauris, 2015); and Muhammad Akbar Notezai, "Iran-Pakistan at the Crossroads?" THE DIPLOMAT, July 9, 2017, https://thediplomat.com/2017/07/iran-pakistan-at-the-crossroads/.

41. In 1998, Iran nearly went to war with the Taliban for killing 11 Iranian diplomats and a journalist. See Douglas Jehl, "Iran Holds Taliban Responsible for 9 Diplomats' Deaths," NEW YORK TIMES, September 11, 1998, https://www.nytimes.com/1998/09/11/world/iran-holds-taliban-responsible-for-9-diplomats-deaths.html.

42. CNN, "1998 US Embassies in Africa Bombings Fast Facts," August 9, 2017, https://www.cnn.com/2013/10/06/world/africa/africa-embassy-bombings-fast-facts/index.html.

43. Oriana Zill, "The Controversial U.S. Retaliatory Missile Strikes," FRONTLINE, PBS, August 1998, https://www.pbs.org/wgbh/pages/frontline/shows/binladen/bombings/retaliation.html; and Al Jazeera, "Taliban Oil," October 8, 2016, https://www.aljazeera.com/programmes/specialseries/2016/10/taliban-oil-afghanistan-161004085739050.html.

44. Los Angeles Times, "Unocal Pulls out of Afghan Pipeline Project," December 8, 1998, http://articles.latimes.com/1998/dec/08/business/fi-51711.

45. Ahmed Rashid, "The Taliban: Exporting Extremism," FOREIGN AFFAIRS 78, no. 6 (Nov. /Dec. 1999): pp. 22–35.

46. Dennis Kux, The United States And Pakistan 1947–2000: Disenchanted Allies (Washington: Woodrow Wilson Center, 2001), pp. 348–49; Human Rights Watch, "Afghanistan: Crisis of Impunity," 13, no. 3 (July 2001), https://www.hrw.org/reports/2001/afghan2/Afghan0701.pdf; and Michael Rubin, "Who Is Responsible for the Taliban?" Middle East Review Of International Affairs (March 2002), http://www.washingtoninstitute.org/policy-analysis/view/who-is-responsible-for-the-taliban.

47. By 2000, no U.S. president had visited India in 22 years, Pakistan in 30 years, or Bangladesh since its independence in 1971. See Richard Haass, "Clinton Should Try to Cool South Asia," Brookings, Opinions, March 17, 2000, https://www.brookings.edu/opinions/clinton-should-try-to-cool-south-asia/; and Rudolph and Rudolph, "The Making of US Foreign Policy for South Asia," p. 705; Kux, The United States And Pakistan, pp. 356–58.

48. Deputy Secretary of State Strobe Talbott and Indian Minister of External Affairs Jaswant Singh met 14 times in seven countries between June 1998 and September 2000. Talbott has documented his experiences in detail in a memoir. See Strobe Talbott, Engaging India: Diplomacy, Democracy, And The Bomb (Washington: Brookings Institution, 2004).

49. President Bill Clinton, speech to Pakistani people, Pakistan TV, March 25, 2000, https://www.c-span.org/video/?156234-1/speech-pakistani-people.

50. Talbott, Engaging India, pp. 200–205.

51. RAND, "Operation Enduring Freedom: An Assessment," Research Brief, RB-9148, 2005, https://www.rand.org/pubs/research_briefs/RB9148/index1.html.

52. Agreement on Provisional Arrangements in Afghanistan Pending the Re-Establishment of Permanent Government Institutions, December 22, 2001, http://www.un.org/News/dh/latest/afghan/afghan-agree.htm.

53. International Security Assistance Force, https://www.nato.int/cps/en/natohq/topics_69366.htm.

54. Shahid Hussein, "Pakistan Welcomes Bonn Agreement," GULF NEWS, December 5, 2001, https://gulfnews.com/news/uae/general/pakistan-welcomes-bonn-agreement-1.431752.

55. Steve Coll, Directorate S: The Cia And America's Secret Wars In Afghanistan And Pakistan (New York: Penguin, 2018), pp. 140–41; and Riaz Khan, Afghanistan And Pakistan: Conflict, Extremism, And Resistance To Modernity (Karachi: Oxford University Press, 2012), pp. 106–8.

56. David Kilcullen, Blood Year: The Unraveling Of Western Counterterrorism (New York: Oxford University Press, 2016), pp. 18–19; Coll, DIRECTORATE S, p. 135. Also see Human Rights Watch, "Afghanistan's Bonn Agreement One Year Later," https://www.hrw.org/news/2002/12/05/afghanistans-bonn-agreement-one-year-later.

57. The Iraq war led to the creation of the Islamic State of Daesh (ISIS). See Zachary Lamb, "Islamic State," CFR Backgrounder, Council on Foreign Relations, August 10, 2016, https://www.cfr.org/backgrounder/islamic-state; Zach Beauchamp, "18 Things About ISIS You Need to Know," VOX, November 17, 2015, https://www.vox.com/cards/things-about-isis-you-need-to-know; and Mehdi Hasan, "Blowback: How ISIS Was Created by the U.S. Invasion of Iraq," THE INTERCEPT, January 29, 2018, https://theintercept.com/2018/01/29/isis-iraq-war-islamic-state-blowback/.

58. William J. Broad, David E. Sanger, and Raymond Bonner, "A Tale of Nuclear Proliferation: How Pakistani Built His Network," NEW YORK TIMES, February 12, 2004, https://www.nytimes.com/2004/02/12/world/a-tale-of-nuclear-proliferation-how-pakistani-built-his-network.html; Ester Pan, "Nonproliferation: The Pakistan Network," CFR BACKGROUNDER, Council on Foreign Relations, February 7, 2005, https://www.cfr.org/backgrounder/nonproliferation-pakistan-network; and William Langewiesche, "The Wrath of Khan," THE ATLANTIC, November 2005, https://www.theatlantic.com/magazine/archive/2005/11/the-wrath-of-khan/304333/.

59. During her Senate confirmation hearing to become the director of the CIA, Gina Haspel stated that the CIA continues to monitor any links between Pakistan's nuclear scientists and extremist groups. See Gina Haspel, confirmation hearing, Senate Intelligence Committee, May 9, 2018, https://www.intelligence.senate.gov/hearings/open-hearing-nomination-gina-haspel-be-director-central-intelligence-agency. Also see Catherine Collins and Douglas Frantz,

"The Long Shadow of A. Q. Khan," Snapshot, FOREIGN AFFAIRS, January 31, 2018, https://www.foreignaffairs.com/articles/north-korea/2018-01-31/long-shadow-aq-khan; and Sahar Khan, "How Haspel's CIA Could Improve U.S.–Pakistan Relations," AXIOS, May 24, 2018, https://www.axios.com/how-haspels-cia-could-improve-us-pakistan-relations-eb12b1ca-11d1-4928-b8ce-49f292083c56.html.

60. Jeffrey Goldberg and Marc Ambinder, "The Ally from Hell," THE ATLANTIC, December 2011, https://www.theatlantic.com/magazine/archive/2011/12/the-ally-from-hell/308730/; Abubakar Siddique, "How Safe Is Pakistan's Nuclear Arsenal?" RadioFreeEurope.com, August 19, 2012, https://www.rferl.org/a/how-safe-is-pakistans-nuclear-arsenal/24681549.html; and Rahmatullah Nabil, "The World Must Secure Pakistan's Nuclear Weapons," NEW YORK TIMES, August 20, 2017, https://www.nytimes.com/2017/04/20/opinion/the-world-must-secure-pakistans-nuclear-weapons.html.

61. Khurshid Mahmud Kasuri, Neither A Hawk Nor A Dove: An Insider's Account Of Pakistan's Foreign Relations Including Details Of The Kashmir Framework (Karachi: Oxford University Press, 2015), pp. 596–608. Also see Ikram Junaidi, "Quality, Capacity, Safety of Pakistan's Nuclear Weapons Better than India's," DAWN, December 28, 2016, https://www.dawn.com/news/1304890.

62. "Obama's Address on the War in Afghanistan," New York Times, December 1, 2009, https://www.nytimes.com/2009/12/02/world/asia/02prexy.text.html.

63. Danielle Kurtzleben, "Chart: How the U.S. Troop Levels in Afghanistan Have Changed under Obama," NPR, July 6, 2016, https://www.npr.org/2016/07/06/484979294/chart-how-the-u-s-troop-levels-in-afghanistan-have-changed-under-obama.

64. Dave Philipps, "Mission Ends in Afghanistan, but Sacrifices Are Not Over for U.S. Soldiers," NEW YORK TIMES, December 31, 2014, https://www.nytimes.com/2015/01/01/us/mission-ends-but-sacrifices-are-not-over-for-us-soldiers.html.

65. CNN, "Death of Osama bin Laden Fast Facts," April 15, 2018, https://www.cnn.com/2013/09/09/world/death-of-osama-bin-laden-fast-facts/index.html; Husain Haqqani, "What Pakistan Knew about the Bin Laden Raid," Foreign Policy, May 13, 2015, http://foreignpolicy.com/2015/05/13/what-pakistan-knew-about-the-bin-laden-raid-seymour-hersh/; and Ahmed Rashid, "Sy Hersh and Osama bin Laden: The Right and the Wrong," THE NEW YORK REVIEW

OF BOOKS, September 29, 2016, http://www.nybooks.com/articles/2016/09/29/sy-hersh-osama-bin-laden-right-and-wrong/.

66. Asad Hashim, "Leaked Report Shows bin Laden's 'Hidden Life,'" Al Jazeera, July 8, 2013, https://www.aljazeera.com/news/asia/2013/07/20137813412615531.html.

67. The Obama administration had begun leaning toward talking to the Taliban in 2010. See Coll, Directorate S, pp. 447–49.

68. Matthew Rosenberg, "Taliban Opening Qatar Office, and Maybe Doors to Talks," New York Times, January 3, 2012, https://www.nytimes.com/2012/01/04/world/asia/taliban-to-open-qatar-office-in-step-toward-peace-talks.html; and Christoph Reuter, Gregor Peter Schmitz, and Holger Stark, "How German Diplomats Opened Channel to Taliban," SPIEGEL, January 10, 2012, http://www.spiegel.de/international/world/talking-to-the-enemy-how-german-diplomats-opened-channel-to-taliban-a-808068.html.

69. Coll, Directorate S, pp. 578–79.

70. DAWN, "Obama Signs Kerry–Lugar Bill into Law," October 16, 2009, https://www.dawn.com/news/913807; and Stephen D. Krasner, "Talking Tough to Pakistan: How to End Islamabad's Defiance," Foreign Affairs 91, no. 1 (January/February 2010): 93.

71. "Advance Questions for Admiral James A. Winnefeld, Jr., USN, Nomination for the Position of Vice Chairman of the Joint Chiefs of Staff," July 2011, https://www.armed-services.senate.gov/imo/media/doc/Winnefeld%2007-21-11.pdf.

72. Remarks by President Trump on the Strategy in Afghanistan and South Asia, Fort Myer, Arlington, VA, August 21, 2017, https://www.whitehouse.gov/briefings-statements/remarks-president-trump-strategy-afghanistan-south-asia/. The chance that the U.S. homeland remains vulnerable to attacks from Afghanistan is actually low. Yet policymakers have consistently engaged in threat inflation. See Benjamin H. Friedman, "Alarums and Excursions: Explaining Threat Inflation in U.S. Foreign Policy," in A Dangerous World? Threat Perception And U.S. National Security, eds. Christopher A. Preble and John Mueller (Washington: Cato Institute, 2014), pp. 281–303.

73. On U.S. mismanagement of Afghan reconstruction, see Phil Hegeseth, "Inspector General Reveals DoD Can't Verify Where $3.1 billion Was Spent in Afghanistan," Long War Journal, March 31, 2018, https://www.longwarjournal.org/archives/2018/03/inspector-general-reveals-dod-cant-verify-where-3-1-billion-was-spent-in-afghan-

istan.php?utm_source=feedburner&utm_medium=email&utm_ca
mpaign=Feed%3A+LongWarJournalSiteWide+%28FDD%27s+L
ong+War+Journal+Update%29; and Clark, "The War in Afghanistan," https://taskandpurpose.com/war-afghanistan-continues-go-
terribly/. On lack of coordination between U.S. troops and ISAF,
see Gopal Ratnam, "Poor Planning, Coordination Cited in Afghan
Intervention," USIP analysis and commentary, United States Institute of Peace, December 16, 2015, https://www.usip.org/publica-
tions/2015/12/poor-planning-coordination-cited-afghan-inter-
vention. For corruption within Afghan domestic politics, see Javid
Ahmad, "Mafia Politics Threatens Afghan Security as Much as Insurgency Does," The Hill, January 4, 2018, http://thehill.com/opin-
ion/international/367414-mafia-politics-threaten-afghan-securi-
ty-as-much-as-insurgency-does.

74. See Fair, Fighting To The End, pp. 103–35; Human Rights Watch,
"Afghanistan: Crisis of Impunity," p. 24.

75. Husan Haqqani, "From Key Pakistani General to ISIS Terrorist
'Killed' in Jihad, the Chilling Saga of Shahid Aziz," The Print, May
27, 2018, https://theprint.in/opinion/from-key-pakistani-gener-
al-to-isis-terrorist-killed-in-jihad-the-chilling-saga-of-shahid-
aziz/63221/.

76. Rubin, "Who Is Responsible for the Taliban?" Colonel "Imam" was
killed by the TTP in 2011. See Jane Perlez, "Onetime Taliban Han-
dler Dies in Their Hands," New York Times, January 24, 2011, https://
www.nytimes.com/2011/01/25/world/asia/25pakistan.html;   and
Rahimullah Yusufzai, "The Implications of Colonel Imam's Murder
in Pakistan," CTC Sentinel 4, no. 4 (April 2011): 18–20, https://ctc.
usma.edu/the-implications-of-colonel-imams-murder-in-pakistan/.

77. Hersh, "The Getaway"; Ayesha Jalal, The Struggle For Pakistan: A
Muslim Homeland And Global Politics (Cambridge, MA: Harvard
University Press, 2014), p. 327.

78. C. Christine Fair, "The Milli Muslim League: The Domestic Politics of Pakistan's Lashkar-e-Taiba," Current Trends In Islamist Ideology, Hudson Institute, May 7, 2018, https://www.hudson.org/
research/14305-the-milli-muslim-league-the-domestic-politics-of-
pakistan-s-lashkar-e-taiba. Also see Stephen Tankel, Storming The
World Stage: The Story Of Lashkar-E-Taiba (New York: Oxford University Press, 2013).

79. Saba Imtiaz, "Militancy in Pakistan and Impacts on U.S. Foreign Policy," International Security Program Carnegie Fellow, New America Foundation, August 2014; Saba Imtiaz and Declan Walsh, "In Pakistan, a Charity Project Points to Official Tolerance of Militants," NEW YORK TIMES, January 28, 2015, https://www.nytimes.com/2015/01/29/world/in-pakistan-a-charity-project-points-to-official-tolerance-of-militants.html; and Saba Imtiaz, "Pakistan's Perpetual Militant Feedback," FOREIGN POLICY, January 25, 2016, http://foreignpolicy.com/2016/01/25/pakistan-india-azhar-pathankot-jaish/.

80. Karzai suspected as early as 2003 that Pakistan was continuing to sponsor the Taliban and Haqqani Network. See Coll, Directorate S, p. 198.

81. United Nations High Commissioner for Refugees, "Pakistan," http://www.unhcr.org/en-us/pakistan.html; and "Pakistan's Afghan Refugees: A Timeline," EXPRESS TRIBUNE (Pakistan), October 5, 2016, https://tribune.com.pk/story/1193771/pakistans-afghan-refugees-timeline/.

82. Imtiaz Gul, The Most Dangerous Place: Pakistan's Lawless Frontier (New York: Viking, 2009), pp. 43–54; Zahid Hussein, "Pakistan's Most Dangerous Place," Wilson Quarterly (Winter 2012): 15-21, https://www.wilsonquarterly.com/quarterly/winter-2012-lessons-of-the-great-depression/pakistans-most-dangerous-place/; and Foreign Policy and New America Foundation, "The Battle for Pakistan: Militancy and Conflict in Pakistan's Tribal Regions," April 19, 2010, http://foreignpolicy.com/2010/04/19/the-battle-for-pakistan-militancy-and-conflict-in-pakistans-tribal-regions/.

83. Shuja Nawaz, "The Pakistan Army and Its Role in FATA," CTC Sentinel 2, no. 1 (January 2009): 19–21, https://ctc.usma.edu/the-pakistan-army-and-its-role-in-fata/.

84. Zafar Abbas, "Pakistan's Undeclared War," BBC NEWS, September 10, 2004, http://news.bbc.co.uk/2/hi/south_asia/3645114.stm.

85. Hassan Abbas, "A Profile of Tehrik-i-Taliban Pakistan," CTC Sentinel 1, no. 2 (January 2008): 1–4, https://www.belfercenter.org/sites/default/files/files/publication/CTC%20Sentinel%20-%20Profile%20of%20Tehrik-i-Taliban%20Pakistan.pdf.

86. BBC, "Pakistan Taliban: Peshawar School Attack Leaves 141 Dead," December 16, 2014, http://www.bbc.com/news/world-asia-30491435.

87. South Asia Terrorism Portal, "Fatalities in Terrorist Violence in Pakistan 2000–2018," http://www.satp.org/Datasheets.aspx?countries=pakistan. (Data Sheets accessed on July 6, 2018.)

88. Seth G. Jones and C. Christine Fair, "Counterinsurgency in Pakistan," RAND, 2010, https://www.rand.org/content/dam/rand/pubs/monographs/2010/RAND_MG982.pdf; and Ahmed Rashid, "Pakistan's Continued Failure to Adopt a Counterinsurgency Strategy," CTC Sentinel 2, no. 3 (March 2009): 7–10, https://ctc.usma.edu/app/uploads/2010/06/Vol2Iss3-Art3.pdf.

89. Counterinsurgency campaigns targeting the Pakistani Taliban began in 2009.

90. Express Tribune, "490 Soldiers, 3500 Militants Killed in Operation Zarb-e-Azb So Far: DG ISPR," June 15, 2016, https://tribune.com.pk/story/1123356/1-dg-ispr-addresses-press-conference-afghanistan-pakistan-border-clashes/.

91. Mehmood Ul Hassan Khan, "Operation Radd-ul-Fasaad and Its Parameters of Success," Ankara Center for Crisis and Policy Studies, April 27, 2017, https://ankasam.org/en/operation-radd-ul-fasaad-parameters-success/; and Hannah Johnsrud and Frederick W. Kagan, "Pakistan's Counter-Militant Offensive: Operation RaddulFasaad," Critical Threats, American Enterprise Institute, August 25, 2017, https://www.criticalthreats.org/analysis/pakistans-counter-militant-offensive-operation-raddul-fasaad.

92. Amnesty International, "Denying the Undeniable: Enforced Disappearances in Pakistan," ASA 33/018/2008 (2008), https://www.amnesty.org/download/Documents/ASA330182008ENGLISH.pdf; Reema Omer, "Forgotten Justice," DAWN, September 25, 2016, https://www.dawn.com/news/1285903; and Umer Farooq, "How War Altered Pakistan's Tribal Areas," Snapshot, FOREIGN AFFAIRS, October 6, 2017, https://www.foreignaffairs.com/articles/pakistan/2017-10-06/how-war-altered-pakistans-tribal-areas.

93. Sahar Khan, "Pashtun Protests Reflect Pakistan's Tensions with U.S., Afghanistan," AXIOS, April 16, 2018, https://www.axios.com/pashtun-protests-reflect-pakistans-tensions-with-us-afghanistan-59a00747-5833-4bb9-a15a-5117697be90d.html.

94. Jane Perlez, Eric Schmitt, and Carlotta Gall, "Pakistan Is Said to Pursue Foothold in Afghanistan," NEW YORK TIMES, June 24, 2010, https://www.nytimes.com/2010/06/25/world/asia/25islamabad.html.

95. Rani D. Mullen, "India in Afghanistan: Understanding Development Assistance by Emerging Donors to Conflict-Affected Countries," Changing Landscape Of Assistance To Conflict-Affected States: Emerging And Traditional Donors And Opportunities For Collaboration, Policy Brief no. 10, Stimson Center, August 2017, https://www.stimson.org/sites/default/files/file-attachments/India%20in%20Afghanistan%20Understanding%20Development%20Assistance%20by%20Emerging%20Donors%20to%20Conflict-Affected%20Countries_0.pdf.

96. Shoaib A. Rahim, "Capricious Afghanistan–Pakistan Trade: Who Wins?" THE DIPLOMAT, May 25, 2018, https://thediplomat.com/2018/05/capricious-afghanistan-pakistan-trade-who-wins/.

97. DAWN, "Trade Route Linking Chabahar Port with Afghanistan a Security Threat," May 31, 2016, https://www.dawn.com/news/1261792.

98. Harsh V. Pant, "India–Iran Cooperation at Chabahar Port: Choppy Waters," CSIS BRIEFS, Center for Strategic and International Studies, April 2, 2018, https://www.csis.org/analysis/india-iran-cooperation-chabahar-port-choppy-waters; Stimson Center, "Strategic Competition in Southern Asia: Arms Racing or Modernization?," event, Washington, May 17, 2017, https://www.stimson.org/content/strategic-competition-southern-asia-arms-race-or-modernization; and Max Bearak and Brian Murphy, "To Sidestep Pakistan, India Embraces an Iranian Port," WASHINGTON POST, May 24, 2016, https://www.washingtonpost.com/news/worldviews/wp/2016/05/24/to-sidestep-pakistan-india-embraces-an-iranian-port/?utm_term=.6d345746961c.

99. For a detailed analysis on CPEC, see Arif Rafiq, "China–Pakistan Economic Corridor: Barriers and Impact," Peaceworks no. 135, United States Institute of Peace, pp. 24–29, file:///H:/My%20Documents/PA/Pakistan--State-sponsored%20Militancy/Arif%20Rafiq--CPEC.pdf.

100. Sahar Khan, "After Kabul Hotel Attack, Pakistan Should Make Clear where it stands," CATO AT LIBERTY (blog), January 23, 2018, https://www.cato.org/blog/kabul-hotel-attack-opportunity-pakistan.

101. All 16 laws are listed in chronological order: (1) the Pakistan Penal Code, 1860; (2) the Explosive Act, 1884; (3) the Code of Criminal Procedure, 1898; (4) the Explosive Substance Act, 1908; (5) the

Punjab Arms Ordinance, 1965; (6) the Qanun-e-Shahadat Order, 1984 (also known as the Evidence Act or Evidence Order); (7) the Anti-Terrorism Act of 1997; (8) the Anti-Money Laundering Act, 2010; (9) the Actions (in Aid of Civil Power) Regulation, 2011; (10) the Investigation for Fair Trial Act, 2013; (11) the National Counter Terrorism Authority Act, 2013; (12) the Protection for Pakistan Act, 2014; (13) the Constitution (Twenty-First Amendment) Act (Act 1 of 2015); (14) the Pakistan Army (Amendment) Act (Act II of 2015); (15) the Constitution (Twenty-Third Amendment) Act, 2017; and (16) the Pakistan Army (Amendment) Act, 2017. The statutes in italics are procedural in nature, whereas the others are substantive laws that define crimes and list punishments for offenses not covered under the ATA.

102. The Anti-Terrorism Act, 1997, http://www.molaw.gov.pk/molaw/userfiles1/file/Anti-Terrorism%20Act.pdf.

103. Huma Yusuf, "Pakistan's Anti-Terrorism Courts," CTC SENTINEL 3, no. 3 (March 2010), https://ctc.usma.edu/pakistans-anti-terrorism-courts/.

104. Charles Kennedy, "The Creation and Development of Pakistan's Anti-Terrorism Regime," in Religious Radicalism And Security In South Asia, eds. Satu Limaye et al. (Honolulu: Asia-Pacific Center for Security Studies, 2004), p. 400.

105. DAWN, "New Regulations Give Legal Cover to Detentions in Tribal Areas," July 12, 2011, https://www.dawn.com/news/643548.

106. Sahar Khan, "Selective Activism: The Role of Pakistan's Judiciary in Counterterrorism," Pakistan Politico, July 9, 2018, http://pakistan-politico.com/selective-activism-the-role-of-pakistans-judiciary-in-counterterrorism/.

107. Mark M. Stavsky, "The Doctrine of State Necessity in Pakistan," Cornell International Law Journal 16, no. 2 (Summer 1983): 341–94, https://scholarship.law.cornell.edu/cgi/viewcontent.cgi?article=1128&context=cilj.

108. Sahar Khan, "Pakistan's Military Courts: The Army's Newest Political Tool," New Perspectives In Foreign Policy, Center for Strategic and International Studies, no. 11 (Summer 2016): 15–23, https://csis-prod.s3.amazonaws.com/s3fs-public/publication/160701_npfp_summer2016.pdf.

109. Declan Walsh, "Taliban Besiege Pakistan School, Leaving 145 dead," New York Times, December 16, 2014, https://www.nytimes.com/2014/12/17/world/asia/taliban-attack-pakistani-school.html.

110. "National Action Plan, 2014," National Counter Terrorism Authority NACTA Pakistan, https://nacta.gov.pk/nap-2014/.

111. Reema Omer, "Objection, Your Honour," Friday Times, August 14, 2015, http://www.thefridaytimes.com/tft/objection-your-honour/.

112. Khan, "Selective Activism."

113. National Internal Security Policy 2014, https://nation.com.pk/27-Feb-2014/text-of-national-security-policy-2014-18.

114. The laws are the Police Act of 1861 and Police Rules 1934.

115. International Crisis Group, Authoritarianism And Political Party Reform In Pakistan, Asia Report no. 102 (Washington: ICG, 2005).

116. Aqil Shah, "Getting the Military out of Pakistani Politics: How Aiding the Army Undermines Democracy," FOREIGN AFFAIRS 90, no. 3 (May/June 2011): 69–82, https://www.foreignaffairs.com/articles/south-asia/2011-04-15/getting-military-out-pakistani-politics.

117. Rebecca Williams, "PCF and PCCF—Similar but Different," Budget Insight, A Stimson Center Blog on National Security Spending, October 12, 2009, https://budgetinsight.wordpress.com/2009/10/12/pcf-and-pccf-similar-but-different/. For a brief history of U.S. arms sales to Pakistan, see Richard F. Grimmett, "U.S. Arms Sales to Pakistan," CRS Report RS22757, Congressional Research Service, August 24, 2009, https://fas.org/sgp/crs/weapons/RS22757.pdf.

118. Julian Pecquet, "Congress Axes Pakistan Counterinsurgency Fund," The Hill, March 22, 2013, http://thehill.com/policy/international/289803-congress-axes-petraeus-backed-pakistan-counterinsurgency-fund. Congress also discontinued the Pakistan Counterinsurgency Capability Fund (PCCF), which was established together with the PCF in 2009, in April 2013. See DAWN, "US Ends Counter-Insurgency Assistance," April 13, 2013, https://www.dawn.com/news/802216.

119. Anwar Iqbal, "US to Withhold $255m from Another Fund after CSF Cuts," DAWN, December 31, 2017, https://www.dawn.com/news/1379904/us-to-withhold-255m-from-another-fund-after-csf-cuts.

120. Sahar Khan, "What Is the CSF and Why It Serves U.S. Interests in Afghanistan," CATO AT LIBERTY (blog), January 5, 2018, https://www.cato.org/blog/what-csf-why-it-serves-us-interests-afghanistan; and C. Christine Fair, "A New Way of Engaging Pakistan," LAWFARE (blog), April 11, 2016, https://www.lawfareblog.com/new-way-engaging-pakistan.

121. Baqir Sajjad Syed, "Anti-Terror Law Amended to Ban UN-Listed Groups, Individuals," DAWN, February 13, 2018, https://www.dawn.com/news/1389042; and C. Christine Fair, "Jamaat-ud-Dawa: Converting Kuffar at Home, Killing Them Abroad," Currents Trends In Islamist Ideology, Hudson Institute, November 4, 2017, https://www.hudson.org/research/13874-jamaat-ud-dawa-converting-kuffar-at-home-killing-them-abroad.

122. Dipanjan Roy Chaudhury, "After FATF Grey-Listing, Pakistan Faces EU Black-Listing Threat," Economic Times, March 5, 2018, https://economictimes.indiatimes.com/news/defence/after-fatf-grey-listing-pakistan-faces-eu-black-listing/articleshow/63161750.cms; and Michael Kugelman, "Now That It's Headed to the Grey List, Pakistan Faces Real Economic Risks Too," THE PRINT, February 26, 2018, https://theprint.in/opinion/now-headed-grey-list-pakistan-faces-real-economic-risks/38036/.

123. Adam Taylor, "Do Sanctions Work? The Evidence Isn't Compelling," Washington Post, August 2, 2017, https://www.washingtonpost.com/news/worldviews/wp/2017/08/02/do-sanctions-work-the-evidence-isnt-compelling/?utm_term=.189ac50970dc.

124. Uzair Younus, "How Will Being on the FATF Grey-List Actually Impact Pakistan?" The Diplomat, March 1, 2018, https://thediplomat.com/2018/03/how-will-being-on-the-fatf-grey-list-actually-impact-pakistan/.

125. For information on Pakistan's anti-money-laundering laws, see Zafar Azeem, "Pakistan's Anti-money Laundering Laws," Business Recorder, June 28, 2012, https://fp.brecorder.com/2012/06/201206281206530/.

126. Madeeha Anwar, "US Designates Pakistani Party Milli Muslim League as 'Terrorist,'" Voice of America, April 3, 2018, https://www.voanews.com/a/us-designates-pakistan-party-milli-muslim-league-terrorists/4331538.html.

127. RadioFreeEurope/RadioLiberty, "U.S. Adds Pakistan's Milli Muslim League to Terror List," April 3, 2018, https://www.rferl.org/a/u-s-milli-muslim-league-u-s-terror-list/29141811.html.

128. Fair, "The Milli Muslim League."

129. Richard G. Olson, "How Not to Engage with Pakistan," New York Times, January 9, 2018, https://www.nytimes.com/2018/01/09/opinion/pakistan-trump-aid-engage.html?_r=3.

130. "China in Talks with Baloch Militant to Secure CPEC Projects, Says FT," DAWN, February 20, 2018, https://www.dawn.com/news/1390520; and Shazar Shafqat, "CPEC and the Baloch Insurgency," THE DIPLOMAT, February 8, 2017, https://thediplomat.com/2017/02/cpec-and-the-baloch-insurgency/.

131. "America's Decision to Freeze Military Aid to Pakistan Won't Work," THE ECONOMIST, January 13, 2018, http://media.economist.com/news/asia/21734461-pakistan-has-more-leverage-over-america-other-way-around-americas-decision-freeze.

132. John Glaser, "Withdrawing from Overseas Bases: Why a Forward-Deployed Military Posture Is Unnecessary, Outdated, and Dangerous," Cato Institute Policy Analysis no. 816, July 18, 2017, https://object.cato.org/sites/cato.org/files/pubs/pdf/pa_816.pdf; and John Glaser, "A Naval Race with China Is Unnecessary and Will Likely Backfire," Arizona Daily Star, June 18, 2018, https://tucson.com/opinion/national/john-glaser-a-naval-race-with-china-is-unnec-essary-and/article_5574f5b4-c381-5d74-b095-5006dfcf6c7f.html.

133. In October 2017, the Trump administration declared the Taliban's political office in Doha, Qatar, as a failed Obama administration initiative. The announcement, however, did not gain much traction and has since disappeared. See Sameer Lalwani, "Putting Peace out of Reach," U.S. NEWS AND WORLD REPORT, October 27, 2017, https://www.usnews.com/opinion/world-report/articles/2017-10-27/closing-the-taliban-doha-office-will-harm-us-aims-in-afghanistan.

134. Sahar Khan, "How Haspel's CIA could improve U.S.–Pakistan relations," AXIOS, May 24, 2018, https://www.axios.com/how-haspels-cia-could-improve-uspakistan-relations-eb12b1ca-11d1-4928-b8ce-49f292083c56.html?utm_source=twitter&utm_medium=twsocialshare&utm_campaign=organic.

Bibliography

Ahady Anwar-ul-Haq. 1991.Conflict in postsoviet-occupation Afghanistan. Journal of Contemporary Asia, Vol. 21, No. 4

Abbas, Hassan 2015. Pakistan's Drift into Extremism: Allah, the Army, and America's War Terror. Abingdon: Routledge.

Afzal, Madiha 2018. Pakistan under Siege: Extremism, Society, and the State. Washington, DC: Brookings Institution Press.

Ahmed, ShamilaKouser, 2012, July. The Impact of the "War on Terror": On Birmingham's Pakistani / Kashmiri Muslims' Perceptions of the State, the Police and Islamic Identities. (Doctoral Thesis, University of Birmingham, Birmingham, United Kingdom). http://etheses.bham.ac.uk/id/eprint/3635

Ali, Murad, 2012.The Politics of Development Aid: The Allocation and Delivery of Aid from the United States of America to Pakistan. Doctoral Thesis, Massey University, Palmerston North, New Zealand. URL: http://hdl. handle.net/10179/3418

Ahmed, Khaled. 2016, Sleepwalking to Surrender: Dealing with Terrorism in Pakistan. Haryana: Viking. Ataöv, Türkkaya (2018): Kashmir and Neighbors: Tale, Terror, Truce.

Abingdon: Routledge. Barfield, Thomas. 1996. 'The Afghan Morass', Current History, Vol. 95, No. 597.

Andrew, Christopher M. and Jeremy Noakes. 1987. Intelligence and International Relations, 1900-1945. Exeter: Exeter University Press,

Ashman, Harold Lowell. 2009. Intelligence and Foreign Policy: A Functional Analysis. Salt Lake City: Ashman, 1974. Association of the Bar of the City of New York, Committee on Civil Rights The Central Intelligence Agency: Oversight and Accountability. New York,

Abshire, David. 2001, "Making the Pieces Fit: America Needs a Comprehensive National Security Strategy." American Legion Magazine,

Ackerman, Wystan M. 1998,"Encryption: A 21st Century National Security Dilemma." International Review of Law, Computers & Technology.

Andersen, Per, Richard Morris, David Amaral, Tim Bliss, & John O'Keefe 2006. The Hippocampus Book, Oxford: University Press.

Anderson, Alan Ross, &Nuel D. Belnap, Jr. 1975 Entailment: The Logic of Relevance and Necessity, Princeton University Press, Princeton.

Anderson, John R. (1983) The Architecture of Cognition, Cambridge, MA: Harvard University Press.

Anderson, John R., & Gordon H. Bower,1973 Human Associative Memory, Washington, DC: Winston.

Anderson, John R., & Gordon H. Bower, 1980 Human Associative Memory: A Brief Edition, Hillsdale, NJ: Erlbaum.

Anderson, John R., &Lebiere, C. 1998. The atomic components of thought, Mahwah, NJ: Erlbaum.

Adams, Thomas K. "Future Warfare and the Decline of Human Decision-making." Parameters, Winter 2001/2002, v. 31, no. 4

Adler, Emanual. "Executive Command and Control in Foreign Policy: The CIA's Covert Activities," Orbis, fall 1979, v. 23, no. 3

Agrell, Wilhelm. Sweden and the Dilemmas of Neutral Intelligence Liaison. Journal of Strategic Studies, August 2006, v. 29, no. 4

Aid, Matthew M. "All Glory is Fleeting: SIGINT and the Fight against International Terrorism." Intelligence and National Security, Winter 2003, v. 18, no. 4

Ast, Scott Alan. Managing Security Overseas: Protecting Employees and Assets in Volatile Regions Boca Raton; FL: CRC Press, 2010.

Ataov, Türkkaya 2018: Kashmir and Neighbors: Tale, Terror, Truce. (Routledge Revivals). Abingdon: Routledge.

Afghanistan Analyst Network (Osman, B.) 18 October 2019, The Islamic State in 'Khorasan': How it began and where it stands now in Nangarhar, 27 July 2016, https://www.afghanistan-analysts.org/the-islamic-state-inkhorasan-how-it-began-and-where-it-stands-now-in-nangarhar/,

Amnesty International, Pakistan: Enduring Enforced Disappearances, 27 March 2019,https://www.amnesty.org/en/latest/research/2019/03/pakistan-enduring-enforceddisappearances/, accessed 15 July 2019

Azam, M., Javaid, U, 2017, The sources of Militancy in Pakistan, in: Journal of the Research Society of Pakistan, Volume No. 54, Issue No. 2 http://pu.edu.pk/images/journal/history/PDF-FILES/13-Paper_54_2_17.pdf, accessed 24 July 2019.

Baloch, H., Peace Talks, ISKP and TTP--The Future in Question, 6 May 2019, ITCT (Islamic Theology of Counter Terrorism), https://www.itct.org.uk/wp-content/uploads/2019/05/Peace-Talks-ISKP-andTTP.

Bell, Paul M. P. 2007, Pakistan's Madrassas – Weapons of Mass Instruction? (Master's Thesis, Naval Postgraduate School, Monterey, United States). URL: http://hdl.handle.net/10945/3653

Bennett, John T. 2014, Bend but Don't Break: Why Obama's Targeted-Killing Program Challenges Policy and Legal Boundaries but Rarely Breaches them. (Master's Thesis, Johns Hopkins University, Baltimore, United States). http://jhir.library.jhu.edu/handle/1774.2/37221

Badalic, Vasja, 2019 The War against Civilians: Victims of the "War on Terror" in Afghanistan and Pakistan.(Palgrave Studies in Victims and Victimology). Cham: Palgrave Macmillan / Springer Nature. DOI: https://doi.org/10.

Bergen, Peter L.; Rothenberg, Daniel (Ed.) 2015, Drone Wars: Transforming Conflict, Law, and Policy. New York: Cambridge University Press.

Bergen, Peter L.; Tiedemann, Katherine (Eds.), 2013, Talibanistan: Negotiating the Borders between Terror, Politics, and Religion. Oxford: Oxford University Press. Brooke-Smith, Robin (2013): S

Bayly, C. A. 1996, Empire and Information: Intelligence Gathering and Social Communication in India: 1780-1880. NY: Cambridge University press,.

Bazan, Elizabeth B. 2008. The Foreign Intelligence Surveillance Act: Overview and Modifications. New York: Nova Science Publishers,

Bailey, David, 1997, A Computational Model of Embodiment in the Acquisition of Action Verbs, Doctoral dissertation, Computer Science Division, EECS Department, University of California, Berkeley.

Baillie, Penny, 2002 The Synthesis of Emotions in Artificial Intelligence, PhD Dissertation, University of Southern Queensland.

Baker, Mark C. 2003 Lexical Categories: Verbs, Nouns, and Adjectives, Cambridge University Press, Cambridge.

Baldwin, J.F. 1986 Automated fuzzy and probabilistic inference, Fuzzy Sets and Systems, vol 18,

Ballard, Dana H., Mary M. Hayhoe, Polly K. Pook, & Rajesh P. N. Rao 1997 Deictic codes for the embodiment of cognition, Behavioral and Brain Sciences 20, 723-767.

Bar Hillel, Yehoshua, 1954 Logical Syntax and Semantics, Language 30, 230-237.

Beck, Melvin. 1984. Secret Contenders: The Myth of Cold War Counter-intelligence. New York, NY: Sheridan Square Publications,

Beichman, Arnold. 1984. "The U.S. Intelligence Establishment and Its Discontents." IN Dennis L. Bark (ed.) To Promote Peace: U.S. Foreign Policy in the Mid-1980s. Stanford, CA: Hoover Institution Press, Stanford University,

Bazai, Fida Muhammad, 2016 Pakistan's Responses to the United States' Demands in the War against the Taliban and Al-Qaeda. (Doctoral Thesis, University of Glasgow, Glasgow, United Kingdom). http://encore.lib.gla.ac.uk/iii/encore/record/C-Rb3258590

Bell, Paul M. P. (2007, March): Pakistan's Madrassas – Weapons of Mass Instruction? (Master's Thesis, Naval Postgraduate School, Monterey, United States). URL: http://hdl.handle.net/10945/3653

Bennett, John T. 2014 Bend but Don't Break: Why Obama's Targeted-Killing Program Challenges Policy and Legal Boundaries but Rarely Breaches them. (Master's Thesis, Johns Hopkins University, Baltimore, United States). http://jhir.library.jhu.edu/handle/1774.2/37221

Bhattacharya, Sandhya S. 2008 The Global Impact of Terror: 9/11 and the India-Pakistan Conflict. (Doctoral Thesis, Pennsylvania State University, State College, United States https://etda.libraries.psu. edu/catalog/7900

Barrett, David M. "Glimpses of a Hidden History: Sen. Richard Russell, Congress, and Oversight of the CIA." International Journal of Intelligence and Counterintelligence, Fall 1998, v. 11, no. 3, p. 271-298.

Barry James A. "Managing the Covert Political Action: Guideposts from Just War Theory." Studies in Intelligence, 1992, v. 36, no. 5 https://

www.cia.gov/library/center-for-the-study-of-intelligence/kentcsi/docs/v36i3a05p_0001.htm

Barry, James A. Bridging the Intelligence-Policy Divide. Studies in Intelligence, 1994, v. 37, no. 5. https://www.cia.gov/library/center-for-the-study-of-intelligence/kentcsi/docs/v37i3a02p_0001.htm

Basile, James F. Congressional Assertiveness, Executive Authority and the Intelligence Oversight Act: A New Threat to the Separation of Powers. Notre Dame Law Review, 1989, v. 64, no. 4

Beres, Louis Rene. On Assassination, Preemption, and Counterterrorism: The View from International Law." International Journal of Intelligence and Counterintelligence, Winter 2008, v. 21, no. 4

Bhattacharya, Sandhya S. 2008, The Global Impact of Terror: 9/11 and the India-Pakistan Conflict. (Doctoral Thesis, Pennsylvania State University, State College, United States). https://etda.libraries.psu.edu/catalog/7900

Clarke, Ryan 2011, Crime–Terror Nexus in South Asia: States, Security and Non-State Actors. (Asian Security Studies). Abingdon: Routledge.

Coll, Steve, 2018 Directorate S: The C.I.A. and America's Secret Wars in Afghanistan and Pakistan. New York: Penguin Press.

Dorronsoro, Gilles. 2012. 'The transformation of the Afghanistan-Pakistan border', in under the drones: Modern lives in the Afghanistan-Pakistan Borderlands. Harvard University Press

Cassirer, Ernst,1942 ZurLogik der Kulturwissenschaften, translated by S. G. Lofts as The Logic of the Cultural Sciences, Yale University Press, New Haven.

Cattell, R. G. G., & Douglas K. Barry, eds. 1997, The Object Database Standard, ODMG 2.0, Morgan Kaufmann, San Francisco, CA.

Ceccato, Silvio. 1961 Linguistic Analysis and Programming for Mechanical Translation, Gordon and Breach, New York.

Ceccato, Silvio,1964 Automatic translation of languages, Information Storage and Retrieval 2:3, 105-158.

Chafe, Wallace L. 1970 Meaning and the Structure of Language, University of Chicago Press, Chicago.

Chamberlin, Don, 1996 Using the New DB2, Morgan Kaufmann Publishers, San Francisco.

Cruickshank, Paul, 2013, Al Qaeda. (5 Vols.). (Critical Concepts in Political Science). Abingdon: Routledge.

Canfield, Robert L. 1992. 'Restructuring in Greater Central Asia: Changing Political Configurations', Asian Survey, Vol. 32, No. 10.

Drumbl, Mark A. 2002. 'The Taliban's 'other' crimes', Third World Quarterly, No. 23.

Daily Times, Police service-challenges and reforms, 6 October 2018,https://dailytimes.com.pk/306595/police-service-challenges-and-reforms/,

Daily Times, Reforming the judicial system, 8 March 2019,https://dailytimes.com.pk/362536/reforming-the-judicial-system/, accessed 17 October 2019

Dawn, 2009: Southern Punjab extremism battle between haves and have-nots, 21 May 2011 https://www.dawn.com/news/630651, accessed 21 July 2019

David, G.J. 2009. Ideas as Weapons: Influence and Perception in Modern Warfare. Washington, DC: Potomac Books,

DCAF Intelligence Working Group, Intelligence Practice and Democratic Oversight – a Practitioner's View. DCAF, Occasional paper no. 3. August 2003.

Dehaene, Stanislas, 2014 Consciousness and the Brain, New York: Viking.

DeJong, Gerald F.1979 Prediction and substantiation, Cognitive Science, vol. 3,

DeJong, Gerald F. 1982 An overview of the FRUMP system, in W. G. Lehnert & M. H. Ringle, eds., Strategies for Natual Language Processing, Erlbaum, Hillsdale, NJ,

Deledalle, Gerard, 1990 Charles S. Peirce, Phénoménologue et Sémioticien, translated as Charles S. Peirce, An Intellectual Biography, Amsterdam: John Benjamins.

de Moor, Aldo, Wilfried Lex, & Bernhard Ganter, eds. 2003 Conceptual Structures for Knowledge Creation and Communication, LNAI 2746, Berlin: Springer.

Deng, Li, & Dong Yu, 2014 Deep Learning: Methods and Applications, Foundations and Trends in Signal Processing.

Dennet, Daniel C. 1987 The Intentional Stance, MIT Press, Cambridge.

Dennet, Daniel C. 1995 Darwin's Dangerous Idea: Evolution and the Meanings of Life, Simon & Schuster, New York.

Dennet, Daniel C. 1996 Kinds of Minds, New York: Basic Books.

Dearth, Douglas H. 1992, Strategic Intelligence and National Security: A Selected Bibliography. Carlisle Barracks, PA: U.S. Army War College Library, http://handle.dtic.mil/100.2/ADA256389

Dearth, Douglas H. and R. Thomas Goodden. 1995. Strategic Intelligence: Theory and Application. 2nd ed. Carlisle Barracks, PA: U.S. Army War College Library

Der Derian, James. 1992. Antidiplomacy: Spies, Terror, Speed and War. Cambridge, MA: Blackwell,

Diamond, John. 2008.The CIA and the Culture of Failure: U.S. Intelligence from the End of the Cold War to the Invasion of Iraq. Stanford, CA: Stanford Security Series,

Dawn, Military courts cease to function today, 31 March 2019,https://www.dawn.com/news/1472947, accessed 3 July 2019

Dawn, Military Courts part of National Action Plan: PM Nawaz, 30 December 2014https://www.dawn.com/news/1154046, accessed 20 July 2019

Diplomat, July 2019,The, Taking Stock of Pakistan's Counterterrorism Efforts, 4 Years After the Army Public School Attack, 21 December 2018, https://thediplomat.com/2018/12/taking-stock-of-pakistans-counterterrorism-efforts-4-years-after-the-army-public-school-attack/,

Economic Times (The), US asks Pakistan to act against Haqqani network, other terror groups, 27 February 2018, https://m.economictimes.com/news/defence/us-asks-pak-to-act-against-haqqaninetwork-other-terror-groups/articleshow/63096010.cms, accessed 17 June 2019

Express Tribune, The Army launches Operation Radd-ul-Fasaad against terrorists across the country,22 February 2017, https://tribune.com.pk/story/1335805/army-launches-country-wide-operationterrorists/, accessed 30 July 2019

Einstein, Albert, 1921 The Meaning of Relativity, Princeton University Press, Princeton, NJ, fifth edition, 1956.

Einstein, A., H. A. Lorentz, H. Weyl, & H. Minkowski, 1923 The Principle of Relativity, Dover Publications, New York.

Einstein, Albert, 1944 Remarks on Bertrand Russell's Theory of Knowledge, in P. A. Schilpp, ed., The Philosophy of Bertrand Russell, Library of Living Philosophers.

Eklund, Peter W., Gerard Ellis, & G. Mann, eds. 1996 Conceptual Structures: Knowledge Representation as Interlingua, LNAI 1115, Berlin: Springer,

Express Tribune (The), Blast hits Hazara community's shoe market in Quetta, 6 August 2019, https://tribune.com.pk/story/2029583/1-least-two-martyred-13-injured-quetta-market-blast/

Elahi, N. 2019 Terrorism in Pakistan: The Tehreek-e-Taliban Pakistan (TTP) and the Challenge to Security. London: I.B. Tauris.

Fair, C. Christine 2014 fighting to the End: The Pakistan Army's Way of War. Oxford: Oxford University Press.

Fair, C. Christine 2018 In their Own Words: Understanding Lashkar-e-Tayyaba. London: Hurst.

Farwell, James P. 2011 The Pakistan Cauldron: Conspiracy, Assassination & Instability. Dulles: Potomac Books.

Feldman, J. A. 1981. A connectionist model of visual memory. In Hinton, G. E. and Anderson, J. A., editors, Parallel Models of Associative Memory, chapter 2. Erlbaum, Hillsdale, NJ.

Fukushima, K. 1975. Cognitron: A self-organizing multilayered neural network. Biological Cybernetics, 20:121–136.

Feigenbaum, Edward A., & Pamela McCorduck, 1983. The Fifth Generation, Addison-Wesley, Reading, MA. Brain and Language 89, 385-392.

Feldman, Jerome A. 2006 From Molecule to Metaphor: A Neural Theory of Language, MIT Press, Cambridge, MA.

Feldman, Jerome, & Srinivas Narayanan,2004 Embodied meaning in a neural theory of language, Brain and Language 89, 385-392.

Feldman, Jerome, Ellen Dodge, & John Bryant,2009. Embodied construction grammar, in B. Heine & H. Narrog, eds., The Oxford Handbook of Linguistic Analysis, Oxford: University Press.

Fellbaum, Christiane, 1998. WordNet: An Electronic Lexical Database, MIT Press, Cambridge, MA.

Feynman, Richard, 1965 The Character of Physical Law, Cambridge, MA: MIT Press.

Glatzer, Bernt. 2002. 'Centre and Periphery in Afghanistan: New Identities in a Broken State', Sociologus, winter issue.

Goodson, Larry. 1998. 'The Fragmentation of Culture in Afghanistan', Alif: Journal of Comparative Poetics, No. 18, Post-Colonial Discourse in South Asia.

Goodson, Larry P. 1998 'Periodicity and intensity in the Afghan War', Central Asian Survey, Vol. 17, No. 3.

Goudarzi, Hadi. 1999. 'Conflict in Afghanistan: Ethnicity and Religion', Ethnic Studies Report, Vol. XVII, No. 1.

Harpviken, Kristian Berg. 1997. 'Transcending nationalism: the emergence of non-state military formations in Afghanistan', Journal of Peace Research, Vol. 34, No. 3.

Haqqani, Husain, 2018 Reimagining Pakistan: Transforming a Dysfunctional Nuclear State. Noida: HarperCollins India.

Hayes, Louis D. 2016 The Islamic State in the Post-Modern World: The Political Experience of Pakistan. Abingdon: Routledge.

Hiro, Dilip, 2012 Apocalyptic Realm: Jihadists in South Asia. New Haven: Yale University Press.

Hussain, Rizwan, 2005 Pakistan and the Emergence of Islamic Militancy in Afghanistan. Aldershot: Ashgate.

Hinsley, F.H. and Richard Langhorn. 1985, Diplomacy and Intelligence during the Second World War: Essays in Honour of F.H. Hinsley. Cambridge, NY: Cambridge University Press

Hitchcock, Walter T. 1991, The Intelligence Revolution: A Historical Perspective: Proceedings of the Thirteenth Military History Symposium, U.S. Air Force Academy, Colorado Springs, Colorado, October 12-14, 1988. Washington, DC: U.S. Office of Air Force History,

Haaparanta Leila, 1994, Charles Peirce and the Drawings of the Mind, in HistoireÉpistémologieLangage 16:1, 35-52.

Harris, Kathryn E. 2015, Asymmetric Strategies and Asymmetric Threats: A Structural-Realist Critique of Drone Strikes in Pakistan, 2004-2014. (Master's Thesis, Virginia Polytechnic Institute and State University, Blacksburg, United States).http://hdl.handle.net/10919/64516

Hoyt, Melanie Raeann, 2014, Decembe. A Game of Drones: Comparing the U.S. Aerial Assassination Campaign in Yemen and Pakistan. (Master's Thesis, Angelo State University, San Angelo, United States).http://hdl. handle.net/2346.1/30273

Hubbard, Austen, 2016, A Study on the Relationship between Security and Prosperity in Pakistan. (Master's Thesis, Angelo State University, San Angelo, United States). URL: http://hdl.handle.net/2346.1/30604

Hussain, Syed Ejaz, 2010, Terrorism in Pakistan: Incident Patterns, Terrorists' Characteristics, and the Impact of Terrorist Arrests on Terrorism. (Doctoral Thesis, University of Pennsylvania, Philadelphia, United States). https://repository.upenn.edu/edissertations/136

Hoffman, Bruce. Lessons of 9/11. Santa Monica, CA: RAND, 2002. http://www.rand.org/pubs/testimonies/CT201/index.html

Hussain, Safdar, and Muhammad Ijaz Latif. 2012. 'Issues and Challenges in Pakistan-Afghanistan Relations after 9/11', South Asian Studies, Vol. 27, No. 1.

Hussain, Shabir, and Syed Abdul Siraj. 2018. 'Coverage of Taliban conflict in the Pak–Afghan press: A comparative analysis', International Communication Gazette.

ICG. 2014. 'Resetting Pakistan's Relations with Afghanistan', International Crisis Group.

Iqbal, Khalid. 2015. 'Natural Allies: TurkeyPakistan-Afghanistan', Defence Journal, Vol. 18. No. 8.

Inderfurth, Karl F. and Loch K. Johnson. 1988, Decisions of the Highest Order: Perspectives on the National Security Council. Pacific Grove, California: Brooks/Cole,.

Ibrahimi, S. Yaqub. 2017. 'The Taliban's Islamic Emirate of Afghanistan (1996–2001): 'War-Making and State-Making' as an Insurgency Strategy', Small Wars & Insurgencies, Vol. 28, No. 6.

Intelligence Services and Democracy. Geneva, Switzerland: Geneva Centre for Democratic Control of Armed Forces, 2002.

Iran: Intelligence Failure or Policy Stalemate? Washington, DC: Georgetown University, Institute for the Study of Diplomacy, 2005. http://www12.georgetown.edu/sfs/isd/Iran_WG_Report.pdf

Jinnah Institute. 2013. 'Sources of Tension in Afghanistan & Pakistan: Perspectives from the Region

Johnson, Thomas H. and M. Chris Mason. 2008. 'No Sign until the Burst of Fire: Understanding the Pakistan-Afghanistan Frontier', International Security, Vol. 32, No. 4.

Jaffrelot, Christophe (Ed.), 2016, Pakistan at the Crossroads: Domestic Dynamics and External Pressures.

(Religion, Culture, and Public Life). New York: Columbia University Press.

Jamal, Arif, 2009, Shadow War: The Untold Story of Jihad in Kashmir. New York: Melville House.

Jan, Faizullah, 2015, The Muslim Extremist Discourse: Constructing Us versus Them. Lanham: Lexington Books.

Jalalzai Musa Khan. May 2018, Pakistan: Living with a Nuclear Monkey, Vij Books India Pvt Ltd, Darya Ganj New Delhi, India,

Judah, Tim. 2002. 'The Taliban Papers', Survival, Vol. 44, No. 1.

Jaffrelot, Christophe, 2016, Pakistan at the Crossroads: Domestic Dynamics and External Pressures. New York: Columbia University Press.

Jalalzai Musa Khan, 22 September, 2015. The Prospect of Nuclear Jihad in Pakistan: The Armed Forces, Islamic State, and the Threat of Chemical and Biological Terrorism. Algora Publishing, Riverside, New York, USA. ISBN-10: 1628941650. ISBN-13: 978-1628941654.

Jan, Faizullah, 2015, The Muslim Extremist Discourse: Constructing Us versus Them. Lanham: Lexington Books.

Kalia, Ravi, 2016, Pakistan's Political Labyrinths: Military, Society and Terror. Abingdon: Routledge.

Kapur, S. Paul, 2017, Jihad as Grand Strategy: Islamist Militancy, National Security, and the Pakistani State. New York: Oxford University Press.

Khalilzad, Zalmay. 1996. 'Afghanistan in 1995: Civil War and a Mini-Great Game', Asian Survey, Vol. 36, No. 2.

Khan, Ijaz. 1998. 'Afghanistan: A geopolitical study', Central Asian Survey, Vol. 17, No. 3.

Magnus, Ralph H. 1998. 'Afghanistan in 1997: The War Moves North', Asian Survey, Vol. 38, No.2.

Maley, William. 1997. 'The Dynamics of Regime Transition in Afghanistan', Central Asian Survey, Vol. 16, No. 2.

Malik, Iftikhar Haider, 2005, Jihad, Hindutva and the Taliban: South Asia at the Crossroads. Karachi: Oxford University Press.

Malik, Jamal, 2008, Madrasas in South Asia: Teaching Terror? (Routledge Contemporary South Asia Series, Vol. 4). Abingdon: Routledge.

Murphy, Eamon, 2013, The Making of Terrorism in Pakistan: Historical and Social Roots of Extremism. (Routledge Critical Terrorism Studies). Abingdon: Routledge.

Murphy, Eamon, 2019, Islam and Sectarian Violence in Pakistan: The Terror Within. Abingdon: Routledge.

Maloney, Sean M. 2015. 'Army of darkness: The jihadist training system in Pakistan and Afghanistan, 1996-2001', Small Wars & Insurgencies, Vol. 26, No. 3.

Mukhopadhyay, Dipali. 2012. 'The Slide from Withdrawal to War: The UN Secretary General's Failed Effort in Afghanistan, 1992', International Negotiation, Vol. 17, No. 3.

Nester, William, 2012, Hearts, Minds, and Hydras: Fighting Terrorism in Afghanistan, Pakistan, America, and Beyond – Dilemmas and Lessons. Dulles: Potomac Books.

Nielsen, Thomas Galasz; Syed, Mahroona Hussain; Vestenskov, David, 2015, Counterinsurgency and Counterterrorism: Sharing Experiences in Afghanistan and Pakistan. Copenhagen: Royal Danish Defence College.

Ollapally, Deepa M. (2008): The Politics of Extremism in South Asia. Cambridge: Cambridge University Press.

Odom, William E. 2003, Fixing Intelligence: For a More Secure America. New Haven: Yale University Press, 2003.

Odom, William E. 2004, Fixing Intelligence: For a More Secure America. 2nd ed.New Haven, CT: Yale University Press, 2004.

Odom, William E. et al. 1997, Modernizing Intelligence: Structure and Change for the 21st Century. Fairfax, VA: National Institute for Public Policy,

Olmsted, Kathryn S. 1996, Challenging the Secret Government: The PostWatergate Investigation of the CIA and FBI. Chapel Hill: University of North Carolina Press,

Olmsted, Kathryn Signe. 1993, Challenging the Secret Government: Congress and the Press Investigate the Intelligence Community, 1974-76. Dissertation. Davis, CA: University of California, Davis.

Pande, Aparna, 2018, Routledge Handbook of Contemporary Pakistan. Abingdon: Routledge.

Rais, Rasul Bakhsh. 2000. 'Afghanistan: A Forgotten Cold War Tragedy', Ethnic Studies Report, Vol. XVIII, No. 2.

Rieck, Andreas. 1997. 'Afghanistan's Taliban: An Islamic Revolution of the Pashtuns' in Orient, Vol. 38, No. 1.

Roy, Olivier. 1992. 'Political elites in Afghanistan: rentier state building, rentier state wrecking', International Journal of Middle East Studies, No. 24.

Rashid, Ahmed, 2008, Descent into Chaos: The United States and the Failure of Nation Building in Pakistan, Afghanistan, and Central Asia. New York: Viking.

Rashid, Ahmed, 2012, Pakistan on the Brink: The Future of America, Pakistan, and Afghanistan. New York: Viking.

Riedel, Bruce, 2011, Deadly Embrace: Pakistan, America, and the Future of the Global Jihad. Washington, DC: The Brookings Institution Press.

Riedel, Bruce, 2013, Avoiding Armageddon: America, India, and Pakistan to the Brink and Back. (Brookings Focus Books). Washington, DC: Brookings Institution Press.

Rubin, Barnett R. 2000. 'The Political Economy of War and Peace in Afghanistan', World Development, Vol. 28, No. 10.

Rubin, Barnett R. 1999. Afghanistan under the Taliban', Current History, Vol. 98, No. 625.

Rubin, Barnett R. 1994. Afghanistan in 1993: abandoned but surviving'Asian Survey, Vol. 34, No. 2.

Schmidt, John R. 2011, The Unraveling: Pakistan in the Age of Jihad. New York: Farrar, Straus and Giroux.

Shah, Sikander Ahmed, 2015, International Law and Drone Strikes in Pakistan: The Legal and Socio-Political Aspects. Routledge Research in the Law of Armed Conflict

Sharma, Surinder Kumar; Behera, Anshuman, 2014, Militant Groups in South Asia. New Delhi: Pentagon Press.

Sheikh, Mona Kanwal, 2016, Guardians of God: Inside the Religious Mind of the Pakistani Taliban. New Delhi: Oxford University Press.

Saikal, Amin. 1996. 'The UN and Afghanistan: A Case of Failed Peace-making Intervention', International Peacekeeping, Vol. 3, No. 1.

Shahrani, M. Nazif. 2002. 'War, Factionalism, and the State in Afghanistan', American Anthropologist, Vol. 104, No. 3.

Schneider, Erich B. 2013, Balancing the Trinity: U.S. Approaches to Marginalizing Islamic Militancy in Pakistan. Master's Thesis, Naval Postgraduate School, Monterey, United States. http://hdl.handle.net/10945/39008

Shabab, Asma (2012, May): Marketing the Beard: The Use of Propaganda in the Attempt to Talibanize Pakistan. Master's Thesis, University of Southern California, Los Angeles, United States. http://digitallibrary.usc. edu/cdm/ref/collection/p15799coll3/id/38217

Shah, Abid Hussain, 2007,The Volatile Situation of Balochistan – Options to Bring it into Streamline. Master's Thesis, Naval Postgraduate School, Monterey, United States. http://hdl.handle.net/10945/10280

Siddique, Osman, 2013, Rational Irrationality: Analysis of Pakistan's Seemingly Irrational Double Game in Afghanistan. Master Thesis, University of Oslo, Oslo, Norway. https://www.duo.uio.no/ handle/10852/37342

Shahrani, M. Nazif. 2001. 'Resisting the Taliban and Talibanism in Afghanistan: Legacies of a Century of Internal Colonialism and Cold War Politics in a Buffer State', Perceptions: Journal of International Affairs, Vol. 5, No. 4.

Shahrani, M. Nazif. 2000. 'The Taliban Enigma: Person-Centered Politics & Extremism in Afghanistan', ISIM Newsletter, Vol. 6.

Tankel, Stephen, 2013, Storming the World Stage: The Story of Lashkar-e-Taiba. Oxford: Oxford University Press.

Topich, William J. 2018, Pakistan: The Taliban, Al Qaeda, and the Rise of Terrorism. Praeger Security International. Santa Barbara: Praeger.

Tripathy, Amulya K.; Pandit, D. Santishree; Kunjur, Roshni, 2016, Understanding Post 9/11 Cross-Border Terrorism in South Asia: U.S. and other Nations' Perceptions. New Delhi: EssEss Publications.

Tarzi, Shah M. 1993. 'Afghanistan in 1992: A Hobbesian State of Nature', Asian Survey, Vol. 33, No. 2.

Verkaaik, Oskar, 2004, Migrants and Militants: Fun and Urban Violence in Pakistan.Princeton Studies in Muslim Politics. Princeton: Princeton University Press.

Vandenbroucke, Lucien S. Perilous Options: Special Operations as an Instrument of U.S. Foreign Policy. New York: Oxford University Press,

Violia, Marc Anthony. 1993. A Spy's Résumé: Confessions of a Maverick Intelligence Professional and Misadventure Capitalist. Lanham, MD: Scarecrow Press

Volkman, Ernest. 1989. Secret Intelligence. New York: Doubleday,

Von Hassell, Agostino. 2006. Alliance of Enemies: The Untold Story of the Secret American and German Collaboration to End World War II. New York: Thomas Dunne Books,

Williams, Brian Glyn. 2014. 'Afghanistan after the Soviets: From jihad to tribalism', Small Wars & Insurgencies, Volume 25, Issue 5-6.

Webel, Charles; Tomass, Mark, 2017, Assessing the War on Terror: Western and Middle Eastern Perspectives. Contemporary Terrorism Studies. Abingdon: Routledge.

Woods, Chris, 2015, Sudden Justice: America's Secret Drone Wars. London: Hurst.

Yasmeen, Samina, 2017, Jihad and Dawah: Evolving Narratives of Lashkar-e-Taiba and Jamatud Dawah. London: Hurst.

Yusuf, Moeed, 2008, Insurgency and Counterinsurgency in South Asia: Through a Peacebuilding Lens. Washington, DC: United States Institute of Peace Press.

Zaidi, Syed Manzar Abbas, 2016, Terrorism Prosecution in Pakistan. USIP Peaceworks, No. 113 https://www.usip.org/publications/2016/04/terrorism-prosecution-pakistan

Zaidi, Syed Manzar Abbas, 2016, Reconstituting Local Order in Pakistan: Emergent ISIS and Locally Constituted Shariah Courts in Pakistan. (Brookings Local Orders Paper Series, Paper 4). https://www.brookings.edu/research/reconstituting-local-order-in-pakistan-emergent-isis-and-locally-constitutedshariah-courts-in-pakistan

Index

About the Author

Musa Khan Jalalzai is a journalist and research scholar. He has written extensively on Afghanistan, terrorism, nuclear and biological terrorism, human trafficking, drug trafficking, and intelligence research and analysis. He was an Executive Editor of the Daily Outlook Afghanistan from 2005-2011, and a permanent contributor in Pakistan's daily *The Post*, *Daily Times*, and *The Nation*, *Weekly the Nation*, (London). However, in 2004, US Library of Congress in its report for South Asia mentioned him as the biggest and prolific writer. He received Masters in English literature, Diploma in Geospatial Intelligence, University of Maryland, Washington DC, certificate in Surveillance Law from the University of Stanford, USA, and diploma in Counter terrorism from Pennsylvania State University, California, the United States.